CHILDREN OF THE STORM

All around the world, children were moved to places of safety at the start of the war. These British children were evacuated from London to the country. For many, this was their first time away from home. Their faces reflect a feeling more of adventure than apprehension. Polegate, England. 1939.

CHILDREN OF THE STORM

CHILDHOOD MEMORIES OF WORLD WAR II

Edited by Charles Perkins

MBI Publishing Company

This edition first published in 1998 by MBI Publishing Company, PO Box 1, 729 Prospect Avenue, Osceola, WI 54020-0001 USA.

MBI Publishing Company books are also available at discounts in bulk quantity for industrial or sales-promotional use. For details write to Special Sales Manager at Motorbooks International Wholesalers & Distributors, 729 Prospect Avenue,
PO Box 1, Osceola, WI 54020-0001 USA.

Library of Congress Cataloging-in-Publication Data Available.

ISBN 0-7603-0214-6

Printed in the United States of America

CONTENTS

FOREWORD

This is a book about children's memories of World War II. The memories have been drawn from almost 200 taped interviews with men and women in nations around the world. A few came to us in written form, a very few have been taken from previously published sources.

The interviews were transcribed and loosely edited. Repetitions and obvious inaccuracies were deleted or emended, scattered ideas were drawn together, a few link words suggested. Great care has been taken to preserve the individual "voice" of each speaker. Some interviewees were asked to expand or clarify certain memories; other than that, the words that appear on these pages are the speaker's own. These are the raw voices of history speaking with force and emotion of memories that have been buried for fifty years or more. Their vigor lies in their directness. Editorial intrusion has been kept to the minimum consistent with clarity.

Similarly, the structure of the book has been organized along loose chronological progressions and on broad-based themes suggested by the common experiences of my generation – food, rationing, grown ups, school, and so on. The book does not pretend to be a detailed history of World War II nor to have covered every aspect of it in a systematic way.

Most of the contributors are identified by name, nationality, occupation, and age. A few persons have asked us to preserve their anonymity, either with a pseudonym or by revealing only their first or last names; others have asked us to withhold their occupation or their age. We have, of course, respected these wishes.

For whatever weaknesses there may be in this book the responsibility is mine, but its strengths have been derived in no small measure from the help and support of others. Nearly 250 people in thirty countries have been acknowledged and thanked elsewhere in these pages. There are three particular persons, however, without whose contribution it is fair to say this book would not have been published.

In the first instance, I should like to thank Robert Perkins for his long service as collator, indexer, and proofreader.

A very special thank you to Brooke Calverley, who, as designer, contributor, creative sparkplug, and patient and long-suffering friend, has been a tower of calm strength throughout.

Most of all I should like to thank my wife whose intelligence and support have touched every page of this book.

For Bundle with love

A three year old and her doll evacuated from
Antwerp to the comparative safety of London. 1940.

THIS IS THE STORY OF A GENERATION – the generation of children who grew up during World War II. Men and women from every walk of life and from nations around the world, have freely given their time and memories to this book. Their experiences were as different as the wide diversity of the war itself. Some lives the war barely touched, others it devastated; to some it was a great adventure, a game, to others an unspeakable tragedy. For some, giving their memories to this book has been the final purging of horrors too long pushed aside. More than a few have broken down as they spoke. But always these memories have been recalled quietly, spoken without anger, without bitterness. One must listen closely for often it is in the pauses, the silences, the words these speakers choose to leave unspoken, that we hear their voices most clearly.

They speak of a simpler time when "people mattered more," when "neighbors cared." With astonishing vividness they recall the sounds, smells, tastes, faces, and words of a world vanished for nearly half a century. The adult memory may play tricks, but the memories of childhood do not. Truth leaps off these pages. No one who reads these words can doubt, "Yes, this is how it was." Effortlessly these speakers weave together a testament to the courage, resilience, and humanity of children everywhere. Indeed, as they speak, it becomes clear that their generation was bound together far more closely by the experience of war and of the way it

touched their lives than they had ever been divided by the barriers of nation, race, and religion.

They are the last generation to tell their story of the war. It is appropriate that they should at last choose to do so. They are now men and women in their early seventies, their sixties, their fifties. Already, in the way of generations, their numbers have begun to dwindle. When they are gone, so too will be gone all living testimony of World War II. The mightiest event of our time will truly have passed into history. Theirs is too important a story to slip away unremarked.

But enough. It is 1939, the warm, languid autumn of the Phoney War*. The children are excited. They have been playing new games, like helping the grown ups fill sandbags, or tape windows, or dig Victory Gardens; they have been learning new skills like how to wear a gas mask, or how to distinguish the sound of an All-Clear; they have heard unfamiliar new words on the wireless – "Blitzkrieg," "Ghetto," "Air Raid;" they have said hasty farewells to adored fathers.

But for now, their work is done. Soon it will be time for bed. They pause for a moment in the growing dark. There are flashes of lightning on the horizon, the distant rumbling of a storm, but far off and harmless. For the moment, they ignore it.

They speak:

* See Glossary on page 152 for explanation of all asterisks in the text.

We were on holiday in Devon in August 1939. There was much talk of war on the radio and between the adults. It seemed to be everywhere. I asked my father what war was. He said, "It's very bad, war. Very bad. But you'll be all right."

My father was like a god to me and if he was sure I'd be all right, so was I. That conviction got me through the Blitz but it didn't quite carry me through the Flying Bombs.* By then I'd had friends bombed out and friends killed. By then I understood what war was and that people could get killed no matter what their fathers had told them.

Anyway, when we got back to London, we heard Mr Chamberlain on the radio announce that we were at war. No sooner had he finished speaking, it seemed, than the sirens started wailing and we all – adults and children – went and stood under the stairs until the All Clear. To my cousin Joyce and me, it seemed like a game.

Jean Holder   *English   Retired Deputy Head Teacher   Aged 6*

When war broke out on 1st September 1939, I considered it a streak of good luck. I am even now ashamed to admit it, but I was nine at the time and in those pre-TV days children weren't as familiar with death, blood, corpses, and ruins as

they are nowadays. Wars were something out of history books, with dates to be memorized and battles enumerated. There had been much talk about war among grown-ups in 1938, then we heard about Chamberlain's "peace for our time," and then the Germans invaded our country. Discussions about war became more and more worried. But on this particular day I had a big problem.

Before leaving for school, my sister and I had a terrible row, something about my having "borrowed" her new crayons and her calling my doll a "disgusting gnome." I was furious and ruined her new schoolbook in revenge. And ran. On my way to school I pondered how to get out of this predicament because I knew that there would be big trouble

Above: During the war, fathers often had to go off to a mysterious place called "The Front." Saying goodbye was a universal ordeal for children. Berlin, 1942. *Left:* "I have a vague memory of my father kissing me goodbye. I remember the khaki and the rough feel of his uniform. I never saw him again." England, ca. 1940.

at home in the afternoon. My sister could, perhaps, be mollified by offers to take up some of her chores and I could buy her a new schoolbook out of my pocket money. But if she had sneaked on me before leaving, then I was in for one of the rare punishments in our family because ruining books was something utterly despicable, as I well knew. "Barbarian" our parents had called it on a similar occasion where the damage to the book had not even been done on purpose.

As it turned out, there were no classes in school this day. Without notice, the Germans had closed both my École Primaire Française and my sister's Lycée Français as of this day, which meant going home even earlier than I had bargained for. Things looked rather grim there. I stole to the

A Princess, a future Queen, and a royal Corgi do their share for the War Effort. Windsor Castle, England, 1940.

kitchen and asked cook as innocently as I could, what was happening.

"War is happening!" she replied and must have thought me a moron when I exclaimed, "Oh, good!" and ran to my room. I was soon to learn that "good" was not the description of what was to come and yet I often remembered the immense relief I had felt at that moment. The book incident was, of course, forgotten and I later found out that my sister hadn't told on me.

Hana Rehakova   *Czech   Administrator   Aged 9*

I was seven years old on Sunday, 3rd September 1939. Our family was having breakfast at the LaFonda Hotel in Santa Fe, New Mexico. We had driven down from Colorado Springs for a weekend vacation. Dad was reading Shirer's Berlin Diary, *rented from the public library at home. He carried it everywhere. Our waiter brought us news that Hitler had invaded Poland and the shock was so great that Dad spilled coffee all over his book.*

"They won't take it back," said Mom, and sure enough that memento was on our book shelves for years, purchased from the library when we got home.

My brothers and I really didn't grasp the situation. Pearl Harbor was two years away. But a thirty-eight-year-

old father who had just changed jobs and had a wife and three sons and extra medical expenses and supported his mother. . . well, on this news his coffee probably would spill.

This was fiesta weekend in Santa Fe, to be climaxed by the burning of Zozobra. In the minds of the Indian natives, Zozobra was a symbol of evil and death, a blend of their own religious beliefs and those of the Catholic fathers sent to educate them. On the last night of the fiesta, we all trooped up a hill on the outskirts of town where perched Zozobra. He was made of painted cloth and paper and filled with fireworks. To the beat of Indian tom-toms he was set afire ending a year's misfortune, sin, and evil.

Thus the Second World War began.

Edward Thomas   *American   Businessman   Aged 7*

On 3rd September 1939 I was almost seven. My mother and I listened to Chamberlain's broadcast in the morning. We were at WAR with Germany. She sent me to tell the men in the factory behind our house that war had been declared. It was a drop forge and made a heck of a noise. My piping voice must have been difficult to hear, but they got the message.

John Bradley   *English   Aged 7*

A West Coast Victory Garden. Thousands of gardens like this one, worked by children, provided vital food supplies and released men for the front. American Girl Scouts are shown how to sow vegetable seeds. San Francisco, 1943.

I was born in my parents' country estate in Poland. The house was old, large, surrounded by a park then forest, prairies, ponds. We were a family of harmony and happiness.

I was nine. It was autumn. On the very edge of the park, a road led from the mill to the avenue of alders. German tanks were coming. We stood on the terrace, taken by surprise, watching. They were looking at us, standing as if on parade. I saw them for the first time: faces, uniforms.

I did not know how to hate. I did not believe it. I could not understand why they should hate the four of us on the terrace.

They fired, aiming, probably on purpose, at a wall. I stood fearless, suddenly humiliated by their violence, helpless in the face of injustice and the impotence of my parents.

At night, partisans would come. Poles. Russians. Very often the same people known to us and friendly. Later, more and more frequently, just robbers. Germans by day. The house exposed us. It ceased to be a shelter. The forest also became alien. I no longer went there to talk to it as before.

Magdalena Abakanowicz   *Polish   Sculptress   Aged 9*

We lived in London's East End, on Cartwright Street opposite St Katherine's Dock. On the first day – just after they declared war – the siren went off. It was only a test. We sat and listened to Mr Chamberlain's broadcast because mum and dad made us and just after that the siren went but there was no air raid shelters built in those days. I'm not sure how long after that, they dug up all Royal Mint Square. There was a big space all covered in asphalt and they dug it all up to fill sandbags with earth. Everyone was digging and digging and then there was a funny, 'orrible smell and they found bones. I think they found a few skulls an' all. What it was, they knocked off then – stopped the digging – and had people come in to look. They reckoned that they'd found a mass graveyard from when there was the plague and people was more scared of that than anything else.

They also dug a lot of sand at the back of Victoria Buildings and the army came with a sand lorry and we made sandbags and when the sand ran out we started digging the earth. When we did that, we started digging up all these bones again. I tell you what I remember – that 'orrible musty smell. I'll never forget that smell. And no one would ever play in Victoria grounds after that.

Lil Mountain   *English   Retired   Aged 9*
Ernie Askins *(Lil's brother)*   *English   Retired   Aged 14*

Russia attacked Finland in November 1939 and declared war a couple of hours afterwards. However, it was not un-expected by then since Finland refused to give in to Russian demands on naval bases. I was seven at the time and at school when the alarm was sounded. We all thought it was a fire engine, so some kids rushed to the window to see it, as they used to (although they weren't supposed to). No fire engine was in sight, and after a while the headmaster came into the classroom and told everyone to go straight home, without stopping anywhere. I lived about three blocks from

---

When Hitler's troops marched into the Sudetenland, they were greeted not as invaders but as heroes. The children of ethnic Germans who lived there welcome them with flowers and the Nazi salute. Czechoslovakia, October 1939.

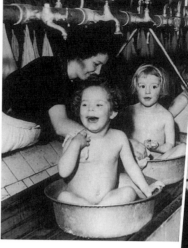

Evacuation. During the early years of the war, children in Britain (and elsewhere) were moved from the cities to the comparative safety of the country. They were often billeted with strangers. Most children were evacuated by train. This fortunate group of under-fives and their dolls (*above*) travelled by private motor car to St Leonard's School in Hertfordshire where places had been found for them.

Inset: Most evacuees travelled with an identity tag around their neck. The group above had identity tags around their ankles. The hands of the Matron, Miss Newbegin, attach an identity band to the ankle of "Miss Clarke." England, 1939.

Above: This group of under-fives are enjoying a daily bath provided by specially trained nurses at a residential school in Windsor. Not all evacuees were so lucky. England, 1941.

A group of British children evacuated to America aboard the liner *Samaria* cheer as the Statue of Liberty comes into view. Their journey was sponsored by the American Committee for the Evacuation of British Children. New York Harbor, October 1940.

the school so I started my walk. There was a policeman running in the street, looking behind him, and I wondered what had got into him.

When I came to the block of flats where I lived, my parents were away at work, as usual, but our neighbors and some of my friends were going into the basement which had been turned into a shelter. One of my friends said, "The war has started." I followed the people into the basement and sat down with them, thinking about what I knew about the war. . . people shooting each other, etc. Suddenly I felt very lonely and frightened and missed my parents, trying to hold back my tears.

Borje Kyrklund   *Finnish   Aged 7*

At the beginning of the war it was recommended that we sleep under the stairs. We didn't have a shelter yet, so we did – with the gas and electricity meters. A pokey little place. Then later on, toward the end of the war, we had one of the Morrison* shelters which we'd eat off of and play on and sleep in.

I can't remember it clearly but I was aware of it being incredibly solid and the flat top was ideal for playing on, particularly jigsaws. In those days, there wasn't much to do in the evenings and jigsaws were a good way to pass the time. So we got bigger and bigger jigsaws and it was good to have a place where you could leave the jigsaw up. We also used to play cards a lot, and a card game called Lexicon, which is rather like Scrabble.

Tom Helcke   *Scots   Biochemical Engineer   Aged 4*

At the end of August 1939 I was a boy scout in what was the Polish province of Galicia (now in the Ukraine). For our summer camp we had gone into the mountains not far from Nowy Targ to help with the older scouts who were doing a gliding course.

As I was not yet thirteen, I had no opportunity for any gliding, as only scouts of sixteen and over were allowed to learn. In those days there were no two seat trainers so "air experience" such as Air Cadets enjoy today was out of the question. The would-be pilot was strapped on an open seat in front of a frail skeleton of a fuselage and wings, which was the primary trainer, which we called Salamandra. Our job was to run with a rubber rope in order to catapult the glider into the air.

Obviously we started on the flat with gentle runs, until the instructor was satisfied that the trainee could control the aircraft, then we would go to the top of a nearby hill and do the same thing, running down the hill pulling this rubber rope, in bigger and bigger teams to propel the glider ever onward as the pilot became more proficient. It was very tiring work. The glider would be pulled back up the hill by an old man with a horse, while we walked back up alongside. The bigger boys used to get warm beer and sausage, but we usually got weak lemonade.

On what was to be the last day of our camp, we were very busy. One boy aged about seventeen had got off in the Salamandra fairly early in the morning, and stayed up for hours. Pretty soon other glider pilots had turned up, and seeing this little speck in the sky hovering almost stationary above our heads, attempted to get off. We pulled and sweated, running down the hill with the rubber rope, then trudging exhausted back up through long grass in the hot sunshine, dragging it back up the hill, while all the modern high performance gliders tacked left then right, losing altitude the whole while, until they flopped disconsolately into the meadow at the bottom of the hill. Nobody else could get up there!

About lunch time we were ordered quite curtly to set out a circle of white canvas on the hill. This was the sign to land immediately, but the scout in the Salamandra, didn't seem to take much notice.

Coaches arrived in the afternoon and we were divided into groups depending on our home towns, awaiting transport home. No one told us what was going on, all the men looked very grim and silent. Finally the lone airborne scout landed, and the chief instructor ran over to him swearing and shouting. "There has been general mobilization. Everyone is to report home. The Germans look as if they are about to start a war!"

The intrepid scout pilot looked shocked. He said nothing, he just stood there with his mouth open. I didn't see what else happened because my name was called and I was bundled into a bus.

When I got home late at night, my mother was dressed in her coat and wearing all her jewelry. Dad was nowhere to be seen. My two sisters were also dressed in coats. "We are meeting Daddy in Bucharest!" said one.

I had never been out of Poland before. I knew that my father had something to do with the Foreign Ministry but I had no idea if he was important. We left our house at about midnight in a black car driven by a soldier. I soon fell asleep on the back seat.

It was still dark when I was awakened by a big bang. There was something burning on the road ahead. I could hear airplanes, but couldn't see anything in the night sky. The soldier ordered us out of the car, and into a nearby wood. We stayed there until mid-morning. We occasionally heard airplanes and heard other explosions, and smelled burning rubber.

When it seemed safe enough to go to the car we found it burned out. All our luggage had been destroyed. The soldier hailed a passing army lorry and left us with the driver, who piled us into the back with two other men in suits and black briefcases. There was nothing to sit on other than the hard wooden floor. We bumped around for hours. It was very painful at times. My sisters who were younger than me just whimpered, but my mother said nothing. Once in a while she would wince when we bumped over a pothole. Occasionally we left the road without warning, and the lorry would wait under the shelter of a tree, and once we drove into a barn, where we waited inside, hearing airplanes going overhead. Sometimes we heard machine guns. None of us knew what was going on.

By nightfall we had reached the Romanian frontier, and were being pushed across through a big white gate by some very anxious looking officials. My sisters were crying, and my mother looked very pale, dirty, and silent. That was the end of the first day of World War II. I don't remember much else, because I fainted! I had not eaten since breakfast at the gliding club the day before. When I woke up I was in a small room with my mother and father. He was talking about getting us to Canada as it wasn't safe even in Romania.

When he saw I was awake, he sat down on the couch where I was lying and told me I must be very brave. He said that the Polish Intelligence Service had discovered that there was a plot for the Russians to help the Germans by executing all Polish government officials and their families. Nobody knew how or when, because Russia had not yet attacked us, but they were expecting it soon. He said that Germany and Russia planned to divide up Poland. Although we would fight, Poland was not strong enough to last more than a few weeks, and that all the Polish Government officials must carry on in other countries. I was to leave with my mother and sisters by train that afternoon. Tonight we would be on a ship for Istanbul, then another to Port Said in Egypt. The embassy had arranged everything. My father was to stay in Bucharest and arrange for the escape of any other official refugees.

I did not know it then, but I was never to see my father again. To this day I have no idea of what happened to him.

Stasek Mihalowicz *Polish   Pilot   Aged 13*

THE LONG PRESTON BLITZ

I grew up in Long Preston, a straggling Yorkshire village on the main road between Skipton and Settle, and a place about as far out of the war as it was possible to get. But, one night, I was fast asleep in bed and was wakened by the throbbing of an aircraft and then suddenly a screaming bomb, the sort of whistling bomb you hear in films. There was a crash and I went straight to the bottom of my bed and hid and I heard by mother rush up and down the landing saying, "It's landed in the garden. It's landed in the garden! It's landed in the garden!!"

And I heard my father say, "Don't be silly. No bloody aircraft could land in our garden."

So then she said, "No, it's not an aircraft, it's a bomb!"

Next morning it transpired, when the milkman arrived, that a German aircraft had off-loaded three bombs to try to gain height as he flew back to Germany. One of them landed in the back lane. That was the screamer. One landed on a hen hut, and another one they found sometime later in the sewage works. It was always rumored by the know-alls that the Germans were attempting to bomb Long Preston railway station, though quite why anyone should want to bomb Long Preston railway station, I can't imagine.

This has been known locally, ever since, as 'The Long Preston Blitz'. The casualties, apart from my parents' nerves, were two hens and a rabbit which at one time was stuffed and put in a glass case in the Boar's Head.

Leo Cooper   *English*   *Writer/Publisher*   *Aged 8*

Laksevag was an important place during the German occupation [of Norway] because the Germans had built a huge concrete bunker for ocean-going submarines which torpedoed the Allied vessels. So, although we were Allies, Laksevag became a target for British bombers.

4th October was a day of warm sunshine. The air raid warning went off at midday. For some reason, my mother and we two young children went up to the [German-built] shelter which was a safe tunnel in the mountain rather than, as we often did, down into the cellar of our own house. The entrance to this shelter is still visible today. My father, who had pneumonia, was left lying in bed because he thought the raid would pass over.

Soon the tunnel was packed with people sitting on top of each other. The first bombs came and were followed by a strong 'drag' in my stomach due to the air pocket which followed the explosion. The lights went out. I remember the drag of the air pocket, the dark – except for small lights – and the crowded people making me feel claustrophobic. My mother was also terrified that something might have happened to my father. I must have fainted. At any rate, I remember a workman giving me tea from a thermos and trying to calm me down. A man who was standing at the entrance to the tunnel called out the names of those who came into the tunnel in the pauses between the bombing raids. Some of them said that the air was black with English planes and that the whole of Laksevag was on fire. My mother has said since that she has never been so relieved in her life as when my father's name was called out at the

entrance to the tunnel. He was unhurt. Later he told us that during a short lull in the bombing he had taken the opportunity of running out of the house without having time to get dressed. The bombs had fallen so near the house that the whole house had shaken and swayed and the lamp had fallen off the ceiling onto the bed. I do not know how many hours passed but at last the bombing raid was over. We came out of the tunnel.

And what a sight met us! In the lovely, warm sunshine the whole air was filled with smoke. Houses nearby were on fire, lay tipped over, or else had large holes in the walls. In the space outside the tunnel there was a huge crowd of people running around and shouting. Soon it was filled with lots of stretchers covered with blankets. Later I understood that under the blankets lay the dead children and teachers from Hole school which was just next to there. Almost two whole classes of children and teachers had been killed when a bomb hit the school and the cellar in the school was not strong enough to protect them. The word "fulltreffer" (direct hit) was a new frightening word which I learnt that day.

Tore Iversen   *Norwegian*   *Aged 5½*

September 1939 brought war, and for our whole family, evacuation. Packing our favourite toys, we took the longest train ride that my twin sister and I had ever experienced, to Newquay in Cornwall, and a way of life very different from our suburban home at Wembley, in north London.

For us children, coming from the city, Cornwall was a wonderland. There were donkeys in the paddock which we were allowed to harness and ride, and a cart which the donkeys pulled down to the sea to collect driftwood. There were horses running free on the common and cows which huddled for shelter near the house wall at night. There were guinea fowl too with lovely spotted feathers. It was a time when I was learning to play with words and the whole place I christened the Land of Now-here.

School was two miles walk away, through lanes with high hedge banks, across fields and farmyards. At school we encountered the local children, boys and girls aged five to fourteen, all in one school, in two classes. "The evacuees from London" were not at first popular. We seemed to know too much for our own good, and soon learned not to be the first to answer up. The school room was heated by two iron ranges. Bottles of milk, 1/3 pint each, were warmed on the top in time for break, then at break we all put our pasties* into the oven to be ready for a communal meal at lunchtime.

On fine days play extended into the afternoon with a free-for-all rounders* game. We were accepted by the local children when we could scale the playground wall to retrieve the ball from the field next door.

When spring came, the walk home from school took longer, as we lingered to pick primroses and violets and, later, cowslips. It was in May 1940, with the cowslips at their best, that we were recalled to London – and the Blitz.

We left Newquay the day the Phoney War ended and Hitler's troops moved into Belgium. The journey home by train was a slow and anxious one. The platforms were crowded at Exeter with soldiers and their packbags on the move we knew not where. I remember my mother's worried face as she watched these troops on the move. She remembered the First World War and the young men who went to war and never returned. "Careless talk costs lives" we had been taught – so no one discussed it much in public.

In the back garden of our home a huge hole was dug to make way for the new Anderson* shelter, a corrugated iron structure that was sunk into the ground. Earth was piled on top and covered with turf to conceal it from bombers. The entrance was securely sand-bagged. Inside we felt extraordinarily safe, if sometimes damp and cold, and it saw us through the worst of the Blitz. It soon proved, however, that the shelter was sunk well below the water table and needed regular bailing out. The wooden floor would float as a trap to the unwary. In time, our Anderson shelter was replaced by the indoor Morrison shelter, an iron structure which replaced the dining table. We learned to play table tennis on it and invented rules for those occasions when the ball bounced off the nuts which secured the steel top to the heavy base. The family cat, Sooty, slept regularly in the middle of the bed underneath, and so did we.

Our homecoming surprised me in the rapturous welcome we received from neighbors who greeted us with open arms, shared meals, and memories; but I was still grieving for Cornwall's cowslips.

Margaret Roake *English   History teacher   Aged 8*

27th May 1940. A Belgian family arranges its own evacuation, fleeing from the advancing troops on a tandem bicycle. The next day, King Leopold ordered the Belgian Army to surrender and his British Allies began a withdrawal to a small coastal town called Dunkirk.

Every inch of space was vital for the War Effort. German children watch the lawn of a municipal garden being cut to provide fodder for horses. Oranienplatz, Berlin. July 1940.

We had a farm near the village of Ceresetto in Bardi di Parma, a remote region in the mountains of northwest Italy. We grew all the staple crops on our farm – potatoes, wheat, maize – and had lots of animals – cows, sheep, horses, a donkey, a goat. We were largely self-sufficient but life was tough, work was hard, and there never seemed to be much left over. The roads in this region were non-existent or impassable, so we went everywhere on horseback or on foot. It took me more than an hour to walk the nine kilometers to school on trails through the mountains; it was twenty-eight kilometers to the nearest train station.

One day in June, 1940, I was out working on the farm. It was a hot day and I was cutting hay. After work I decided to go down to the village, to the osteria [cafe], and have a drink. Lemonade maybe because of the heat. The osteria was cool inside, with marble table tops, and out of the sun. When I came inside I found about twenty people sitting around the radio. There weren't many radios in our village. My brother was there, my uncle, cousins, friends. Some old people. They all looked serious. There was military music playing. Then the news came on again saying that Mussolini had just declared war.

The old people were very upset. "A terrible thing," they said. "We could be starving soon. How will it end?" There was a man from Naples there. A pensioner who sometimes came to our village on holiday. He had been to America. He knew a lot more about the world than most of the villagers. "Mad," he said. "Completely mad. We have no chance." Everyone agreed that Mussolini must have gone crazy.

Tony Sidoli   *British / Italian   Ex-Restauranteur, Scrap Merchant Aged 14*

One thing that seems strange today was that I heard so little news. My father was in the Royal Naval Reserve, a Commander on the armed merchant cruiser Corfu. *My mother was evacuated with my brothers to a farm in Montgomeryshire and I was evacuated to South Wales, where I lived with mining families. I can't remember if all the families I lived with had a radio, but I know that in one household it was only the man who was allowed to put it on. He worked shifts, so this meant it was only if he was working nights that we might hear news at some point during the day. They took a newspaper in that family but it was kept for "Father."*

I thought about my father who was on North Sea Patrol. They told us at school about the sinking of the Rawalpindi, *which was the ship my father had expected to be*

Thousands of families spent the first weekend of the war filling sandbags. Men, women, and children joined in. Sometimes they dug up unpleasant surprises. *(See Lil and Ernie's story, page 11.)*

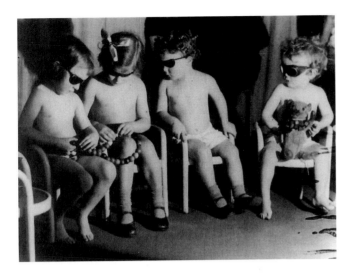

Nursery children bask under sun-ray lamps. Partly from spending so much time in shelters, and partly from the limitations of their diet, it was feared that the health of English children would suffer unless they received sun-ray treatment. London, 1942.

sent to, orders only reaching him to go to the Corfu *at the last minute. He had known most of the crew on that ship. I had never thought my father could die, any more than any of us expected parents to die in the Blitz, being young enough to see them as being immortal, but the fate of the* Rawalpindi *changed that for me.*

On holiday with my mother and brothers in Montgomeryshire, there were no newspapers delivered to our remote farm but we had an old battery radio and listened twice a day. Batteries were expensive and heavy to carry into the nearest market town when they needed to be recharged so the news of battles at sea, the sinking of the convoys my father's ship was guarding, came to us faint and far away like whispers from a lost, ghostly world. My mother and I sat in the window seat of the room she had rented in an old farmhouse, our eyes on the chicken field below and the blue mountains beyond and our ears pressed to the cold bakelite of the old brown radio, and listened to incredible tales of U-boats and drowning sailors, ships on fire, the sea burning. When the news was finished my mother would switch the radio off with more force than was needed, and say, "That's enough of that for today. Let's all go up to the Bent Hill and pick whinberries." [blueberries]

Nina Bawden *English   Writer   Aged 13*

I was born in Singapore, just before the Japanese advance. My mother and I were evacuated to Australia but my father stayed behind as a member of the Straits Volunteer Reserve Force. Sometime after we left, he was captured and interned in Changi Prison. Later, he and other prisoners were transferred to Burma to work on the railway that spanned the Bridge on the River Kwai.

My mother and I lived in Australia until I was about a year and a half old, then moved to South Africa. I remember none of this of course and all my early memories are of growing up in South Africa. My very earliest memory of all is of playing in the garden one day. It was a lovely garden – big trees and a fire where we used to bake potatoes. Like most days in South Africa, it was bright and sunny.

At any rate, I went into the house for something – a drink maybe – and my mother was there with a friend. My mother was sitting in an easy chair or maybe a settee; she was holding a telegram and crying. The friend said, "Your mummy is very upset," and asked me to go back out and play in the garden – which I did. Years later I realized this was the telegram confirming that my father had died in a Prisoner of War camp in Burma. That telegram in my mother's hand is my only memory of him.

Tony Anholt   *English   Actor   Aged 3*

*J*ust after I was born, my father went out to Persia [Iran] on a short contract working as a technologist for the Anglo-Indian Oil Company [now British Petroleum]. Once he got there, war broke out and he couldn't get home again. He had to stay in Persia for the duration. He wasn't able to leave immediately after the war either, because he was essential personnel. So all through the war there was just me and my mother. My only knowledge of my father was from letters – sometimes received as long as nine months after they were posted. I remember that the letters had British stamps over-printed with "Bahrain" and that they were often criss-crossed with blue wax pencil by the censor.

I never actually saw my father until I was nine years old and when I saw him at last I was sort of startled. He didn't appear as I thought he'd be. He was. . . fatter, I guess. Older, maybe. And of course he had very different ideas from my mother about what a son should be like. It took a few years and plenty of patience on both sides to get used to each other.

Tom Helcke   *Scots   Biochemical Engineer   Aged 9*

My father was called up for military service at the beginning of the war. I think that he died on the Eastern Front in 1942. I don't remember anyone in our family receiving a telegram saying that he was dead, but we were told officially that he was "missing," which on the Eastern Front meant that nobody was going to see him again. Most of my school colleagues had already lost their fathers.

Wilhelm Schultzki   *German   Night Watchman   Aged 9*

My first hazy memories were of my father going off to fight in France in 1939. I also clearly remember my mother singing at the top of her voice when, after weeks of frantic uncertainty, a telegram arrived saying my father was safe home from Dunkirk. She was so excited she weeded half my aunt's garden. The syringa was in bloom. Even today if I breathe in its sweet heady smell, it triggers off instant euphoria.

I also remember my mother disappearing into a great bear hug when she met my father at Leeds the next day. She expected him to be haggard, but he had never looked better; tanned almost black by the French sun and sea air, and two stone [28 pounds] lighter from not eating.

A modest man, he talked little about the ordeal of Dunkirk except to describe one ludicrous instant. Waiting endlessly for a little boat, he suddenly noticed the rocks were covered in tar and instinctively, despite bombs and bullets falling round him, removed his tin helmet and sat on it, so his trousers wouldn't get dirty.

Jilly Cooper   *English   Writer   Aged 2-3*

Helsinki, 1940. An air raid, burning buildings, a mother and her frightened child – this scenario was to be repeated many times in the war years that followed.

Although I am American, on 3rd September 1939, I felt that I and my family were also at war. This must have stemmed from my childhood reading which was composed almost entirely of British literature. Intellectually, at a very young age, I felt strongly linked with Great Britain. We read English poetry and studied it at school. We read British children's books and were as conversant with the British kings and queens as we were with the presidents of the United States.

The other students at my private day school felt much as I did. We all set to work knitting squares to be sent to Britain which were later made into blankets. We became very proficient at knitting since we spent much time at it, later tackling more difficult knitting projects; our ultimate accomplishment was Balaclava helmets for British sailors who manned the ships on that most brutal of all convoy routes – the North Atlantic. I had some sense of the sacrifices those British and, later, American crews were making so that I could continue to live comfortably in an apartment house safe from bombing, cold weather, wave, and wind.

We all worked for "Bundles for Britain," an organization which collected money and clothing for Great Britain during the long winters when bombing in London and other British cities was taking its toll. Pictures in the *New York Times* and the *Herald Tribune* showed us (in that pre-television age) the damage that was being inflicted.

We all listened, hardly daring to breathe, while Edward R Murrow told us what it was like to be in London while the bombs were dropping. Being fully aware of the consequences should Britain lose the war and the Nazis take over, we were paralyzed with fear when the British Expeditionary Force waited on the beaches of France hoping to be rescued. We thrilled when the BEF was taken back to England. We listened while the Battle of Britain unfolded and our fears almost outran our pride when Britain held firm against a possible Nazi invasion.

One December afternoon, I was watching a [gridiron] football game at the Polo Grounds. The loudspeaker said that the leaves of all American sailors and soldiers had been cancelled. The announcer also called for the publisher of *The Philadelphia Inquirer* to go at once to a telephone. We knew something had happened but we did not know what. We assumed that the Nazis had declared war on the Americans. In the event, the Japanese had bombed Pearl Harbor, and a few days later the Germans declared war on us. America had entered World War II.

Joan Challinor   *American   Aged 12*

FRITZ GAUERT WAS HIS NAME

When I was fourteen, I went through a stage when I did a lot of sport so that I actually knew more boys than girls. We went cycling and swimming together but... of all those friends, I think only two or three came back.

I had a particular friend who lived round the corner, the only son in a very close family. When he was seventeen, he went into the army. Before he went – I think he was very fond of me – he gave me a ring that his parents had given to him for his confirmation and a bracelet. One day his mother came to me, crying bitterly, and told me that he was missing.

She asked me if I would let her have the ring back, which, of course, I did. But I've still got the little bracelet he gave me. It's nothing very valuable, just some little carved ladybirds [ladybugs], but I still treasure it. In Germany ladybirds are supposed to be lucky. They never found out what happened to him. Fritz Gauert was his name.

Rosemarie Pottell-Rasch   *German Principal Dancer, Hanover State Dance Company   Aged 14*

Upper picture: Rosemarie Pottell-Rasch. At fourteen, already an accomplished professional dancer, she danced before von Ribbentrop and other high-ranking Nazis. After the war, she married a British soldier.

Lower: Rosemarie Pottell-Rasch holds the ladybird bracelet she has treasured since before the war. Some of the linkages have perished through time.

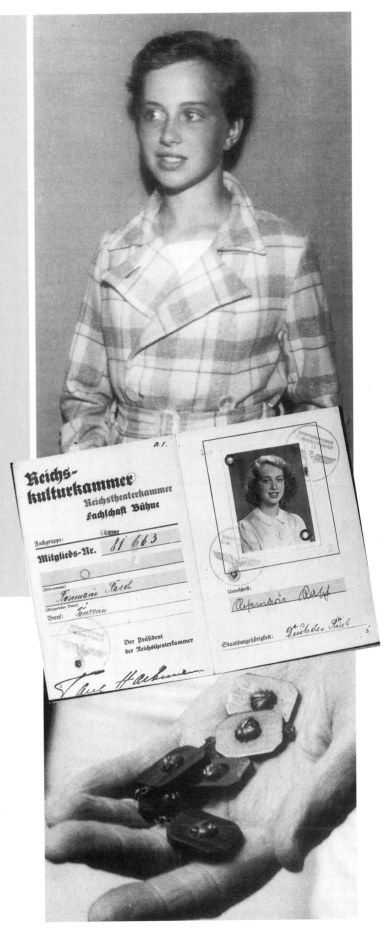

Early in March 1942, the city of Soerabaja, East Java, in which I lived, was under siege. The Japanese were bombing the town. We could hear the explosions in the distance. My father was a volunteer in the Home Guard and was trying to hold one of the main bridges into town but failed.

On Sunday, 8th March, the Japanese Army entered the city. The streets were deserted. Everyone stayed indoors. It was deadly quiet. We all felt something was about to happen.

At midday we heard a faint humming noise in the silence. The humming quickly grew louder. Nobody dared go outside so we stood at the window; a few seconds later round the corner appeared the invaders. They were riding on tiny bicycles. I remember it well because to my great surprise the bicycles were about the same size as mine – which of course was a child's bicycle.

They rode past in silence except for that humming sound. Khaki uniforms, caps with flaps down their backs, rifles strapped to their shoulders, their eyes looking everywhere. It was an amazing sight, ominous but also somewhat comical. Little men on little bicycles.

After they had passed, we all looked at each other, stunned. We sat down and were very quiet. I had expected more. A military show of some sort. I remember thinking, "That's an invading army?" But somehow the lack of show made it all the more sinister.

Els Huss-van Ham   *Dutch   Housewife   Aged 10*

We lived in London all during the war, right near the gasworks in Vauxhall. My brother, sister, and I used to go up on the flat roof near our 'ouse and watch the raids with binoculars. Planes and searchlights and guns going off. After the raids we used to run out and pick up pieces of shrapnel for souvenirs.

One night we was at 'ome. It was about eight o'clock and a big old land mine come down in a parachute. We was living in some back-to-back terrace 'ouses with small gardens. We 'ad an Anderson shelter in the garden. As the land mine come down, we run into the shelter. Just made it. It 'it and blew up nine or ten of the 'ouses on our block. Just destroyed 'em. Our own 'ouse, all the windows was gone, the ceilings fallen down, the back cracked.

Later on, a Nazi pilot come down in 'is parachute. 'E come down right on the corner of the Kensington Oval*. Almost landed on the cricket pitch. The women got 'old of 'im, really piled on, kicking 'im, 'itting 'im, biting. I've never seen nothing like it. I reckon 'e was glad to see the wardens come and arrest 'im.

The first contingent of Polish refugee children from the Polish-German border disembark from the *Warszawa* at Mark Brown's Wharf in London. Four days after their arrival, their country was invaded and World War II began. London, 29th August 1939.

After the Germans 'ad flattened most of our street, the Council used German Prisoners of War to build little pre-fabricated 'ouses for the people 'oo'd been bombed out. The 'ouses are gone now but I reckon there are still lots of people living around Vauxhall 'oo remember that Nazi pilot coming down. An' wherever 'e is, I bet 'e does too!

John Bedford   *English   Maintenance Engineer   Aged 12*

My earliest memories were of the "May Blitz" when the Germans were trying to destroy the docks in Liverpool. Being the baby of the family, I always slept on the bottom bunk and every time the person above me moved, a shower of rust fell into my eyes which made me cry.

My mother and older brother sat with us in the shelter. My father was out on his Home Guard* duties. There was a paraffin* heater and they played cards by candlelight and made cocoa. I still remember the way the candlelight touched their features. Like a painting. The atmosphere was quite cosy. We never felt frightened and once we got into the shelter we felt quite safe. I always look back on the shelter as kind of a happy memory. There was discomfort and cold sometimes, but not that much fear. A feeling of safety even in the middle of a raid.

Beryl Stephenson   *English   Schoolmistress   Aged 4*

Above: When danger threatened, families fled any way they could by whatever means they could find. These Czech refugees made their way to the Romanian border town of Sighet in a farm cart. Romania, 1939.

Left: A Philippino family flees with its possessions from Cavite, Mindanao, after a bombing raid. Their means of transport is home-made but clearly serviceable. The Philippines, 1941.

My father had an Irish passport. I believe that he may have had an English passport as well but I don't know that for certain. In the 1920s he came to Kobe in order to look after some business interests for a variety of European companies. He had learned Japanese from a Jesuit, and married a Japanese girl who, unusually, was a Catholic. I was born in 1931.

By 1939 many of the Europeans had left Kobe, (which had an historic foreign quarter where we all were supposed to live), because the Japanese were conducting a vicious war in China and confronting British, American, and Russian interests there. As Ireland was neutral, father thought that he could gain an advantage by caretaking any European interests.

My earliest clear memories were of a very polite Japanese officer, no more than twenty years old, who used to come to the house once a day, with copies of foreign newspapers and telegrams, and ask my father to translate them. Father did not master all the complexities of the Japanese alphabets, so he enlisted Mummy's help. They would work together all day, while the officer would take me for a walk, and talk to me in Japanese.

I was not allowed to speak to other Japanese children, as many foreign children had been bullied in Japanese schools for "not accepting Japanese thought." I was not afraid of the Japanese children, I felt sorry for them. All of them were in uniforms, meekly trotting in large groups from one place to another. Most of them looked underfed. The teachers were mostly young women or old men, many of whom looked ill themselves. If a party of soldiers was walking along, the children were shooed out of the way by the teachers, who seemed to be frightened of any military uniforms.

One day the young officer came to our house. He was very red, which usually meant that he had been drinking. He kept shouting that Japan had attacked America, and that this would mean victory for the Asiatic peoples. He then did a funny thing. He knelt down in front of my father and burst into tears.

Francis O'Brien   *Irish /Japanese   Diplomat   Aged 10*

Officially neutral at first, America entered the war after the attack on Pearl Harbor on 7th December 1941. Most American children on the mainland heard the news on the radio and have never forgotten the impact it made on them. Redding, California, 8th December 1941.

During 1940 President Roosevelt ran for a third term and his Republican challenger, Wendell Willkie, mounted a strong challenge. At one point during the campaign, FDR said, "Mothers and fathers of America, I assure you again and again, your sons will not fight on foreign shores." My father, who was a staunch Republican, often quoted this speech in the years afterward as an example of FDR's hypocrisy. He believed that FDR secretly wanted to maneuver the country into war. When FDR entered into a lend-lease agreement to allow England to use forty US destroyers and later imposed an oil embargo on Japan, my father believed his suspicions were confirmed.

On 7th December 1941, when I was eleven years old, I came into the dining room and saw my two older brothers, Richard and Allan, and my parents gathered around the radio.

Allan said, "The Japs are bombing Pearl Harbor." I remember my shock and dismay that something like that could happen to the country.

The next day, FDR gave his "Day of Infamy" speech, condemning the "dastardly attack" of the Japanese, and requesting Congress to declare war against the Japanese. Once war was declared, my father ceased to criticize FDR and we all put our minds on winning the war.

Gil Upton   *American   Lawyer   Aged 11*

[Eighteen miles away, Mr Upton's future wife heard the same broadcast in another rock-ribbed New England Republican home].

Grandmother hated FDR. Her hero was Republican candidate Wendell Wilkie. A picture of Wendell Wilkie hung in her bedroom along with an American flag. In her window was a small flag with a blue star (for Uncle Arthur, an Air Force officer stationed in England). Grandmother was intensely patriotic and wrote campaign songs for every Republican candidate who ran against FDR. [Sings] "Wilkie crusader / Wilkie the brave / Spirit of the land / That the Founding Fathers gave / We'll back him loyally / Wilkie is the spirit of democracy."

Grandmother's singing while accompanying herself on the piano rang through the house, imbuing us all with the "spirit of democracy" both during the 1940 election and throughout the war years that followed.

One day, about a year after FDR had (despite grandmother's songs) been re-elected, she and I were playing the piano when my father called in from the living room asking us to "Quiet down. I can't hear the radio."

When we continued to play, he shouted, "Stop playing. We are going to war. I want to hear this." It turned out to be Franklin Roosevelt addressing Congress.

I was terrified and began to cry. "Are we going to be bombed?"

"No," he said as I crawled into his lap. "The fighting will be far away, on the other side of the ocean." From the comfort of his lap, I felt a great relief.

Penelope Upton   *American   Psychotherapist   Aged 10*

We lived on Alewa Heights, which commanded an unparalleled view of Pearl Harbor. I remember getting up well before my parents one morning, as six-year-olds love to do, and hearing loud explosions. A Lieutenant (j.g.) John York, assigned to the battleship USS Nevada, *was spending a weekend furlough with my family. John also was up at an early hour, and the two of us ran to an upstairs balcony where the viewing was best. By that time my mother was up, and in response to her concerns, Lt York assured us that the military was only conducting "maneuvers." The activity seemed too realistic, however, to be merely practice, and it wasn't long before everyone realized that Pearl Harbor was being attacked. I remember great fireballs and plumes of black smoke, and soon the picture was so chaotic that, from our vantage point, Pearl Harbor was almost obscured.*

Later, on 7th December 1941, I learned that my father had gone to play golf on the windward side of the island, leaving even before I was stirring. When they were playing the fourth hole, Japanese warplanes swept over at treetop level. It was then that the golfers realized that something extraordinary was happening as they dove for cover. Between nines, they heard over the clubhouse radio that Oahu had been attacked by the Imperial Japanese Navy. The radio report also mentioned that all roads on the island had been closed. So what else was there to do but go out and play another nine?

Bob McCorriston   *American   Retired Personnel Executive Aged 7*

"WHY ARE THERE MANEUVERS ON SUNDAY?"

At dawn on Friday, 5th December 1941, I crept into my parents' dressing room in our home in a valley above Honolulu. At 5$^{1}/_{2}$, I was a typically curious child, and I do not now remember what I had in mind, but climbed up on the dresser. Boldness then gave way to panic and I tumbled to the floor. A rigid ceramic ornament also fell, shattered, and cut into my stomach just above the navel. The commotion aroused my mother, who was stunned when confronted with the bleeding chaos. I was immediately hustled next door to the home of Dr Ralph Cloward, a young but already prominent neurosurgeon. We sped to a hospital downtown and into an operation room where Dr Cloward meticulously sutured the gash after partially drugging me.

This trauma remains vividly in memory, but was severely overshadowed by events two days and two hours later. I was in bed, still in some pain, when I heard my father shouting, "Why are there maneuvers on Sunday? Look at all the planes!" Then he was interrupted by the dull thumps of the bombs dropping on the United States Pacific Fleet, about twelve miles away. Somehow I made my way downstairs and out onto the driveway. My two older sisters were looking at the sky, pointing and talking excitedly. Several planes from the east flew over us, their round orange insignia clearly visible. I cannot measure how long it was between that sight and a gigantic explosion followed by tremors similar to those of an earthquake. We learned much later that the blast was the result of a bomb dropping into the smokestack of the destroyer *USS Shaw* and detonating in the engine room in the bowels of the ship.

Cellars were, and are, few and far between in Hawaiian houses, but my father was originally from New York, and had installed one in ours. He shooed the rest of us – mother, grandmother, sisters, me – down into it. A radio was with us, and a nervous announcer was shrieking confirmation of the attack. As a combat veteran of World War I, my father said he had to try "to help" and rashly jumped into the car and headed toward the harbor. He was back within twenty minutes; a defective anti-aircraft shell had plunged into the street and exploded 100 yards ahead of him so he turned around.

By this time, the Japanese had completed their second and final wave of attack and were returning to the carriers, but we obviously did not know that, so huddled in the cellar for most of the rest of the morning. At around noon, a half-dozen cars appeared in the neighborhood, carrying people fleeing Hickam Field, the air base adjacent to Pearl Harbor.

The evacuees stayed for the rest of the afternoon. Their comments, and what other limited communication existed, led to speculation and rumours of all kinds. The Japanese had landed. No, they had not landed. Would there be another attack? Maybe they would invade less-defended neighbour islands first. And so on.

The "Day of Infamy" was over, but the war had begun for us. It remains, quite simply, the singular event and most important influence in my life of fifty-nine years.

Paul Wysard   *American   Retired school administrator; part-time teacher and writer   Aged 5$^{1}/_{2}$*

Bare feet and wooden rifles do not dim the patriotism of these young Hawaiian Islanders when their homes are threatened. As the sharpness of their formation suggests, they were drilled and trained by local Coast Artillery soldiers. Despite official fears, every group in Hawaii's rich racial melting pot shouldered its fair share of the war's burdens and responded patriotically to their country's needs. Oahu, Hawaii, 1941.

The attack on Pearl Harbor began one Sunday before Sunday School. We children were herded into a concrete garage across the street, while the adults stood out on the lawn watching the action. I felt cheated that I didn't get to watch any of the aerial dogfights but, more importantly, at least I got to skip Sunday School!

Nearly all my friends in school were either of Japanese or Chinese descent. We all equally hated "the Japs" and responded the same way as other American children to the propaganda about Tojo, Hirohito, Mussolini, and Hitler.

Chiang Kai-Shek* was regarded as somewhat of a hero in our house. Only when I was in college did I find out that the father of one of my Japanese friends had been placed in a relocation camp.

Duane Yee *Hawaiian-American of Chinese descent School Principal Aged 6*

My first recollection of the Japanese attack on Pearl Harbor was awakening early Sunday morning to find my parents and brother watching explosions in the water around a ship off of Honolulu Harbor. My father commented that they appeared to be awfully close for what we believed to be military practice. We soon learned from a friend listening to the radio that this was not a practice exercise and that we were under attack. Soon thereafter, we saw Japanese Zero* aircraft fly very low up the valley where we lived during the war years. The airplanes were just above the tree tops and we could clearly see the Rising Sun emblems and the faces of the pilots as they flew by. My brother ran and got his .22 caliber rifle and started shooting at the Japanese aircraft. This made me nervous, as I thought that it might make the pilots turn around and strafe or bomb our house. Apparently his aim was not good, as no aircraft turned around. They were headed for Kaneohe Naval Air Station on the north side of Oahu.

The day of the attack was frightening, as among other things going on, shells were whizzing around the valley and exploding on impact instead of in the air, apparently from the failure to set the fuses to explode at a certain altitude. My best friend's neighbor, a Mrs White, was killed by one of these shells approximately one mile away from our house. That night, and those to follow, were scary without lights and the rumors going around about an imminent invasion.

Robert M Chapman *American Businessman Aged 10*

On 7th December 1941, I was living with my mother, step-father and two older brothers (ten and thirteen) at the Kaneohe Naval Air Base. My two brothers and I had just stepped out the door to go to church when the first wave of Japanese planes flew over our heads. As I looked up, I was able to make eye contact with one of the pilots. In a matter of seconds, the air field had been bombed and strafed. It was total chaos! I have often wondered if that pilot would have tried to kill us children had his mission not been to attack the ships and planes.

My father left for the airfield immediately and we ran indoors and hid under the stairwell. Later that evening, my step-father returned home covered with blood from casualties and had my mother soak all of his white uniforms in vats of coffee so they would act as camouflage.

Loretta Hoapili Arnold   *American   Office Supervisor   Age 9*

My first real memory of the war was on a Sunday outing to a lake some miles from our Massachusetts home. I was very sad and slightly outraged when Mum told the three of us children that this would be our last trip to the lake. She explained, of course, that gas was to be rationed and we would not have enough coupons to make the trip until war's end.

Joan Perry Morris   *American   Administrator, Florida Department of State   Aged 6-10*

My family had a very strict routine that we followed every Sunday. First, church, where my father sang in the choir. Then, home, and a large Sunday dinner. On this particular Sunday I was sitting in the living room, still in my church clothes, listening to the radio when it was announced that Pearl Harbor had been attacked.

I went running into the other room and blurted out the news. Someone, it may have been my mother, (whose flare for the dramatic was always better than her geography), replied, "If they keep coming, they'll be here [northern New England] in twenty-four hours."

I immediately burst into tears.

Malcolm Swenson   *American   President, Swenson Stone Consultants   Aged 4*

One of my most vivid childhood memories was of the day Pearl Harbor was bombed. After church, we went down to the little town of Wilson in Lynn County [Texas], to my grandfather's farm. It was off a dirt lane that led to an unpaved country road, and produced fine cotton during the

rainy years of the early 1940s. Yet Sunday, 7th December, was a clear sunny day like those you often get in that country in early winter. Just after the noontime dinner, I was out in a little lane between the fields, rolling an old metal cultivator wheel for the hell of it, when my mother came to the front door of the farm house and hollered for me to come inside. There, everyone was sitting around the wind-charged battery radio (a tall console affair), listening to news of how the Japanese had attacked our fleet at Pearl Harbor, Hawaii.

Grandpa said, "If they are in Pearl Harbor, it may not be long until they get to California!"

My auntie replied, "No. . . they won't come to this country. We have never been invaded."

To which Grandpa said, "Oh, yes, indeed we have been invaded! Pa told me time and again how he hid under the bed when the Yankees invaded us back in 1865. It could happen all over again."

After the news broadcast, my mother told me to play quietly and not go far from the house, for to do otherwise would be disrespectful. 'Funeral behavior' was called for during the remainder of what had begun for me, as a pleasant day on Grandpa's farm.

Lee Johnson   *American   Archaeologist   Born 1936*

We lived in Hawaii on a sugar plantation in a house that was elevated off the ground to prevent flood damage. But one particular Sunday in December there was a drainage problem, and I was under the house, playing with little boats and helping fight the water at the same time. Suddenly, my brother appeared and said that we were at war with Japan.

One of the first American victims of the war was this young child. He was killed on Pearl Harbor Day, not by Japanese bombs and bullets, but by the motor car in the background. Its frantic driver had fled in a panic from the raid. Hawaii, 1941.

My father was *issei* – first generation of American-born Japanese. There were Japanese flags in our house and in friends' houses, but these were quickly hidden or burned over the next few weeks. The supply of sake [rice wine], which came from Japan, was cut off so for the first time people started making it in Hawaii. The principal of the Japanese language and cultural school nearby was sent to an internment camp in California, despite the fact two of his sons were casualties in the US Army and stars hung in the windows of his house as they did in the windows of all Americans who served.

Norman Hondo   *American   Country Club Manager   Aged 11*

Seven o'clock Mass was dragging on for me on 7th December 1941. The church was especially cold and the short pants my mother made me wear did not help. My mind usually wandered in church and that Sunday I was staring out the window, preoccupied with the hundreds of little black puffs that suddenly appeared in the early morning sky. Where were they coming from? The mystery was soon solved when we returned home and the radio was turned on. The radio announcer kept repeating "This is the Real McCoy – the Japanese are bombing Pearl Harbor." The puffs were our anti-aircraft shells bursting.

Douglas Philpotts   *American   Retired Financial Executive   Aged 10*

I really didn't know what I was in hospital for, but at seven years of age I was more concerned about missing school and the chance to play with my classmates than about the reason for my hospital stay.

The nurse came in just before six o'clock. "Time to wake up," she said as she drew open the curtain and let the winter sun into my my hospital room. Usually she would turn on the radio and say, "Let's have some happy music," or some other cheerful thing, but that day she said, "I think you should listen to the six o'clock news this morning. Your mother would want you to do that, I'm sure."

She tuned in the solemn voice of a newscaster. Young as I was, I knew his ominous tone was one reserved for only the most grave occasions. Perhaps because of it, I never forgot his exact words: "Announcement by the Imperial Supreme Headquarters: early dawn today, the eighth,[†] the Imperial Army and Navy fell into a state of combat on the southern Pacific Ocean with the nations of Great Britain and the United States of America."

Mamoru Mitsui   *Born Japanese, naturalized citizen of the United States of America   Architect   Age 7*

†[Because of the difference in time zones, the Japanese learned of the attack on Pearl Harbour on 8th December 1941].

Japanese-American mother and child on their way to a "relocation" camp. Hawaii remained integrated throughout the war. On the US mainland, tens of thousands of Japanese-Americans were interned. USA. March, 1942.

THE WAR IN TURKEY, TEXAS

My name is Curtis Dale Tunnell. I was born in Turkey, Texas on 24th January 1934, during the Great Depression. My father, Curtis Oliver Tunnell, ran a service station on the main street in Turkey. The station was called the "Downtown Station," and sold Texaco products. During the war years, I worked at the station every afternoon after school and all day Saturday. In the summer months, I worked full time.

I did a variety of jobs around the station, from cleaning out the grease pit to hand-pumping gas up into the old glass-globe gas pumps. But my primary job was fixing flat tires.

Every afternoon after school when I arrived at the station, there would be a tall stack of "flats" to be fixed. In those days, we fixed them by hand with tire-irons and a hammer. Rubber tires and tubes were strictly rationed during the war, and everyone had a hard time getting them. As the war went on and on, I had more and more flats to fix. Often I would take an old red-rubber inner tube out of a tire and it would have sixty or seventy rubber patches on it. I was putting patches over patches, and trying to make them hold air pressure. We used Schaler hot-patches to repair the thorn and nail holes. These consisted of a soft rubber patch attached to a metal pan filled with a combustible material. After clamping the patch against the tube, I would light the combustible material and it burned with a hot flame, producing a cloud of acrid smoke. After a while I learned to like the smell of the smoke. After peeling the metal pan off the tube, the rubber patch was welded into place. Sometimes I got to know "old friends," and would recognize the same old tube coming in week after week for repair of another leak.

Tires were another matter. People wore them completely out and then continued to use them. Often the tires had two or three oval spots which were worn through the layers of cords. In the center of these spots would be holes as big as your fingernail with the tube showing through. I would use a heavy rubber "boot" as big as a pot lid, and glue it inside the tire over the hole, after scarifying the rubber. I also grew quite fond of the smell of rubber cement.

An even bigger problem were the large tires off of farm tractors. Farmers often filled these with water to give more traction to the tractor, and they weighed hundreds of pounds. I had to get all the water out of them, through the little valve stem, before I could handle them and make repairs. This was cotton country and cotton was needed for the War Effort, so lots of tractor flats were brought into the station.

I would often work until 10:00 o'clock at night in order to finish all the flats brought in during the day. After handling all those dirty tires and tubes, I would be about the same color as them. Although I pulled cotton, collected scrap iron, flattened tin cans, and collected grease to help the War Effort, my primary contribution was fixing thousands of flats, and helping people milk a few more miles from their old tires and tubes.

Curtis Tunnell   *American   Executive Director, Texas Historical Commission   Aged 7-12*

Pictures: The "Downtown Station" in Turkey, Texas during the war. Note the old glass-globe pumps. Curtis Tunnell's father stands on the right of this picture; Curtis Tunnell (*insert*, with his dog, Snow White) was in school when the main photograph was taken.

A rehearsal for evacuation. William, Margaret, John, and

Eileen Brown arrive for a practice evacuation at Compton

Road School, Clerkenwell, with knapsacks made by their

father. A few days later, their practice became the real thing.

London, 28th August 1939.

When I was a girl we lived in a house right on the edge of the Yorkshire moors. The powers-that-be decided this would be a good place for a parachute invasion so they showed all the local people what to do. You know, how to fight back.

I know this sounds crazy, but apparently the first thing paratroopers want to do after they land is to use the toilet. Being Germans, and orderly about such things, the authorities assumed they'd head straight for the nearest house and crowd three or four into the toilet. So we were shown how to put a bomb in the cistern which would explode when they pulled the chain.

The other thing was, if the Germans had tanks, we children were supposed to spread out dinner plates on the road, face down. The Germans would see the dinner plates, think they were mines, get out to inspect them, and then be shot by the adults. That was the theory at least. I don't care how daft all this sounds. I promise you it's true.

Valerie Brooke-White   *English   Radio New Zealand*
Aged 6   (Emigrated to New Zealand in 1966)

I grew up in Kedah, a small village about 100 kilometers from Penang in Malaya. It was a farming village, growing mainly rice, and we were very poor. In our culture, when you are poor and there isn't enough food to go around, male children are given a larger share of meat or whatever else there is. Male children were considered more important than females and this always made me angry even as a very little girl.

One day, Japanese soldiers came to our village. One of the soldiers entered our house and put his helmet on the table while he looked around. He didn't speak Chinese. He just went through our house helping himself to whatever he wanted, particularly food. This made me very angry. Maybe it had to do with my brother always getting the meat. It was bad enough that my brother got a bigger share. It didn't seem fair that a stranger should get it too.

Anyway, when no one was looking, I stole the soldier's helmet, ran out to the chicken house, and hid it under sacks and piles of rubble. The soldier was angry. He shouted at us. The soldiers searched our village but they never found the helmet. The chicken house was very smelly and they didn't even go near it.

After they had gone, I told my father what I had done and showed him the helmet. He was very angry. "You are dangerous," he said. "You will get us killed. They will shoot you. They will shoot us. You have to go away."

I never saw the helmet or my village again. The next day my father sent me to live with my sister in Penang and that is where I spent the rest of the war. We didn't get meat

very often in Penang but, when we did, my sister shared it equally with me.

Lena Tang   *Malaysian Chinese   Copy Shop proprietor   Aged 5*

Berlin wasn't really a Nazi city in the same way that Nuremburg was. Many people talked about Socialism, and were critical of Hitler, but only among friends. It didn't pay to have critical conversations overheard.

After one of the early air raids, some Luftwaffe officers came to see the damage with Reichsmarschall Hermann Goering who turned up a little later in a big white Mercedes. He was wearing a white uniform, and was beaming away at the small crowd which had gathered round a pair of junior Luftwaffe officers. He stopped smiling when he heard that the people were complaining to them about the air raids.

One old woman shouted, "That fat fool Goering said we could call him 'Meyer' [used by Goering as a generic Jewish name in an ill-considered boast] if one enemy bomb fell on the Reich. He is worse than a 'Meyer.' Even Jews could do a better job!"

Goering looked shocked. I'll never forget his face. He was only a couple of meters from me. His aides turned him round and shoved him back into the Mercedes. They drove off at high speed. I think they were afraid that he would be attacked.

Wilhelm Schultzki   *German   Night Watchman   Aged 10*

A bomb in the back garden of our suburban London home prompted my dispatch, as an eight year old, to live with my grandparents in Wales.

They were pillars of the Baptist church in Llandrindod Wells, and almost as soon as I arrived I was scrubbed and polished and taken to the Sunday evening service.

That evening I saw the first black people I had ever laid eyes on. Several rows of them, sitting behind the minister, eyes and teeth sparkling from the gloom and mahogany. They were GI's, the Baptist choir from the American army camp that had been established down the road at Builth Wells.

The congregation at our chapel regularly sang their hymns with all the serious fervour that the Welsh can manage. But those Negro Spirituals (as we called them then) were something else! This was godliness with a rhythmic beat, devotion with a smile. Our minister's usual preoccupations were fear of the devil, hellfire, and damnation. Those black men syncopated a message of joy. Heaven was as likely a possibility as hell. God could even be

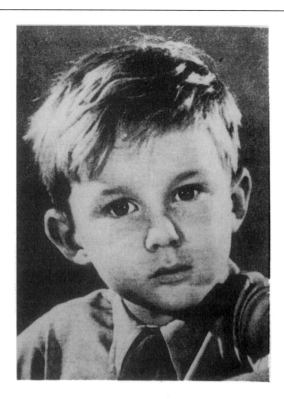

" Johnnie was questioned on his way home from school "

A little chill of fear runs through the family, a sudden stillness falls upon the tea-table.

What might the little chap have said that could be twisted ? What exactly was he asked ? . . .

Don't keep saying it couldn't happen here ! It happened last week to the little son of that nice restaurant proprietor in Brussels, it will happen to-morrow to the daughter of that jolly old fisherman at St. Malo. (And the next night Daddy doesn't come home from work.)

It will happen here—if you let it.

Put up your barrier now ; a barrier of shot and shell, plane and tank, for which the eager hands reach out. Pile in your money with both hands for the one thing that matters — security.

What else can you use your money for that is one half so precious as the freedom to love and laugh and grouse out loud, as your father did before you ?

   ★   ★   ★

Put every penny you can scrape together into--War Savings !

Issued by the National Savings Committee

The innocence and vulnerability of children was exploited by all nations. This British National Savings Committee Advertisement appeared in *Illustrated* magazine on 25th April 1942.

gently teased – in four-four time.

That night, the GI choir came home with us to supper. I was later to learn that the chapel elders were shocked at this. At the long pine kitchen table we ate pigeons and wild duck shot by my grandfather and baked in clay parcels in the embers of the kitchen range. And afterwards they sang again, foot tapping on a slate kitchen floor as black and shiny as they were. It was a night to remember.

Bruce Marshall *British Publisher Aged 8*

I lived most of the war in Wales. There was an American base nearby and all the children in town used to chase after them shouting, "Got any gum, chum? Got any gum?" I can still remember the GIs laughing and smiling and throwing us gum from the backs of their lorries [trucks]. Years later I was talking with a friend who grew up on the south coast, near Portsmouth. He told me he used to shout the same thing to the Yanks. "Got any gum, chum?"

J L Jones *Welsh Miner Aged 10*

A boy waves Polish and British flags. His hat carries the plaintive street cry of British children throughout the war: "Got any gum, chum?" England.

I was born 5th April 1939 in Asia, Texas. My father was Edwin Read (a fourth-generation Texan), and my mother was Pearly Krzywonski (daughter of Polish immigrants).

The very day that Pearl Harbor was bombed, my dad's leg was amputated. He had a type of bone cancer that then had a survival rate of about two percent, and he was given less than five years to live. So, we moved from east Texas back to Lockhart to be close to my mother's family. About a year after the United States entered the war, my dad was *able to function on crutches, and he went to work at a small air base, doing aircraft engine repair, and he continued to work on the line until the end of the war. He had worked on every kind of engine there was, from cars to railroad engines, and he had an absolute genius for it.*

At one time during the war, I remember he had worked so many consecutive shifts that he developed a serious insomnia problem, and he had to get medication from the doctor in order to be able to fall asleep. And once, he was working with a crew on an airplane that caught fire. The guys ran off in all directions and when they gathered their wits they looked around for their "handicapped" co-worker. My dad said he was at least fifty meters farther away than them, because he had left his crutches on the plane and hopped on one leg – and outran them all! I guess the point of this story is the courage of my dad, who, living with the expectation of imminent death and walking on one leg, still felt that he should contribute whatever he could to the War Effort. And he did it without ever complaining, then or later. I think he, and other civilians like him, contributed as much to the War Effort as anyone. And there were no veterans benefits for them, no memorials. After the war, no one would hire my dad to do aircraft engine repair because they said it was too dangerous for a handicapped person to do that work while on crutches. My dad, who was stubborn enough to carry tools and engine parts around while he walked on crutches, was also stubborn enough to live to the age of eighty.

Helen Simmons *American Editor Aged 5*

In Germany, teenage boys joined the Hitler Youth. Heini Volker, above, was voted the most popular boy in Germany after appearing in a propaganda film, "Hitlerjunge Quex".

I must have been an extremely impudent child, because my parents kept warning me that my cheek would get me in big trouble some day. As it was, in one tremendously important instance, it did exactly the opposite. My mother was a Jew and my father a Roman Catholic, but religion never was an issue in our family and it therefore came as a surprise when my mother decided to enrol me at the age of seven in school classes on Judaism. She probably just didn't want me to roam about the school garden while other children attended lessons of their respective religions, which is why I resented the idea from scratch.

On my first – and incidentally also last – day of religious education a stern looking, elderly man (probably a rabbi) told me where to sit and took no further notice of my existence. He did, however, when he heard my exclamation of "Jesus and Maria!" at something which had surprised me. Both in Czech and in German this was an idiomatic expression of astonishment, nothing to do with religion or so I thought until he started to teach me otherwise. When he ranted on and on how I could and why I shouldn't, I interjected that he could hardly expect me to exclaim

"Moses and Maria!" He ordered me out and out I went in a huff. At home my parents thought it might be better not to send me back.

When two years later Nazi Germany invaded former Czechoslovakia, the infamous Nuremberg racial law came into force in our country too. And according to these every person with two Jewish grandparents (whom I had) but not practising Judaism was categorized as "first-class mongrel" (Mischling erster Klasse was the German expression). Attending religious lessons was considered practising and in such a case the person was considered to be a Jew. The difference between the fates of Jewish and half-Jewish children was tremendous and often it literally was the difference between life and death. However serious the question was, our family often joked about the "chutzpah" (which is the Yiddish word for impudence) big enough to turn a Jew into a mongrel. Because according to religious laws every child of a Jewish mother is considered a Jew, anyway.

Hana Rehakova *Czech Administrator Aged 9*

THE LOSS OF TATIANA

W*E LIVED AT A STRANGE LOCATION. The borders between Russia, Ukraine, and Poland were somewhere in the neighborhood, but there was little agreement as to where they were. My parents had a farm, and a few tenants, clustered around. The place looked more like a fort surrounded by marshes, scrubby trees, and low lying fields. Nobody knew their way around except us, which is perhaps why we were left alone until late 1939.*

We had heard on the radio that the Germans had attacked Poland. Everyone became very worried, as we all thought that the Russians would join in. News was strictly censored at that time, so we had to guess at the real meaning. The English call it "reading between the lines."

I do not remember the exact date, but one morning a local peasant who cut reeds came running in. He told my father that we all must hide, as he had seen some Russian soldiers looking for a crossing point over one of the many slow rivers.

Mama said that all the menfolk must hide, but she and the old women would look after the farm until we could return. There were no young women of marriageable age, and at twelve, we all thought that my sister Tatiana would be safe. My parent's generation remembered all the atrocities of the 1921 Russo-Polish war.

Papa was very worried, saying that the Russians might set fire to the farm, but Mama said that they might steal some pigs, but we all spoke Russian, so there shouldn't be a problem.

We took some sausage and dried hams with us, and followed the peasant. There was my father, two young laborers, an older farm hand, his wife, and ten year old son. They had left their three younger children with my mother, as we thought that living off the land would be too dangerous for small children.

Fortunately the weather was dry and still warm. We went deep into the reedy marshes. The mosquitoes and midges swarmed all over us, and soon my face was raw and painful. It was even worse for the younger boy. He must have tasted very sweet to those insects.

We spent the night in a small hut perched on stilts above the water. Our clothing and packs were wet through. I couldn't sleep as all through the night millions of frogs kept croaking, shrieking, whistling, and murmuring. The sound was deafening. Nobody could understand what it was like until they had experienced it for themselves. The insects kept on biting us as well!

The next morning was very misty. Standing on the platform outside the hut, my head and shoulders were in sunshine, but my back and legs were quite cold and damp, in a pool of low lying fog. As the sun climbed higher the mist began to rise forming thin low clouds that began to disperse as they rose. It was like being in a cold steam bath.

We all were wondering what to do next, when we heard a low rumbling noise in the east. We had only ever seen about half a dozen airplanes in the whole of our lives. This noise was being made by hundreds! They took ages before we could see them. They looked like masses of black dots high up in the sky moving very slowly. Nobody knew if they could see us, or whether they would attack. They just kept rumbling on. The air itself seemed to vibrate. It took well over half an hour for them to pass overhead, and disappear in the direction of Poland.

There was some argument as to whether it was safe to stay where we were. The peasant said that there was nowhere else to go to. Papa was very unhappy about the younger boy whose face was very puffed up. His lips were swollen and split, and it looked as if he had a temperature. We had to drink the water, which tasted all right, but we should have boiled it. Everyone was afraid to light a fire in case the smoke was seen by the Russians. By the next evening I was feeling very ill, and had bad diarrhoea. I had to wade some distance from the hut, to find some reeds to use as a bathroom. Soon everyone was wandering off to find private clumps of reeds. Only the peasant seemed to be unaffected.

Poland, near the border with Russia and the Ukraine. Two Polish refugee children, adrift on the tides of war, seek to solace each other. Poland, 1941.

After another terrible night, it was agreed that the peasant would sneak back to the farm and see if the coast was clear. He left in the early morning while it was still misty. All through that day the young boy became more and more ill. His mother was crying, and his father kept straining water through a cloth into a tin mug for the boy. I felt so weak, that I couldn't face the thought of going back to my own reedy "bathroom." My father had to carry me at least four times. I could not face any food.

The peasant came back shortly after sundown. He was punting a long flat-bottomed boat, with some bales of reeds in it. He looked very upset. He told us that the coast was clear, but there was nobody around. He had waited for a couple of hours then left without seeing anybody. There were no dead bodies, so he thought that the Russians hadn't shot anyone. We all made ourselves as comfortable as possible in the boat, and the peasant punted off. I don't know how he found his way back. There was no moon or stars, and the frogs were once again deafening. It started to rain lightly which gave us a little relief from the insects. I think it was about midnight when we got back.

There were no lights to be seen, and there was no sound of any animals. Papa called out for Mama and Tatiana. Suddenly my mother was there. When she saw my father she started to cry.

"We thought you were Russians coming back!"

Tatiana was not there. When we got into the kitchen, my mother closed all the shutters then lit an oil lamp. Other people, some of whom we did not know, started coming into the kitchen from other parts of the house. We later learned that most of them had been fleeing the Germans, then found the Russians firing at them. There were no wounded, they had either died soon after being hit, or were too ill to be moved. One said that the Russians were using "dum-dum" bullets which splintered when they hit you. He told me that once you were hit, you were as good as dead, as you quickly caught gangrene!

I kept asking what happened to Tatiana, but my mother just burst into tears. Much later I learned that the Russians had turned up at the farm demanding a guide through the marshes. They had chosen my sister. Mama had dressed her up in her finest Sunday clothes, and pretty headdress, thinking that if she looked sweet and appealing that the soldiers would treat her well. She did not see her again. Some of the other refugees had found a young girl about an hour's walk away later in the day, stripped and bayonetted to a barn door. My mother had gone with the old people to find the body. They found instead a little mound of earth with a rough cross on it, and hanging from the cross was Tatiana's bonnet. She had no idea who had dug the grave.

"I don't even know if she had been violated!" My mother kept sobbing this for the next couple of days. My father looked very old all of a sudden.

Alek Smirnow-Wisniak   *Polish   Engineer   Aged 10*

MAN WIRD DOCH DER GESTAPO ERKLÄREN KÖNNEN. . .

"I wept and sulked, both of which show in the passport photograph taken for the occasion." Hana Rehakova's unused passport. Before she could leave the country, Czechoslovakia had been invaded.

To stay or to go – that was the question for all Jewish or part-Jewish families we knew between 1935, the year of the Nuremberg racial laws, and 1939, the year when German armies marched into Czechoslovakia. "All we have is here" was the argument for staying; "children must be brought to safety" the main one against. One solution seemed to answer both: the offer to ship off Jewish or part-Jewish children to England, organized I do not remember by whom, but it was the one our parents chose for me and my sister. She was twelve at the time and I was eight. To leave everyone and everything we loved in exchange for hypothetical safety seemed a lousy bargain. I wept and sulked, which both show in the passport photograph taken for the occasion. I still have the passport, pristine and never used, because – bearing the date 17th April 1939 – it came much too late. The Germans marched into Prague on May the 15th of the same year. The reason why I kept my passport was probably the fact that my next one was issued a full twenty-nine years later, the Communists being as stingy with passports when they came to power, as the Nazis had been.

Back in 1939, I was happy that the plan did not come off. Since we were fortunate enough to survive the war, I may have been right in refusing to leave. But so many others weren't! Friends of my parents – a nice, elderly, childless couple we have always remembered, were among them. He was a retired doctor and the pride and love of his old age was a beautiful library, which took up the major part of their flat in Prague's Old Town Square. He couldn't bring himself to leave it. His wife loved and understood him. Once, while rolling out the pastry for one of her famous strudels, she clinched the final discussion on emigration and said, "Man wird doch der Gestapo erklären können. . ." which means that, "After all, it would always be possible to explain to the Gestapo that. . ." (I don't know what).

Of course, at the time people already knew about anti-Jewish terror in Germany, knew about books being burned. The sentence was so pathetically naive that it later became a grim joke in our family. They were both deported soon after the first transports of Jews started leaving Prague for concentration camps. On the day they said goodbye, he told my mother, "If we survive this, I am going to tear page after page out of every book as I will read it. Because I never, ever want a library again." But they never came back.

Hana Rehakova *Czech Administrator Aged 9*

Sünching, the Schloss,* is a very large octagonal mansion in Bavaria, belonging to my maternal grandmother, who during the war took in all the many relatives and friends who fled Eastern Europe, including us. We learned later that the Schloss had been a valuable landmark for the Allies on their bombing raids of Dresden and other German cities on account of its peculiar shape, like a giant Kugelhupf, [doughnut] which was clearly visible from the air.

On 28th April 1945, the Americans marched into the Schloss to occupy it. It was a cold, snowy day, and I remember the soldiers entering our bedroom, where the youngest of us were having our afternoon sleep. The blankets were pulled off us, and we had to hurriedly dress to leave the Schloss. Imagine the soldiers' surprise and merriment when several little children leapt out of cots and beds and stood there in Swastika nighties! My grandmother had refused to fly the regulation Swastika flag on the Schloss flagpole, and being a resourceful woman had had the flags converted into nighties and handkerchiefs. The hankies were very coarse and hurt our noses.

I remember our walk from the Schloss into the village. My Tante [Governess] had to be conveyed by wagon, as she was seriously ill with a blood disorder called "erysipelas." We were taken in by various villagers, my family being housed in the barn of the local baker. At one point a large tank came into the baker's yard and friendly American soldiers handed us chocolate bars. I recall that I believed all soldiers to be enemies and refused to take a chocolate.

The Americans only occupied the Schloss for three days, then they went away to free the concentration camps in Theresienstadt. But then they came back to stay for another three months. Their Headquarters was in Regensburg.

Some of my brothers and sisters and I sneaked back up to the Schloss occasionally and watched the American soldiers emptying what looked like delicious cakes – and other food delicacies we had forgotten existed – into large tin drums in the courtyard.

Another time my older sister dared us to walk through the Schloss. You could enter through one large door, walk through the courtyard and out the front entrance. As we did this, a soldier happened by. I do not know whether he was joking but he pointed a gun at us and told us to "Scat!" or he would shoot us. We were totally petrified, and my sister urged us not to run, but to walk away slowly otherwise, she warned, he was bound to shoot. It seemed to take an eternity to walk slowly and reach the garden gate with a gun pointing at our backs. The incident still makes me shiver today.

I remember an American General taking a liking to me. I was told that I reminded him of his daughter back home, who was of a similar age, with similar curly hair like mine. He would send me food parcels, and one came with a wonderfully colorful clown, which I treasured for many years. I do not recall the general's face, as I only came up to his knees and being very shy I only looked at his knees. But I later heard that it was General Patton.

Countess Hanna Jankovich-Besan *Hungarian Therapist Aged 4*

Above: Hanna Jankovich-Besan, at age 4; just tall enough to reach General Patton's knees.
Right: Hanna Jankovich-Besan (in foreground) and her sisters scamper across the bridge over the old moat. In a few short months, an American soldier would order them to "Scat!" across this same bridge, or he would shoot them!

Schloß Sünching.

Top centre: Sünching, the Schloss. The distinctive shape of Sümching Schloss made it a useful landmark for Allied airmen during the war. Rebuilt in 1668 after the original was burnt down during the Thirty Year's War, Sünching is one of the most beautiful castles in Bavaria. *Above:* The Hall of the Schloss. Ceiling paintings by Mathäus Günther.

I grew up on a farm in Karelia near Lake Laatokka, a beautiful area in the east of Finland that borders Russia. In 1939, Russia declared war on Finland and invaded our country. This was the so-called Winter War. Refugees flooded into our area from further east as they fled the advancing Russians.

The snow was heavy that year. Russian airplanes were constantly flying over us so we all wore white sheets on our way to school and if we heard planes we threw ourselves flat on the ground. I was seven and had just started school, but after a short time, the school had to be closed because there were so many refugees crowding into the schoolhouse. They were living there because they had no place else to go. Our parents became concerned as the Russians came nearer. "The day will come when we also have to leave," they said. My mother told us children (I was the eldest of five) to leave our clothes every night on hooks where we could find them easily if we had to leave suddenly. And, of course, we didn't obey.

One evening there was heavy bombing with fires and lights from cannons. The Russians were coming very close and at midnight there was a knock on the door. It was the man in our village appointed to take care of the

Above: "We had. . . to make our escape using horse and sledge." Sirkka-Lüsa Rantanen's family must have looked much like this as they fled westward that fateful winter. The only possesssions they had were those they could carry on the sledge. *Center inset:* "We all wore white sheets on our way to school and if we heard planes we threw ourselves flat on the ground." *Right:* "The roadsides were full of animals which had frozen to death. . . there was a lot of meat to eat." As the Russians invaded Karelia from the east, the Finns fled west. Many tried to take their cattle with them. A winter of minus 30⁰ centigrade proved too severe even for hardy Finnish livestock. Karelia, Finland, 1939.

evacuation. He said my family was to report at once to the school where buses were waiting to take us to the west.

Of course none of us could find our clothes. I had all kinds of shoes including good, warm leather boots but I was so shocked and afraid that I pulled on a pair of rubber boots – in a temperature of minus thirty degrees centigrade. My grandfather was so upset that he put both socks on one foot only and the other foot was bare. The one thing I did remember was my doll, Ritva. Ritva stayed with me all through the war but I don't remember what happened to her after.

When we got to the schoolhouse, there were no buses so we had to return to the farm and make our escape using horse and sledge – in fact, we had two horses and two sledges. Perho was the name of one of our horses but I can't remember the other. We fled westward on the sledges wearing white sheets for camouflage until eventually we found some buses for refugees. My mother and the other children got aboard, but I got sick on buses so I stayed with my father and we set off on a sledge journey of several hundred kilometers.

It was a bitterly cold winter, minus thirty degrees or more, and of course the snow was very heavy. Everywhere in Karelia, the roads were filled with people fleeing. They tried to take their animals with them so all the roadsides were full of animals which had frozen to death or had to be killed

because of the cold. I remember seeing them stacked on top of each other like a woodpile. This meant there was a lot of meat to eat of course so we were not hungry but very cold. The nights of the journey seemed to blur together. One night I remember my father slept on chairs in a minister's house. I slept under the table because otherwise there was not enough room. Another time we slept in a factory. We were one or two weeks on this journey. And there were incidents that stay in my memory like when one family's horse slipped down the hill and the mother got a heart attack from the shock.

Eventually, I was evacuated to the town of Ylitornio in the north of Finland where I was moved onto a farm and where I went back to school. I felt funny at first, like an outsider, but quickly made a friend. I only had one awful coat that I'd managed to take with me and I confessed to my friend that I was afraid that the other children at the school would laugh at my coat. So this girl went to the other pupils and said, "If you laugh at her coat I will hit you!" So they didn't.

And I still had my rubber boots. The wife of the farmer wanted to give me other shoes because it was so cold. "Here," she said to me, "here. You have a nice pair of warm shoes." They were Lappish shoes, made of reindeer skin. They looked so awful that I didn't want to put them on because I thought they would make people laugh at me. But when I went to school, everybody was wearing exactly the same kind of shoes. And my feet were warm!

Later, in 1942, the Finnish Army pushed the Russians out of Karelia and we were able to return to our farm. We have a word in Finnish – "Ryssa." It's not a nice word – an insulting racist word, like you say in English, "Nigger." That is what we called the Russians. Ryssa. When we came back to our farm we found that the Ryssa had destroyed everything. They had kept chickens in our house and there was excrement all over. My uncle had cleaned up a bit so that wasn't so bad. What was worse was that everything had been taken away. Everything. No furniture, nothing. We had lost everything. Every house in the village was like that. Empty. Some of them had been burnt. We never knew if it was the Ryssa who did this or other Finns.

There was no one left in Karelia except women, children, and old men. Grandfather had died some place way up in the north. My family had to work three different farms just to get enough to stay alive. There was never enough food. I had constant nose bleeds. Our bread had bits of husk in it and was not very good. Worse, we had to walk twenty-five kilometers to find yeast. In school, we had no books but our teachers read to us and tried to teach us that way. We had nothing but gradually we began to build a life again.

Sirkka-Liisa Rantanen *Finnish   Aged 7-9*

JOIN BIG BILL CAMPBELL'S WILD WEST CLUB TO-DAY! See Page 13.

Popular entertainers such as Arthur Askey and Tommy Handley did much to maintain the morale of British children – and of British adults. Arthur Askey, among others, was so popular that he had his own comic strip.

[In 1939, June Cross was evacuated to Devon. She returned to London to take up a place in a grammar school in September, 1940].

I was in Devon for eleven months and about two nights before I came home, the Blitz started. We slept in Anderson shelters in the garden. After a few nights, my mother and brother and I went to join a neighbor in their shelter – just for the company.

*There was one-ten-year old boy there of that family. I can't remember his name, but every time a bomb came whistling down and exploded he would say, "Aye **thenk** you!"*

This was a catch phrase of Arthur Askey's.* I can't say

it quite how Arthur Askey used to say it. Every time a bomb went off nearby, maybe ten times an evening, he'd say it. I must have heard him say it hundreds of times: "Aye **thenk** you!"

*We didn't laugh but I think our parents marvelled at the spirit of their children. I don't think we realised even in the middle of a raid that our lives were actually in jeopardy. "Aye **thenk** you!"*

June Cross   *English   Teacher   Aged 11*

I spent the war years in Clapham, south London, near the Common. There used to be anti-aircraft guns on the Common and they all made different noises when they were being fired. We gave them names according to the noises they made. "Peggy Pop Gun," made a quick, light sound; "Marjorie Mobile" got moved around to different positions on the Common; "Nausea the Naval Gun" made a deep roar.

I got the name "Nausea" from Arthur Askey's* programme. My favourite radio show of the time, however, was called ITMA ("It's That Man Again"). The man, of course, was Tommy Handley.* There was a character on his show called Colonel Chinstrap who when spoken to always replied, "Gin and Tonic and I don't mind if I do." Another character, Herr Funf, was supposed to be a German spy. His catch line was to say in a thick German accent, "Thiss iss Funf speaking."

We heard at some point in the war that Princess Margaret had phoned her father on the secret royal state phone and said to him, "Thiss iss Funf speaking." Do you suppose that's true? I'd like to think it was.

Jean Holder   *English   Retired Deputy Head Teacher*
Born 1933

I was very young and at home with a baby-sitter while my parents had gone with my brother to his school concert. I remember thinking of the baby-sitter as being very old and grown-up, but she was probably only in her teens. During the evening, the air raid sirens went and we had been told to go into the cellar if this happened. However, the baby-sitter insisted on our sitting at the top of the cellar steps, although I never knew why, and this is where my parents found us when they returned a short time later. It wasn't until years afterwards that I discovered she was more afraid of going down into the cellar than she was of the bombs!

Dame Judi Dench   *English   Actress   "Very young."*

All published material seemed to be largely in black and white. Or it might occasionally have a little bit of red in it. If one managed to find an old magazine, pre-war, that had a few color plates in it, it always created great interest among one's friends. Then of course the GIs came over. And American comics were in tremendous demand. We had our own comics like *Dandy*, *Beano*, *Knock Out*, printed largely in black and white with maybe little bits of red. For an American comic in full color we used to trade about twenty *Dandys* or *Beanos*. And they would be old ones too – not American comics in mint condition or anything.

The other thing I remember is that my grandfather used to subscribe to the *National Geographic*. During the summer holiday we used to move up to Scotland and spend the summer there with my grandparents. The thing I loved was the smell of the glossy paper in the *Geographic*, just the smell of the stuff, and the color, and things like advertisements for Coca-Cola, and American cars, these great American limos. I used to love to look through the color plates and ads and everything.

Some part of my mind when I was a child always associated the general blackness of printed things with the black outs. I don't know why.

Tom Helcke *Scots* *Biochemical Engineer* *Aged 8*

"Things like advertisements for Coca-Cola and American cars, these great American limos." For those fortunate enough to obtain copies, American magazines such as the *National Geographic* offered children around the world glimpses of an exotic world where unheard of luxuries were still plentiful.

Work has temporarily halted on the construction of these new bomb shelters. What could be more natural than that these Danish children should convert the shelters into a playground? Copenhagen, 1939.

The bombs started dropping in 1940 and on 10th September Peabody's* got hit. We were staying in our sister's flat which had all the windows boarded up. It was on the ground floor and mum lived on the next floor. When Peabody's got hit we could hear stones and shrapnel hitting against the woodwork; the furniture shook and the pictures came off the wall. We thought the ceiling was coming in on us.

Our old man [father] had been outside and he come back and said, "Peabody's been hit."

Mum said, "We've got to go to the shelter." So all of us went into St Marks School under the railway arches. We squeezed in under the arches with our old gran [grandmother] and everything. We had the pram* with us too, all piled up. There were hundreds of people in there and I think I must 'ave fallen asleep because the next thing I know, mum was dragging me out. The back of the shelter was alight. They led us from there into a little brick shelter. There were no lights in it and you had to stand up it was so crowded and you couldn't see anyone it was so dark.

Anyway, dad turned up to see where we were and he said, "Come on let's get out of it." You couldn't stand it there were so many people, and my sister was nine months pregnant besides and we had the pram an' all. Anyway, we started walking down Derby Street past the building that had been hit the night before. Mum put her hands over my ears in case we heard any screaming. My gran was holding my arm and there were planes and guns going everywhere. It was a terrible night, wasn't it, Ernie?

Mum said to me, "Run, run as fast as you can." But my gran wouldn't let me go. Mum said to her, "You've had your life, let her have hers." But gran held on to me she was so frightened. There were search lights and you could see the planes. All of a sudden you could hear, "Whaaam! Boom!" Someone said it was an anti-aircraft gun in the Tower; it was a mobile gun and it shook the place and it done more damage than the bombs did. No, it really did. When that bomb landed it was more of a swoosh – you heard "swooosshh" and then a thud. It wasn't at all like a "Boom, boom!"

The land mines you didn't hear, they just floated down. They used to say that if you couldn't hear it, it wouldn't hit you but if you just heard the whistle, you'd 'ad it! But that night I can remember feeling the pressure of air and the bomb fell just behind us. We did hear the Peabody's bomb. One hundred and ninety people were killed in Peabody's. Most of the kids had been evacuated but there were a couple of girls, the Baileys, who was made orphans that night – their mum, dad, and little brother got killed.

The next night dad found a shelter in Savage Gardens by the Tower. We went to shelter there in Pepys Street and were all of us in there when the docks were burning. They burned for months. I suppose it must have been the third or fourth night after we was in there and we couldn't get back

home because the heat was so terrible, that the people in Savage Gardens told us that the landlord of the Cheshire Cheese pub was going to pay for a lorry to take us out of London. So we had to go back to the street to get our things but the police stopped us.

Our mum said, "We're going away and we have to go to collect our clothes." So we got through the police lines and out came the old pram again. It was my sister's pram for the baby and we piled it up with everything we could. There was a chap who lived down the street who was in the fire brigade and he got the petrol out of a fire engine for the lorry because petrol was rationed of course, and his family was going an' all. The Andersons, Watkins, and Popes was all going. We didn't know where we was going and I

THE CHAIRS TOBACCO BUILT

I grew up in a little Quebec village called St Leon de Standon, about forty miles from Quebec. There was a lot of rationing in Canada during the war – butter, eggs, Crisco, all the usual things – and we had a very large family. Twelve children in all; much larger than the standard ration allowed for. Fortunately for us, my father had some friends who were farmers. The farmers didn't need coupons so my father was able to buy their spare coupons and use them to get enough of the basics for us all.

A barter system developed in rural Canada during the war. A neighbor who could not find a job came over to our house to ask my father to help him find work in order to support his wife and two children. He was a good carpenter and furniture maker. He also loved to smoke but he could never get enough tobacco.

So my father agreed to give him tobacco, sugar, butter, plus fifty cents every week. (Fifty cents was a lot of money in those days). In return, the neighbor made us some beautiful kitchen chairs, which, as you can see from the photo, we still use to this day. He didn't have much to work with – just a knife and some primitive tools. He made six chairs in all so I assume he must have been a very heavy smoker!

My father and the neighbor passed on after the war, but every year for as long as she lived the neighbor's son would come to visit my mother and bring her a basket of blueberries that he had picked.

Françoise Chouinard *Teacher Canadian Aged 7*

Still smiling. Bomb damage to their home the night before cannot wipe away the cheeky smiles of London's East End children. September 1940.

remember we was all in the back of this lorry. It was night-time by then and I always remember sitting at the back of this lorry, which was open at the back, and looking out at all the fires. The lorry went up a big old hill somewhere. We was up so high and behind us all of London seemed to be on fire.

Lil Mountain   *English   Retired   Aged 9*
Lil's brother, **Ernie Askins**   *English   Retired   Aged 14*

Because we used our bomb shelter so often, I used to keep toys there, including my Teddy. It was blue, I think. Maybe pink. Anyway, one day it disappeared from the shelter. I was very upset. My mother explained that it must have been stolen by a child but I secretly believed that somehow the Germans had got it.

Beryl Stephenson   *English   School mistress   Aged 3*

There was a porter at Long Preston railway station known as "Nine Bomb Charlie" because when the Germans were bombing the Rolls Royce works at Clitheroe and Manchester he'd always say [Yorkshire accent], "I 'erd nine bombs last night." The total was always the same. Nine bombs. So he became known as "Nine Bomb Charlie." And that was our war in Long Preston.

Leo Cooper   *English   Publisher/Writer   Aged 11*

In Vienna we stayed at the Bristol Hotel and my siblings and I once watched the bombs drop onto Vienna from the balcony of our suite, until the sirens blared and we were hustled down to the air raid shelter. I remember the claustrophobia I felt wearing a gas mask which was too big for me and the horrible smell of rubber. It was weird being packed into a shelter with masses of strange people including one man who had a cockatoo on his shoulder.

Hanna Jankovich-Besan   *Hungarian   Therapist   Aged 4*

In 1939 air raid shelters started to be delivered, courtesy of the Home Office. Several local families pooled their materials, and with the assistance of a builder friend, there was assembled in my father's aunt's yard a considerable underground fortification with bunks and suitable equipment which could have been a prototype for Hitler's bunker in Berlin.

Not too long after it was finished, the night raids began in earnest. London, the ports, and the big cities took a pasting. I have never understood why the Germans virtually ignored the Black Country* towns which were in fact one large factory engaged almost 100% on war work. We didn't escape entirely however. One bomb fell across the way from The Old Park, and killed one poor old chap whilst seated on the lavatory. A land mine then demolished All Saint's Church on the Walsall Road about 400 meters away. I saw the ten meter crater the next morning and All Saint's had just disappeared into it. All around were terraced* streets with several thousand people, and although many of the houses were damaged I don't remember anyone being killed.

The sirens were a regular feature of life in the night-time and we were bundled into blankets and carted off down the road to the bunker. I remember the men standing at the door staring at the red glow in the sky, the night that Coventry was bombed, thirty miles away.

At school there was a long air raid shelter built in St Joseph's Presbytery grounds, and a number of times our caucus disappeared into it to sing hymns until the All Clear sounded. Aged eight, I was made an altar boy, and turned up regularly for 8.00 a.m. mass after being awake sometimes during the night.

A side show was the collection of shrapnel from bombs and our anti-aircraft guns the morning after a raid. Boys (mostly) competed for the most impressive samples and swaps and trading were a regular feature of our school days. A nose cap from a shell was prized and I did find one once. Where is it all now?

John Bradley   *English   Aged 8*

I was at London docks the day they were bombed by the Germans. It was the biggest raid up until then. My uncle had taken me there over the Saturday to visit his mother and we went out and saw the planes coming over and then the actual flat was sort of swaying with the impact of the bombs and then we saw the English fighter planes coming over and we could actually see the bullets going straight past. They must have been either Spitfires or Hurricanes coming across and fighting and shooting. They were shooting tracer bullets so that I could see them coming over. It was very frightening and even more so that the sky was absolutely red, caused by the burning docks. I can still remember it vividly. It was absolutely red like a beautiful autumn when the sun comes down in the evening and it was just like that.

Mike Barnett   *English   Science Teacher   Born 1933*

Quite a few bombs fell around us because we lived near Feltham [Middlesex] where there were some enormous marshalling yards which of course the Germans were anxious to destroy. There were also some reservoirs which supplied central London. Still do. And they dropped bombs to try and breach the walls of the reservoirs. Altogether quite a few bombs fell around the area. I still remember the bombs coming down, whistling like they do in films and the sirens going off and then the All Clear which was a kind of continuous droning.

Later we had the Doodlebugs* which made a throbbing-chugging noise until they'd cut off and then down they'd come. Not many came near us but when they did out I'd go to collect pieces of shrapnel. In 1944, we moved to Ashford which is sort of a dormitory suburb of London near what is now Heathrow Airport. At about four o'clock one morning, I was wakened by an enormous bloody great bang. There was a feeling of air rushing through the house, and the light bulbs exploded, and windows were sucked out. I jumped out of bed and ran to my bedroom window (which was still intact). Our house backed onto a school playing field. Towards where the school was we could see a great cloud of debris and soil falling to the ground like an enormous fountain.

I realised a bloody great bomb had gone off. It turned out to be one of the first V-2 rockets that fell on London. Anyway, I quickly got up and went over to the crater because one of my pastimes was collecting bits of shrapnel. I was lucky on this occasion to pick up some particularly fine specimens of the outer casing of the rocket, complete with printing in German. It gave me quite a funny feeling to think of a German hand painting those words on the casing, knowing that he was helping make something which could have killed me. It made the war personal in a way that just dropping bombs on me hadn't. I was very pleased with these additions to my collection but unfortunately my mother was friendly with one of the ARP* wardens and, because this was one of the first V-2s, I had to surrender my shrapnel to the Wardens. I always remember that and seeing that enormous crater and smelling the brick dust and the rubble.

About thirty people were injured or killed. A terrible tragedy. It was about 400 meters from my house. I could still go there and show you where the house was and where the bomb fell.

Tom Helcke   *Scots   Biochemical Engineer   Aged 8*

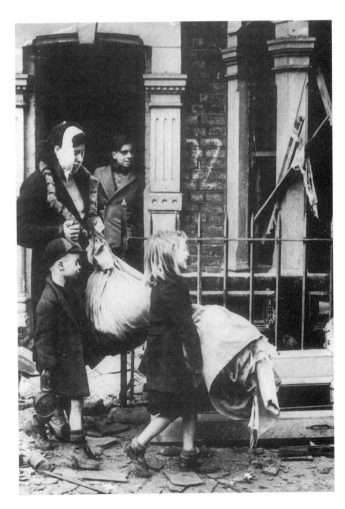

A wounded mother and her children, their home shattered by bombs, have salvaged a few belongings. London, September 1940.

school and blow a whistle. I also had a big rattle which I wound round as fast as possible. The school would be telephoned by the civil defence centre, which gave us a warning of about twenty minutes. I was supposed to take cover with the other children, but sometimes I was disobedient.

If the sky was clear, I could see the contrails high in the sky. They always seemed to be ruler straight, like plough furrows in the sky. They didn't always come from the same direction, I suppose that the Allies varied the run depending on the wind and flak disposition, which used to change from week to week. The flak didn't open up until about five minutes before the bombs fell. If I was very lucky I could see our fighters attacking. They left much shorter contrails diving steeply through the bomber formations. The air vibrated like a drum with the noise of all those bombers. Sometimes I would see a bomber drop out of formation. The contrail would curve down, then I was able to see a smoke trail. Damaged aircraft would always turn away from the flak towards the open country.

Above: Children in London's East End play a game that reflects the reality around them. The child in the foreground has put a play bandage on her head as she and her friend tend a wounded doll. Stepney, London, 1941.

Right: Bombs were no respecters of non-combatant status. A French mother and her children flee the ravaged countryside. France.

I was a very junior air raid warden in my school in Berlin. School routine became more and more impossible once the daytime air raids got going in 1943. We had got used to British night-time raids. They dropped mostly incendiaries over whole areas of the city. We used to spend all night in large air raid shelters, hundreds of people sitting quietly in this large underground bunker. These daytime raids were different, there was more high explosive. The outskirts of the city used to get the worst of it at first. I think they must have been aiming at the Charlottenburg gas works, or the railway marshalling yards.

My job was to go outside the

German children help clean up after an air raid. Germany, 1944.

I saw parachutes once or twice, but they drifted far away before they got low enough to see the air crew dangling beneath them.

When the flak opened up, the noise was deafening. The sky would be full of what looked like ink smudges. The shrapnel used to rain down like hail hitting all the roofs. It was not safe to stay out. I used to shelter under an arch, trying to see as much of the sky battle as possible. Once I saw a bomber disintegrate in an orange puff of flame. It disappeared, leaving white smoking fragments that went in all different directions. It was very high up. One piece spiralled round and round leaving a thin trail of smoke. It hit a tenement block further down the road and destroyed it as effectively as a bomb!

I went to summer camp by the Kossinsee, to the east of Berlin, in July 1943. When I came back after almost two

months away I did not recognise anything. We had heard the explosions in Berlin even at Kossinsee, and had seen the glare of fires at night-time. I was expecting to see nothing but rubble in my neighborhood. We lived not too far from the Museen Insel where all the famous antiques and art collections were housed. We did not think that our area would be so heavily bombed. It was a shock to see everything devastated.

The night bombing became much worse that autumn. I heard that the RAF called these "Thousand Bomber Raids." Even people in shelters were no longer safe. I once saw a fire whirlwind wander down the street to a shelter entrance which was where I should have been. I had slept so deeply that I hadn't heard the air raid alarm, and my mother was out working as a volunteer nurse, so there was no-one to wake me until the bombs did. I didn't dare go outside. This fiery column made a roaring noise, seemed to lick down the steps of the shelter then went out. Later we found that everyone in there had suffocated. I wanted to help get the bodies out but I was told to stay away as I was too young.

When the spring came in 1944, I was a volunteer Beobachter [observer]. I had a small observation post on the top of a concrete tower, on the outskirts of Berlin, not too far from Schonefeld. I would cycle there at six o'clock every morning. I had a big compass rose on a table mounted with a rotating sight, a tin hat, binoculars, and a telephone. I was to report any aircraft going down, where they were headed, and if there were any parachutes. I was supposed to note the bearing, and estimate the distance. My duties included noting the location of any bomb bursts in a ledger. It was like doing your homework in the middle of an air raid.

It was during that spring that I knew we had lost the war. For the first time I had seen single contrails weaving above the bombers. Sometimes they would break off and form circles as they had dogfights with our fighters. It was obvious that the Americans had fighters to protect them all the way from England to Berlin. Our fighters could not shoot down the bombers. I didn't go home after that. I would sleep at the post. With the RAF night-time *"Terrorflieger,"* and the US daytime bombers coming over at every hour of the day and night, I would not have a home any more.

Wilhelm Schultzki   *German   Night Watchman   Born 1929*

The indomitable spirit of children. Russian children hard at work in the ruins
of their Leningrad school. Russia, 1943.

After the attack on Pearl Harbor, schooling returned from frantic dislocation to business as usual. In my school, private and privileged, the all-female faculty would spend a few moments each day stressing the importance of the war and its aims, but then would shift to pleasant but firm and rigorous emphasis upon the "Three R's." There were three Americans of Japanese Ancestry (AJA) in my class. One is now my dentist, and his father was fighting with the famous 442 Regimental Combat Team (all AJAs) in Italy. The racial situation in Hawaii was nowhere near as sensitive as an uninformed observer might think. All us kids had been together since infancy, and, although our parents rarely socialized, there was mutual respect and never, ever, an iota of doubt regarding the loyalty of our Japanese friends.

There were two words, however, that were never used: "internment" and "Jap." The former was an embarassment for everyone; if Japanese in Hawaii had been herded into camps, (as had happened on the mainland) the free population would have been reduced by a third and the economy would have come to a standstill.

The father of my childhood friend (and current dentist) returned from Italy, moderately wounded, in May 1944, and brought his son a souvenir. The son brought it to school for "Show and Tell." It is probable that only in Hawaii at that time could such a scene have taken place; an eight-year-old boy of Japanese ancestry, holding up high, for all to see, a German combat helmet captured by his father.

Paul Wysard   *American   Retired Administrator; part-time teacher and writer   Aged 5-9*

Booth was a small, owlish, bespectacled young man who was known in the school as "The Professor." He had a father who was a Prisoner of War. I don't think Booth actually remembered his father much because has father was captured at Dunkirk which, as you know, was in 1940.

We all knew that Booth's father was a Prisoner of War, although we didn't understand the implications of that. Anyway, I remember towards the end of what was our last term (because the school was evacuated up to the Yorkshire

Children were quick to adapt to the most unlikely circumstances. A class in gasmasks calmly proceeds with its lesson. England, 1942.

Dales from Broadstairs in Kent), the news came that Booth's father had been released from prison camp and as a special privilege was coming to visit him. Booth was allowed to take one person with him to enjoy this reunion and so I was chosen by Booth because presumably I was one of his best friends. (One's best friend changed from day to day but that day I was his best friend).

I remember waiting in the hall of this strange Victorian mansion and eventually I think it was a horse and cart turned up with a strange, pale little man in battle dress. I think he was in the RAMC.* I can't remember exactly; I may be wrong there.

Nobody could think what to do because it was still wartime. There was nowhere to go. Nobody had cars, but the Headmaster had the bright idea that we go for a row on the lake in a rowing boat. We had two rowing boats called *Swallow* and *Amazon* and so we traipsed up the hill to the lake and Major Booth, as I suppose he was, thought this was a good idea. Booth and I sat in the stern and Major Booth took the oars and we rowed out into the middle of the dank lake, surrounded by dripping trees and all the hills and dales of limestone and we got out into the middle of the lake and there was me sitting next to Booth. I don't like boats anyway. (I didn't really like Booth that much either).

At the start of the war, I was evacuated from London. Then my mother, who was pregnant, decided that if we were going to die, it would be better if we all died together so I was brought back home. There were no state schools open so I was sent instead to the local Catholic school. I was C of E*, of course. There were several other pupils who were also non-Catholic. We were taught the same as the Catholic children except for Religious Education when we were put to one side of the classroom and called "The Heretics."

Each day the Catholic students began school with Catechism lessons. We "Heretics" weren't assigned other work during this time, so we used to listen to the Catechism lessons. Fortunately, or unfortunately, I had a very good memory and without realising it I picked up the Catechism very quickly.

One day the school was visited by a Monsignor. No one had advised him that Heretics were seated on one side of the classroom so, when he began testing everyone for their knowledge of the Catechism, he included me. As it turned out, I won first prize but they wouldn't give the prize to me after he left because it was a statue of the Blessed Virgin Mary and I was a Heretic.

When the air raids started, all the children felt a great deal of stress. We were taken to the downstairs cloakrooms, which had bricked-up windows, and older girls would read poetry and prose to us while the raid was going on. Say what you will, things like "Pericles' Oration over the Dead at Marathon," and "Queen Elizabeth Reviewing Her Troops at Tilbury" are a wonderful way to keep one's mind off an air raid.

Paper was very scarce. To save paper, we had to write on the covers of our exercise books, inside and out. In the wide margins at the top of the page we had to draw extra lines. At home, if you received an envelope, you sliced it open, reversed it, and made it into scrap paper.

We also used to have a map of the war on the wall at school – after we began winning that is. The children in the class used to take it in turns to move the pins indicating the front lines and the places that Allied troops had captured. Everyone liked being in charge of the Russian map because their front had started moving earlier and it was moving faster!

We lived in Clapham [south London] at that time which was on the direct route to the south coast. During the build-up to the Normandy landings, long convoys of lorries and big transporters carrying armored vehicles used to pass through Clapham. These convoys would take two hours or more to pass one spot and, being military convoys, of course they wouldn't stop for anything.

Knowing this, we'd cross the street and walk to school on the side opposite the one school was on. We always hoped a convoy would come along because if one did we wouldn't be able to get to school for a couple of hours.

Jean Holder *English* *Retired Deputy Head Teacher* *Born 1933*

Jean Holder, Heretic, Aged 10. Story in text.

Left: Coventry. A few months later the school of these children was destroyed by a raid on Coventry on 10th April 1941. They search for books among the ruins.

Below: Students of St Mary-of-the-Angels Song School, Addlestone, Kent, were evacuated to Leigh-on-Sea after their school was destroyed by fire. Boys and their teacher leave with books and belongings rescued from the charred remains of their school in the background. England, 1941.

His father kept on looking at his son who as I described above was the most *unprepossessing*-looking little creature. I mean, he'd presumably last seen him as a small baby and then, to my horror, Major Booth suddenly laid down the oars and, as he was staring at his son, just burst into tears.

I was acutely embarrassed. The only way out was to throw myself over the side but I couldn't swim. I was acutely aware of this terrible, terrible sadness. It may have been disappointment at how his son had turned out, or it may just have been over-emotion, but it's been in my heart and in my mind ever since.

The last I heard of Booth, he was a very senior consultant at a Hammersmith Hospital. I did actually bump into him about ten years ago. He presumably didn't remember the incident. I suspect it may have been much more poignant to me than it was to him. I was acutely aware of the atmosphere. I think it must have been just after VE* Day. It was dank and rainy. Mid-summer. Cricket season, of course.

Leo Cooper   *English   Publisher/writer   Aged 12*

Two changes at school reminded us that we had enemies. The first was that in addition to fire drills, we now practised air raid drills, kneeling under our desks and covering our heads with our arms, waiting for the All Clear signal.

The other was that the way in which we saluted the flag was modified. Instead of stretching out our arms toward the flag, we kept hands over our hearts throughout the Pledge of Allegiance. The change was because of the similarity to the Nazi salute!

Penelope Upton   *American   Psychotherapist   Aged 10*

During the raids, school began at 10:30 a.m. Much of our learning was by rote and improvised lessons in the shelters were the rule. We chanted our tables, learned and recited long poems, and much time went on savings campaigns, encouraging thrift to support the War Effort. Christmas presents from aunts and uncles were invariably savings certificates, enclosed in a card that reminded us of the great mission in which our country was involved.

Margaret Roake   *English   History Mistress   "Aged 8 at the start"*

In school from time to time you used to be given spoonfuls of malt extract. They also gave us milk from a great churn which they ladled out into the little white enamel cups we used to carry attached to our gas masks. On the cups there was a piece of elastoplast or sticky tape with our names on them. I used to feel about reconstituted milk like other people felt about powdered eggs. I still remember how revolting it was. I just couldn't get it down. In fact, it was several years after the war before I could tolerate drinking real milk.

Tom Helcke   *Scots   Biochemical Engineer   Aged 8*

One of my very early memories of the war was being made to eat everything on my plate. "Remember the starving children in England," my mother would say.

Years later, as it happened, I married an English girl. I once asked her about the war. As it turned out, she grew up on the edge of the Yorkshire Dales. Her father knew lots of farmers so she spent most of the war pigging out on bacon, eggs, sausages – just about anything she wanted.

William Ansel *Canadian   Teacher   Aged 4*

We used to eat tulip bulbs during the war. For a time, it was all we had. Today, I often drive past big fields of tulips. Other people see flowers. . .colors. For me, sometimes I see the war.

Sjoerdje Daumme *Dutch   Housewife   Aged 8*

We ate lots of beans. My mother had a way of boiling up ham bones with navy beans or kidney beans that tasted just great to me. This recipe has survived in our family, though with more ham these days. I recall that we also ate Spam. When my uncle came to visit us after the war, my mother served some up for him. He couldn't eat it though, apparently because he'd had quite enough in the Navy on Okinawa.

Wayne L Hamilton *American   Geologist, retired   Born 1936*

Whilst I don't remember being hungry, I do recall fetching flour from a large bin for my mother and on opening the lid finding it crawling with maggots. We used the flour anyway. I also have an abiding hatred of rhubarb, as it appeared all too frequently at mealtimes.

Hanna Jankovich-Besan *Hungarian   Therapist   Aged 4*

What I remember most was eating tulip bulbs. There was a. . .how you say. . .bitter little bit in the middle that we weren't supposed to eat because it would poison us. In the end, we got so hungry that we ate it anyway. It didn't kill me so very much, I guess.

At de Kleijn *Dutch   Bookseller   Aged 8*

I was the bird boy at my prep school.* That meant that you put out the crumbs in the morning for all the birds so you could bird watch. I used to go to the common room kitchen to collect the crumbs but of course they were in this tin with pieces of cherry cake and buttered scones and things like

that. So I used to eat them. There must have been a lot of very thin birds flying around Yorkshire during the war.

Later, at Radley,* we used to eat whale meat and something called snoek. I believe snoek had their heads cut off because they otherwise looked too frightening. It was a sort of rubbish fish which was all we could get and whale meat which was absolutely disgusting. I don't really remember too much about the food except that there was never enough.

We were allowed two sweets a day. Quite how we survived I'm not sure. I don't remember anything about the prep school food except that being bird boy I got to eat all the buttered scones.

Leo Cooper *English   Publisher/Writer   Aged 11*

I was very young during the war. I can't remember much about it except my first orange. I'd wager that every English person my age can remember his first orange, his first banana, and his first piece of chewing gum.

Thomas Potter *English   Librarian   Aged 5*

I remember the first banana that I was given shortly after the war – I can still taste the taste and feel the texture if I close my eyes!

Neil Kinnock *Welsh   European MP, former Leader of the Labour Party   Aged 4*

What I still remember most of all was my first banana. It was, oh, wonderful. So. . .sweet! An American gave it to me. What was odd was that I knew exactly what to do with it. I mean I hadn't even *seen* a banana before but I just took it, and peeled it, and began eating. The American knew it was my first banana so he looked surprised and asked me how I knew what to do. It took me a moment to work it out. Then I remembered. I'd seen Cheetah peel one in a Tarzan film.

Julia Thomas *English   Housewife   Aged 7*

I can't remember my first banana exactly but I remember standing in queues with my mother when the first consignment came in. The queues were enormous. Then all of a sudden all the people were running out of the shop as fast as they could because the bananas had come in these long wooden crates – a whole stem of bananas – and, as they were opening one up, a snake slithered out. It cleared the shop very quickly.

Oranges were very rare. I remember people saving up orange peels in the linen cupboard and when they had enough they would soak them and cut them up and make them into a kind of marmalade.

We also used to eat things like whale meat and snoek which was a fish that came from South Africa. And we'd get food parcels from Canada. And Spam. But we were lucky having a grandfather living in Scotland because he used to send us rabbits and the odd pheasant or two. Of course by the time they reached us they were quite gamy which is why even today I like to eat game in a fairly gamy state.

When we went up to Scotland, we children used to get paid to collect rose hips. We'd get a jam jar or something and go out collecting. They used to make rose hip syrup out of them which was good for babies. We'd get about a penny a jam jar. It was part of an official government programme.

Tom Helcke   *Scots   Biochemical   Engineer   Aged 8-11*

There was food rationing in America during the war but, of course, nothing like people were suffering elsewhere. There were dozens of things you couldn't get. Chocolate, for example. Meat was rationed too but you could get as much of certain things – like horse meat – as you wanted. I thought horse meat was delicious by the way and wouldn't hesitate to eat it again. At one point we tried eating animal spleens – 'melts,' I think they were called – but they were so repulsive we gave it up. Lard was rationed, and so was butter. In fact, if I'm not mistaken, that's how margarine came to be developed. Because there wasn't enough butter.

The margarine used to come in quarter pound blocks that looked like white soap. There was a little button of food coloring and you used to have to mix them together in a bowl. Somehow this became my job. Since I didn't wash my hands any better than most little boys my age, this always struck me as a curious choice. I still remember the way the margarine used to ooze out from under my nails for days afterwards.

Sometimes, if we'd just got a new order in, and were in a hurry, we'd eat the margarine without mixing in the coloring. I shudder to think what E-additives must have been in that yellow dye, but I'll tell you a curious thing; I know food colouring is tasteless, but there's absolutely no doubt that margarine *with* yellow dye tastes better than margarine *without.*

George Kaplan   *American   Printer   Aged 7*

I don't know why the three of us were with mum that day. Probably a visit with my aunt and her children, a stop at the library in Worcester, and a little shopping in the stores there were on the schedule before we reached the butcher shop, on the way back home. My younger brother David and I stayed in the car, but my older brother Bob went in with mum, even though I'm sure she would have been happier if he hadn't. When they came out, Bob acted like the "cat who had swallowed the canary."

That night the house smelled of roast for the first time in a long time. But, when we sat down at the table, mum continued to "fuss" in the kitchen and Bob just pushed the meat around his plate, not really eating. Daddy realized that something was up and extracted the information that the butcher had convinced mum to try horse meat. Daddy, Dave, and I had been happily cleaning our plates until we learned we were eating PONY meat. Mum apologized and daddy asked her not to buy it again, but we're all pretty sure she did.

Joan Perry Morris   *American   Administrator, Florida Department of State   Aged 6-10*

There are lots of cheery memories too. We used to have coal fires in those days and we'd grill bread on forks in front of the fire. And we used to get beef dripping which was about the only kind of meat we could get, and spread it on the toast with some salt and pepper. And I loved that. Still to this day I have it quite often and occasionally a flash of the war will come to me. I'll think of all those coal fires long gone.

Tom Helcke   *Scots   Biochemical Engineer   Aged 9*

An American ration card. Most countries introduced rationing at some point in the war.

As far as meat and things were concerned, my mother always used to give us her ration. I don't recall being undernourished because my mother was like that.

Leo Cooper   *English   Publisher/Writer   Aged 11*

Without having memories of pre-war conditions, I didn't recognize many wartime practices as being departures from normal. I remember, from a birthday party at Patty Stafford's, the first cake I ever saw that had frosting [icing] on the sides as well as on top. "Jimmy knows there's a war on," said one of the adults. I, of course, had not made the connection; I regarded it merely as something unusual, somewhat as I might regard polishing the bottoms of one's shoes today.

James Pringle   *American, living in Canada   Taxonomist   Born 1936*

In London, though we didn't have much, we somehow managed to hoard things. We ate endless vegetable pies and fried Spam, but in the kitchen cupboard I remember line after line of hardening blue packets of sugar, our ration which we bought but never quite finished, and powdered milk tins. Once we were given a real box of chocolates, perhaps from the American PX. My parents insisted on saving these for a special occasion, and when at last we untied the bow and lifted the padded lid, they were all covered with a pale grey mould.

Helen Fletcher   *English   Schoolmistress   Aged 3¹/₂*

In Japan, life did not change very much for about eighteen months. We soon ran out of tea, and mummy was cooking all sorts of strange things, as rice was very difficult to get. We never saw milk. I used to go out on my own looking for anything that we could eat. Sometimes I would bring back fungi, some of which mummy would identify in a big book, then cook in a thin soup. Others, she would just throw away, saying that these were poisonous.

Francis O'Brien   *Irish/Japanese   Diplomat   Born 1930*

Other items that looked like collectibles, but which we weren't allowed to collect, were the ration points, which looked rather like small stamps. These had to accompany cash when one purchased rationed food items. There were several colors, including red, green, and the less often seen black, for different categories of food. Toward the end of the war, these were replaced by OPA* tokens, which were thin but stiff discs about a centimeter in diameter, in red and blue.

They were accompanied by a game board so they could be used like checkers. My mother kept them on a shelf in the kitchen, in a dish that otherwise contained assorted bolts, nuts, paper clips, and other such items the might come in handy. The few tokens left over after rationing remained there for the next twenty-five years or so.

James Pringle   *American, living in Canada   Taxonomist   Born 1936*

In the early 1940s our family lived in Texas. My father was in an Army Engineer unit there prior to his service in the European Theater later in the war. Like everyone else, each member of the family was issued ration books periodically to buy scarce commodities. My younger brother Jon generated a great commotion one night when he was discovered in the act of rendering his already small stamps into even smaller fragments of paper. Apparently their small size and the perforations in the ration books fascinated him with the

starving people in far off places was accentuated by wartime children's awareness of suffering overseas. My brother Jon's habit of leaving bread crusts uneaten stopped abruptly when he was reminded of hungry kids in Europe and Asia. He never again left a crust, in fact, hardly a crumb. After the war, when we moved north in 1946, the center drawer of the dining room table was removed to lighten the table for transport. Only then was the mystery of the crusts revealed. The drawer, which was quite wide and long, was packed with crusts from several years' worth of breakfasts.

Peter S Marshall   *American   Aged 9*

There were shortages of many things during the war, including shoes. Aside from my mother's driving, one of the matters of domestic dispute between my parents was one that arose, indirectly, because of the shortage of shoes. The direct cause was a billy goat that my dad acquired and brought home to live in the backyard as a family pet. My mother despised the goat from the beginning, but the goat

Above: Methods to make the best of rationing are taught in Home Economics class in McKinley High School. A student points out the importance of fresh fruits and vegetables as a way of conserving ration points. Washington DC, 1943.

Right: Children in this American grade school are taught how to shop with ration stamps. It made the teaching of Mathematics almost painless! Fairfax County, Virginia, 1943.

concept of miniaturization. Anyway, my three brothers and parents and I worked long into the night trying to find and then puzzle-piece the fragments back into recognizable, legal-looking ration coupons. We were thereafter more impressed with how precious each stamp was in terms of units of meat, butter, coffee, etc.

The traditional parental warning that wasted food would have been vital to

Collecting shrapnel and spent cartridge cases was a universal preoccupation for children of all nations. England.

was banished after it ate my leather shoes, which I had left on the back porch. Mom took her ration coupons to town and bought me another pair of shoes, but there were no more leather children's shoes. The ones we got were red cloth-and-cardboard sandals that quickly fell apart after the first good puddle jumping. And, in one of the many small but important instances of sharing during the war, one of my mother's friends gave up her shoe coupon so I could have shoes to wear.

Many would say that of the minor domestic and personal problems caused by diverting goods to the War Effort, one of the most inconvenient was the scarcity of rubber, which made it almost impossible to get tires for the family car. Not so. Absolutely the worst of all problems caused by the rubber shortage was the synthetic that replaced rubber in the elastic used in children's panties. When you started down the street, you never knew when the elastic in your drawers would go and your drawers would fall down around your ankles. You never went to school or walked to town without a safety pin to keep your britches from falling

down when the elastic failed without warning. It was humiliating to a little kid when that happened. Fortunately, I don't remember how those failures felt to older girls.

Helen Simmons *American   Editor   Born 1939*

*I*t was considered unpatriotic to grow garden flowers. Every inch of space was put to use to grow food. The lawn was dug up and potatoes planted. Beetroots and carrots decorated the front borders. After a heavy raid we would search the garden early for pieces of shrapnel. Broken shell-cases still smelling of cordite were taken to school as trophies, proving we were all in the front line in this war. My father had an allotment too, where the local cricket club had relinquished their ground to the War Effort. We cycled to it on our bikes called Spitfire and Hurricane to "Dig for Victory."

Margaret Roake *English   History teacher   "Aged 8 at the start"*

The meat shortage led to saving rationing stamps then splurging if a piece of meat could be found. One day, after my mother had stood in line for a long time, she was able to buy a ham which she took home and put in the refrigerator. She then went out to complete her shopping but phoned and told me that I was to start boiling the ham for the evening meal. I did this as quickly as possible, as her call had interrupted my listening to "Jack Armstrong, the All-American Boy" on the radio.

During dinner, everyone wondered about the disgusting taste of the ham. My father mentioned that he also had stood in line and, amazingly, had managed to buy a leg of lamb, something we hadn't had for many months. The end of the story is that everyone wondered how a twelve-year-old could be stupid enough to mistake lamb for ham, and the consequence was that I would have to have weekly cooking lessons given by Laura, our maid. I don't recall the first cooking lesson, but Laura threatened to quit if she had to give me another one.

Also because of the meat shortage, my parents bought twenty-five baby chicks to be raised by a farmer who lived nearby. In this way we were assured of roast chicken every Sunday plus chicken sandwiches, chicken salads, chicken stews, and so on. This may explain why my brother became a picky eater.

Like most families we had a Victory Garden. Ours consisted of four long rows on the edge of the garden of a farmer friend. Primarily, we grew potatoes. In addition, my brother raised beets and I raised carrots. The potatoes we harvested were about the size of small lemons. We were extremely proud of our produce, however, and took a bushel of small, greenish potatoes to my maternal grandmother who expressed much pleasure and praised our efforts.

Raising potatoes was a challenge because Japanese beetles had to be removed constantly from the foliage. My brother and I were assigned the job of picking beetles and putting them in cans of kerosene. I was repulsed by the beetles wriggling on my finger tips and complained a great deal, while my eight-year-old brother fought the scourge of the Japanese beetles with enthusiasm as he believed that they had been sent in balloons from Japan. I was very happy to let him win his contests of who could collect more beetles.

Penelope Upton   *American   Psychotherapist   Aged 12*

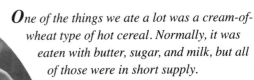

Two young American-Japanese girls await internment by their countrymen on grounds of national security. Los Angeles, USA. 1942.

One of the things we ate a lot was a cream-of-wheat type of hot cereal. Normally, it was eaten with butter, sugar, and milk, but all of those were in short supply.

Sometimes we would eat it with just margarine and sugar, or just with milk. When we had none of those we just ate it straight and it was dreadful to childish tastes. But it was better straight than oatmeal was. My dad, I remember, quite happily ate either with salt alone.

Both of my parents were dedicated coffee drinkers, but we kids were not allowed to drink coffee because it would "stunt our growth." During the war they couldn't get coffee and had to switch to Postum, a sort of powdered coffee substitute. It must have had little or no caffeine, because we kids were allowed to drink it. But, as soon as the war was over, they went back to drinking coffee, and we went back to not drinking coffee.

Helen Simmons   *American   Editor   Born 1939*

My earliest memory of the war is first grade. We used to have drawing time each week. The girls would draw houses, flowers, school, that sort of thing. The boys all drew pictures of airplanes with machine gun fire coming out of their wings.

To make the lines of bullets they used to tap out lots of little dots with their pencils. We had wooden desks and with twenty boys all tapping on them at the same time it sounded like a flock of woodpeckers gone insane. Plus a lot of the boys were also sub-vocalizing various sounds – machine guns, planes diving, explosions, etc. It was bedlam. And kind of spooky. They were all so intense about it. In the end, it got so bad that Miss Center said the boys couldn't do any more machine gun fire.

Cynthia Harper   *American   Secretary   Aged 6*

One curious fact has always stuck in my mind. At the start of the war, American military planes were marked with a small red circle in the middle of a white star on a blue field. Then, quite suddenly, the red circle disappeared so there was just a white star in a blue circle.

This struck me as odd. Later on I read somewhere that

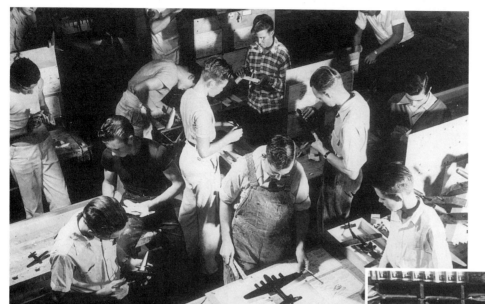

American pilots were seeing the red circles and shooting down our own planes thinking (because of the red circles) that they were Japanese. At first this kind of made sense, but then I began to wonder why the English weren't shooting down their own planes.

Billy Cannon   *American   Store Manager   Aged 8*

I know World War II was a terrible thing. All that death and suffering. Terrible. All the same, to a child, it could be very exciting. I used to love the machinery of war. The tanks, the ships, the planes – particularly the planes. Particularly the fighters. Pursuits, they called them then.

P-38s, P-39s, P-40s, P-47s, Lockheed Lightnings, Bell Airacobras, Grumann Avengers, Thunderbolts, Tomahawks, Spitfires, Hurricanes. I could go on and on. I think I knew by name and silhouette every pursuit aircraft of every country in the war. My favourite was the P-51 Mustang. I once saw one do a long slow barrel roll over an airfield. It was beautiful. Their lines were so. . . well. . . in a strange way there was almost a purity about them. A clarity. They were beautiful the way a shark is beautiful, but without the ugly mouth. Do you know what I mean?

It may make me sound like a warmonger to say so, but I still think the P-51D Mustang is one of the most beautiful objects ever created by the mind of man. And I have an

English friend I know who feels the same way about Spitfires.

Mark Gordon   *American   Assistant Professor   Aged 7*

During those first few years at school, there were some boys who would always dash to the window at the sound of a plane. Ordinarily, the teachers objected, but, if the plane turned out to be a "Flying Fortress," i.e., one with four motors (which I assumed for a while was the basis of its name, not having heard the word "fortress" before), the event might be considered significant enough to justify everyone having a look.

The war also provided collectibles. For a short time, among the best collectibles were the pictures of planes (Piper Cub, Grumann Widgeon, Flying Boat, Sikorsky Autogyro, etc.) that came with Wings cigarettes. Relatively few smokers cared much for that brand, but Al Fisk (brother

of Bill), proprietor of the Western Auto Store, was one who did, and every once in a while my father would bring home a bunch of these cards donated by Al, which I cherished and pored over repeatedly. Eventually, however, Wings cigarettes disappeared from the market.

James Pringle *American, living in Canada   Taxonomist*
Born 1936

In Finland, during the war and just after, the most popular thing for boys was to make model airplanes. We made them out of balsa wood and paper and glue. Thousands of boys all over Finland did this. Different parts of the country had regional contests, Helsinki and the rural districts, and then the winners would fly their airplanes against winners from Norway and Sweden. Some of the airplanes were gliders,

others had propellers. It's strange to think how important these model aircraft were to us once. My brothers and I had many aircraft at home and we constructed many new ones and were very enthusiastic. After the war, I don't know. The hobby just didn't continue. You get older. You leave them at home. You give them to younger brothers. They get broken or lost.

Vesa Lyytikäinen *Finnish   Born 1929*

I was always fascinated by the sound effects in war comics. "AAAIIIEEE!" and "ARRGGGHHHH!" were always popular choices when someone got shot. And I remember some poor devil falling out of an aircraft going "AAAEEEI-IOOUU!!!" Ordnance made sounds like "KA-BOOM!" or "BARRROOOOM!" (artillery) and "RAT-A-TAT-TAT!" (machine gun) "BEEYONGGG!" (ricochet), "CLICK-CLICK!" (weapon being cocked or safety being slipped), "BEEEYOWWW" (sometimes aircraft pulling out of a dive, sometimes bombs whistling down), "TRAMP, TRAMP, TRAMP, TRAMP" (marching), and "VRRRMMMM!" or "BRRRMMMM!" (heavy machinery of any sort – usually tanks).

Japanese soldiers had only one word, "BANZAI!!!" They all had buck teeth, glasses, and always fastened up the chin straps on their helmets. German soldiers had two words: "ACHTUNG!" and "SCHWEINHUND!" British soldiers called everyone "old man" and were always drinking or demanding tea under the most unlikely circumstances. Americans never fastened their helmet straps and they wore their helmets pushed back on their heads. They usually had a cigarette dangling from their lips. In those unenlightened times, no one bothered to warn combat soldiers that smoking could damage their health!

Lloyd Jameson *American*
Aged "tennish"

"We made them out of balsa wood and paper and glue." Model aircraft making was an obsession amongst Finnish boys during the war. Two young Finns test fly their latest model. Finland, 1945.

MEAT, GREASE, AND IRON

My grandfather, Jud Tunnell, worked in the cotton compress until he was in his eighties. Every year he raised two fat hogs to be slaughtered in the fall. During the war this was especially important because meat was rationed and grease was needed for the War Effort. (I never quite understood why). We never had to use the meat stamps in our ration books, because of the hogs.

In November, when the first cold norther blew in, we would all know it was time to kill hogs, and it was an exciting family affair. Everyone would bundle-up in coats and double pants and gather in Grandad's back yard. The hogs were killed in the afternoon and scalded in large wooden vats built by my father. Then the carcasses were hung up to drain, and all the bristles were scraped out of the skin with tin can scrapers. We stayed up all night in the frigid wind, butchering with cotton-sampling knives and sugar curing by the light of kerosene lanterns and a big bonfire.

Ears, snouts, skin, entrails, and trimmings were put in a great iron pot for rendering into lard. Buckets of white lard would be cooling in a row by morning. Lye was added to the "cracklins" left over from the rendering, and resulting large blocks of brown lye-soap would be used for laundering clothes all year. Us kids would eat the hot brown cracklins at every opportunity to help us keep from freezing.

Hams, shoulders, and bacon slabs would go into the big wooden meat box on the back porch. Mama (grandmother) used some of the meat to make sausage, which she put up in white muslin sacks about three inches in diameter and two feet long. Fresh backbones were prized by neighbors for making soup. Chunks of tenderloin were taken to sick folks around town. The meat would be enjoyed by many people into the following summer months, when it finally played out.

Lots of grease resulted from the fat pig meat. During

the war, I went around with syrup buckets and collected bacon grease and sausage grease from neighbors and family. Every woman had a stoneware grease jar on her stove, and they would all empty them into my cans as I made my rounds.

I also had an often repaired red wagon which I used to collect scrap iron for the War Effort. Scouring the neighborhood, I would collect plough points, old hand tools, bolts, chain, hinges, rusty nails, pieces of pipe, cog wheels, flattened cans, parts of old cars, antique end-irons, and many other useful and useless items.

Every few weeks, I would make a trip down to Mr Butler's Feed Store with a load of grease and iron to help fuel our War Effort. The grease was surrendered with no reward, but I received a penny-a-pound for the scrap iron. I would feel that I had a big load of iron, but when it was thrown on the huge pile beside the feed store, it looked insignificant. By the end of the war, I had dug-up and pried-off every bit of iron in our neighborhood.

Curtis Tunnell
American   Executive Director,
Texas Historical Commission
Aged 7-12

Children of all nations made an invaluable contribution to their nation's War Effort by collecting items as varied as scrap metal, grease, waste paper, saucepans, savings stamps, tinfoil, milk weed pods, juniper berries, rose hips, and much, much more. These children in Roanoke, Virginia have been collecting scrap metal by pony cart. 1943.

PART FOUR

INTO THE DARKNESS

Strangely enough, death was still off the scale of my own experience on 13th December 1942 – the day my grandfather committed suicide. To me he had always been the solid, safe authority figure, more than my parents had. He was a gentle man, a doctor loved by all his patients. War was in its fourth year at the time, but I had never heard him complain about all the hardships and ignominies which life with the Jewish Star of David badge had brought him.

When the summons for deportation to concentration camp, which we had feared for over two years, finally came, he invited us all to announce his decision. This was, that at the age of seventy-three, he could not be expected to survive and that he flatly refused to leave. As a doctor he had always kept a dose of poison as his private "final solution." We gathered in the tiny room in one of the Jewish "communal flats," where three families lived while waiting for deportation. We, that is his only daughter (our mother), his son-in-law, and my sister and I, his two granddaughters aged seventeen and thirteen.

His decision had been, as we were later to learn, a wise one. The family respected it, but I probably was not old enough to understand. To this day I am ashamed how cowardly I behaved. I tried to cajole him into changing his decision, wept, told him how much I loved him and please, please not to die. What seemed so horrible was knowing beforehand, knowing the hour when he would die. I know how many worse tragedies occurred during the war, how terribly people suffered. He was old and his death was after all merciful. But all this I did not understand. I do not remember how we left the flat. I know I prayed the whole night, for the first time in my life, but I did not know how to pray, because I had no religion. I have never prayed since that night.

Hana Rehakova *Czech   Administrator   Aged 13*

Two Hungarian orphans share their meagre rations with a stray kitten. Budapest, 1945.

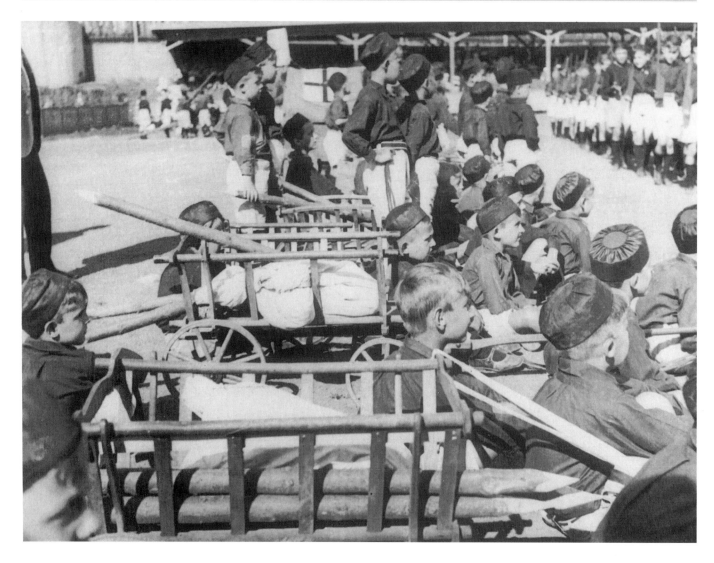

Young Czechs train with wooden "rifles" and "transport wagons" loaded down with wooden "machine guns." Their country would all too soon know the harsh realities of invasion and occupation. Prague, 1939.

They were bringing the wounded from Warsaw. The hospital was in the school and in some other buildings and barracks. I went there to help. Taller than my contemporaries, nobody could tell that I was only fourteen. I carried water and stretchers. I remember one day they brought someone with his face completely burned. He screamed all the time from his open mouth while on the stretcher, and later, when laid on the floor, until he died. Constantly new people, always horribly wounded. There were neither analgesics nor disinfectants. Lice thrived. I killed them on a comb. They were everywhere; everybody had them. Lack of beds. Too many damaged people. A crowd. I do not think I talked to anyone. I did not know how to. Frightened that someone might ask a question and I, as during school lessons, would not have an answer.

Only once was it different and this has stayed with me. I remember it still so precisely that even now I could draw the face and the hands of that boy. He started talking to me as soon as they had brought him in. He had fever and flushed cheeks. I sat on his bed. I felt that I should listen quietly. Jurek Godlewski – that is a pseudonym. Soldier with the Home Army, he was eighteen. He talked about what he wanted to do in the future and of the time when he was small and lived with his parents. I listened, hiding my chapped hands under my apron. He talked to me as if he knew me, looked at me, and smiled as if I were someone close to him. Afterwards, I came to sit at his bed every day. On leaving him, I thought about him joyfully and in my dreams he was with me in my childhood forest. I do not remember how many days passed, such long days, filled with words and dreams. When he died, he seemed very small: both his legs had been severed by shrapnel.

Magdalena Abakanowicz   *Polish   Sculptress   Aged 14*

The war didn't touch us very much in Bardi di Parma. We were in a very remote village with few roads. It was nine kilometers to school, twenty-eight kilometers to the nearest train station. We always had enough to eat; no one bombed us or shot us.

The main signs of the war we saw were soldiers from Italy and Bulgaria using our area for training. From about 1943, we saw Germans sometimes and more often soldiers from overseas wearing German uniforms. They were used by the Germans to catch deserters, ensure civil order, that sort of thing.

One thing we did see a lot of was planes flying overhead. Planes of all nationalities. They seemed a long way away. But then one day, the war came crashing into our little village. A Canadian reconnaissance plane dropped down out of the sky. It just missed the top of a mountain but then followed on down the line of the slope like it was trying to land. It sheared off the tops of trees for more than a mile then crashed with a terrible noise. Everyone in our village and the next village went to see.

The fires were out by the time we got there but there

was wreckage everywhere. One of the engines had been ripped off and thrown for more than 400 meters. Six young fliers had been killed. Two of the bodies had been thrown up into the trees. Another body was legless.

People were respectful at first, then some of the men from the other village began to take things from the bodies – rings, watches, money. They cut open the flying jackets the men were wearing and found lots of French, German, and Italian money hidden in the lining. In the meantime, someone had called the police, then the Italian Army, then, finally, the Germans. When the Germans arrived they laid the bodies out in a row and asked for interpreters to help them read the documents that were with the bodies. There was no shortage in that area of people who spoke and read English. Many of them had left Bardi to find work in the US or UK and then returned to Bardi to live out their days. Perhaps as many as one in five could speak English but no one told the Germans this!

Eventually, the villagers came with coffins and took the young men to the church where they blessed and buried them. I was very upset. It is not the kind of thing one likes to see. I had older brothers and sisters living in both the US and the UK. It could have been them.

Tony Sidoli   *British/Italian   Ex-restauranteur, Scrap Merchant Born 1925*

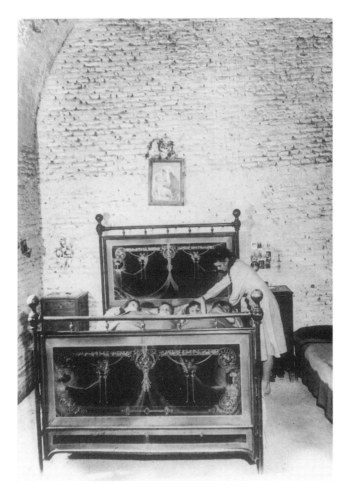

"War makes strange bedfellows. . ." Four children are tucked away in the one bed saved from the ruins of their bombed out home. The bed was reassembled in the vaults of this wine cellar. Italy, 1943.

I was born on 15th March 1939 in Kvalsund, thirty-five kilometers from Hammerfest in northern Norway. My first memories are of when the Germans came. At the start they got lodgings in private houses. They slept on the floor in our house packed close together. I had just learnt to walk and had to climb over all these green-grey clad men. I was not frightened; only surprised.

It became worse later during the war. They built a fort a few hundred meters above our house. The last year of the war, before the evacuation, (forced evacuation), there was more war activity. Englishmen came with their bombers to destroy the fort which had anti-aircraft artillery. We often had to leave the house. Nearly every night we had to go down into the cellar when they bombed. It even happened that when we children were out playing in the middle of the day, the planes came without warning and started shooting. One day I didn't manage to get home and lay in a field during an attack. I suffered from dreadful anxiety, something which haunted me for many years after the war.

When the Russians came over the border at Pasvik near Kirkenes, the Germans prepared their retreat and commanded all the local people to evacuate their homes at a few day's notice. They started to burn all the houses, killed the farm animals, and drove the people away. We had to

Above: Young Lapps, fleeing the Nazi armies retreating from Russia, stare apprehensively into the future. Their mother, on the left, wears traditional Lappish dress. Sodankylä, Lappish Finland, 1944.

Below: Norwegians in occupied Norway were not permitted to celebrate their National Day (17th May). These third generation American-Norwegian children, (plus a few evacuees born in Norway), celebrate it for them. Brooklyn, New York, USA. 1944.

travel on a fishing vessel southwards. It was filled with petrified people.

I remember the first evening when my father took me on his arm. We stood and watched all the houses which had been set on fire by the Germans – a large bonfire was visible in the dark all the way out the Vargsundet towards Altafjord, and my father said, "Look, Grete, they are burning our home. You must never forget this."

Grete Eliassen *Norwegian Born 1939*

A party of men, who may have been soldiers at one time, turned up and told us to pack and follow them. They said that we stood no chance of survival where we were. We left the next day and, after three hours walking, we joined several hundred other people who were just walking along a dusty road. I had no idea where we were going. At night we just slept in a field, then carried on walking. I don't remember feeling hungry. I think we were all too numb. After a while we were told to walk at night then hide during the day, which we all did without question. The men would disappear, then come back a few hours later with food, and water. This went on for about a week.

One morning we were all issued with sheets of paper with some official looking Russian on it, and what must have been a German translation under it. Mine described me as a Polish boy suffering from TB and therefore of no military or economic significance.

The next day we started walking in the early afternoon. We just did as we were told. Everyone was too dejected to argue. Later we were stopped by some soldiers. They looked very rough, more like muggers than soldiers. They weren't bothered about any papers. They took watches, brooches, and any bright silver coins. They did not bother with paper money, which was fortunate for one man, who I later learned had one hundred and fifty US Dollars on him. He said that the soldiers were illiterate.

We were told to assemble that night and wait for transport by one of the ex-soldier looking men. I had not seen him when the guards were raiding us. He just seemed to melt away then reappear. I think that he must have been from some underground organization.

We were marched, but those too weak to carry on walking were taken by a number of horse-drawn wagons, to what must have been a Displaced Persons camp. It was just rows of tents, with Red Cross workers

running a soup kitchen, and some terrible, inadequate, and messy wooden latrines. Nobody seemed to know where we were. Some thought it was Bulgaria, others Romania. The Red Cross workers didn't seem to speak any language any of us had heard before. There was no sign of our mysterious ex-soldiers, (if that is what they were; I never did find out).

The next two years were spent being moved from one camp to another. At one time I am sure we were near the Crimea as I could see the sea in the distance, we saw the occasional warship. We always seemed to be moved on, usually at night, often by train, to bigger and bigger camps. Some of these were well managed with schooling and officials who wrote out forms, always in Polish.

I remember particularly a fine autumn morning. We were not too far from another camp, which I later learned was a temporary barracks. Out of the blue we heard a loud whining noise and saw a Stuka pulling out of a dive leaving three dots which carried on in a graceful arc, hitting the other

camp with a puff of smoke followed by a loud triple bang. Our camp guards just stood there with their mouths open, then they ran off. It seems that the Germans had just attacked the Russians!

Things moved very quickly after that. I was issued with some more forms, and an army cap with a red star. A Polish official told me to wave the cap whenever any Russians saw me, in order to fool them into thinking I was a volunteer. The Polish underground was arranging for us to be evacuated to Palestine which would take three weeks overland. The Russians expected that all Poles were to join the Red Army, under an amnesty signed by Stalin, but we had other ideas. From that time on, I was part of a military machine that was eventually going to take me to England, even though I was only fifteen years old.

Alek Smirnow-Wisniak *Polish   Engineer   Aged 13-15*

The largest human migration in history. The entire population of this Polish village fled the approaching armies. Alek Smirnow-Wisniak (above) was one of the millions displaced by the war.

*I*n January 1945, when the front line reached our little village of Keserves near Rimavská Sobota, a small German unit stayed in our house for three days and then took position on a nearby hill and for more than one month held

its post against the vastly overwhelming Russian troops. The Russians transformed our kitchen (about 36 square meters) into their field hospital. I had seen scenes I cannot ever forget: wounded soldiers without their arms, legs, eyes, and faces. The floor was covered with amputated extremities and the horrible stink was penetrating everywhere.

I remember a Russian soldier who climbed up the high stack of straw and in a moment he was shot into his head by the German sniper from the distance of about one kilometer! The Russians were attacking the hill almost every day but without success and the frozen corpses were carried away on the hay-wagons. About fifty corpses were stacked like sheafs in one hay-wagon.

My worst experience was in that night when I slept with my younger brother in the stable and suddenly a drunken Russian soldier came in. He started to embrace me and I was screaming hard, full of dread. A Russian officer appeared and he wanted to shoot the drunken soldier at once. My father pleaded for the culprit because he knew that a vengeance of the others would be falling on our family.

Our house had been shelled by the Germans at times but no member of our family was wounded and after some five weeks, this part of the war was over for us.

Emilia Krajclová   *Slovakian   Farmer   Aged 14*

Under Danish flags on either side of the altar, two young Danes find refuge in a church in the north. Straw on the floor provides a bed; the solid walls provide a safe haven for their dolls. Denmark, 1945.

YOU'RE NOT GOING TO SHOOT MY MUM!

When I look back I realise I didn't know who my dad was. I remember the letters but I don't know who he was as a person. The letters were on some kind of vellum paper – grease paper – with great chunks cut out of them and they were reduced in size. Tiny writing and great chunks crossed out, and that was all I knew of my father really. He wasn't a real man in my life. He was an image. We were living at that time in Newcastle-upon-Tyne – 44 Neanton Park View – a flat, a ground floor flat. I can see it now – a central corridor. Everything. Anyway, one day my mum told me my dad was coming home and I was very excited. I told all the kids at

Sheila Wallett and her dad.

Chillingham Road School, "My dad's coming home."

He came in the middle of the night. And I just vaguely remember the fuss and bustle and how pleased they were to see each other. Suddenly there was this man in the house who was my dad and I remember watching him shave that morning and then don't remember anything after that except when he started to unpack. While he was unpacking he brought out a pistol and I rushed over to my mum who was kind of on the other side of the room and put my arms around her and said, "You're not going to shoot my mum!"

Sheila Wallett
English   Teacher   Aged "6 or 7"

I grew up in Ireland during the war, although in Dublin we didn't really know that there was a war – who was fighting who or whatever. My family never took newspapers and there wasn't any English news in them anyway. We had a radio but every night we kids were sent to bed right after tea at about six o'clock. The radio wasn't switched on until later after my father came home so we never heard the radio news either.

Once I overheard a friend of my father's telling him that the Germans had bombed Ring's End the previous night. Ring's End was a part of Dublin quite close to where we lived; it's also the part of Ireland nearest to England. It's where the ships came in to Dublin. The Germans had apparently bombed it by mistake. It makes you wonder a bit that they couldn't tell the difference between England and Ireland!

We lived right on the edge of Dublin Bay, and sometimes at night we could hear the drone of German aircraft dropping bombs on England across the Irish Sea. Although we were off the direct sea lanes, many times the tide washed pieces of the war right up onto our beach – life buoys, wooden wreckage from ships, cheeses, boxes of oranges, coal, biscuits, tins of corned beef. We picked the tide line almost every day, collecting the wood and coal to make fires for our homes. That was one of our jobs.

The Irish Army patrolled the beaches, on guard against an invasion although we were never sure who they thought was going to invade. The soldiers would give us bits of chocolate if we ran errands for them – went to the shops or whatever. These were about the only sweets we had until after the war was over. I still remember that chocolate. Black. Very hard. The best chocolate I've ever had. One time I remember a big old mine was washed up onto the beach. A massive great thing with spikes sticking out of it. The army blew it up.

Because of the war, there weren't many deliveries to Ireland from overseas so there was a shortage of some kinds of food and other goods. There was no meat. No sugar. No bread. No tea. No oranges or bananas. Tobacco was in short supply. We had ration stamps but with four children there was never enough and we had to look for ways to feed ourselves. One thing we did was rabbit hunting. Another was that two or three times a week, when the tide was out, we'd take a fishing line about 100 yards long with baited hooks every few feet and stake it down on the sand. The tide would wash over it and when it drew back again we'd have a nice little catch of flatfish and mackerel – enough to share with the neighbors. That was something about those times. People looked after each other more then. Shared things. Everybody seemed to work together in those days.

I wore short trousers throughout the war. They had patches on top of patches but neighbours handed on clothes to us when their own children had outgrown them just as we did with clothes my sisters had outgrown. My own clothes were too worn out to pass on. My dad used to patch the soles of our shoes from old car tires. When we'd go walking on the beach, we'd leave tread marks behind us like a motor car. Mostly I remember how bloody heavy my shoes always seemed!

My father also had a garden to supplement our food supply. He grew tomatoes, beans, cabbages, carrots, lettuce. We also had chickens and had our own supply of eggs so although there was rationing, and we didn't have much money, at the same time we didn't seem to miss much either. We children lived a very strict life. We'd get up. Go to school. Work hard. Do as we were told by the nuns and priests. Come home. Collect wood and coal from the beach. Go hunting for rabbits or service the fishing lines we'd staked out in the bay. Do our exercises from school. Have tea. Go to bed. At school we were given gas masks and shown how to use them and how to do air raid drills but we didn't really understand what they were about and I don't think we took them very seriously. It was a strict Catholic school where they used the cane and the strap pretty freely so we just did as we were told without asking questions or thinking about it too much. We just assumed that carrying gas masks was the normal thing to do. Everyone we knew did it.

Generally speaking we didn't get many presents. At Christmas my sisters used to get dolls. I was the only boy in our family and I used to get a Ludo set one year and Snakes and Ladders the next. This happened for several years. But once, for my birthday, I got a cowboy outfit. A gun, hat, and vest. My heroes at the time were from American cowboy movies so my friends and I used to go into the woods near my home and play cowboys and indians. Naturally, I was always Hopalong Cassidy or Gene Autrey.

Sunday was a special day. I still remember Sunday

Short trousers, patches on top of patches, and a carrot from his father's garden. Les Foreman may once have looked much like this.

breakfast which was about the only time in the week when we'd have meat. I don't know how my father got it. But we'd all get up and the house would be warm from the big wood burning range in the kitchen. It was alight twenty-four hours a day with the coal or wood we'd picked up from the beach and the kitchen would be warm. My mother would be bustling about with an apron on and we'd have a huge family breakfast of tea, bacon, sausages, eggs, black pudding*, white pudding*, tomatoes, and potatoes. Potatoes were one thing we had plenty of. I always remember that feeling of warmth and of my stomach being full; the smell of the fire and the cooking and knowing that after the meal we'd be off to Church. And after Church I might get a chance to go with the other boys to see a football game or some hurling*. My favourite team at the time was Donnegal. Sundays were special. Looking back, the war seemed very faraway from us in Dublin. I didn't know when the war began; I didn't know when it ended. We hardly knew it existed. It affected our lives – but then again it didn't.

Les Foreman   *Irish   Sign-maker and Printer   Aged 5-7*

By the second year of the war, there wasn't much food around but it was dangerous to say so. We had heard of a government official who had been arrested for speaking out about civilian conditions in a way that suggested the military could make mistakes. Our own position was very vulnerable.

We were the only foreigners around. I was regarded as a foreigner, even though I was half-Japanese. My Japanese mother was very ill. Sometimes she would burst into tears and sit on the floor. I couldn't help her up, and I would have to fetch my father. When she started falling over, my father sent for a doctor, who was a nice man with big soft brown eyes. When he came, he spent some time looking at Mummy, while my father sat with me in the garden.

At last the doctor came out into the garden and talked to my father and me. "She is dying. There is nothing I can do. There are no medicines available. When she dies there will be nothing to keep you here. Life will be very difficult for you. The Americans have bombed Tokyo. I don't expect you have heard this. Nobody knows how they reached us as their air bases are too far away. Feeling is growing against all foreigners. You will be better leaving here if you can."

Mummy died a few days later.

My father kept having lots of meetings with many different people, and one day we walked out without any luggage, just in the clothes we wore. He took me to the station and we left Kobe. Just like that. No explanation.

Two days later we left from some port, I don't know where, in a very crowded ferry which took us to a small port in what is now Korea. All the Europeans (about ten of us, most of whom were old men and women) were put in a railway carriage with an old man who acted as some sort of servant. He spoke Chinese and Korean. From the look of him I think he must have been Indian.

A food queue in Tokyo. During the war, rationing and long food queues were a daily reality for city dwellers. This mother and her children patiently wait their turn. On this day, only beans were available.

We spent three days in the train. We ate dried thin biscuits, and drank water from a tea urn that was brought to us whenever the train stopped. There was no lavatory so we all rushed outside at these stops. Finally we were ordered to leave the train and march on our own without any escort up a road leading over some low hills. After a couple of hours of slow walking, we saw a lorry coming down the road to us. It had a big red star on it, but the man driving it was British. "Welcome to Russia. I am a British Army Major and it is my job to see to your repatriation."

We saw very little of Russia. There was a guard in the corridor who spoke only Russian. The Major would speak to him and give him a cigarette if we needed something, and the guard would go away for a while, then return with anything from a bowl of soup to a cup of black tea. There was a lavatory and wash basin compartment on this train, but no soap, and the water was brown and salty. We spent about ten days in the train with blackout curtains pulled down. We were forbidden to look outside and the Major advised us not to do anything to annoy the guard. You know, in ten days, I never once saw that guard asleep.

Finally we seemed to stop for ages, then we were taken out and we were standing on a very cold dockside where the Major took us over to some British sailors. We left Russia on a destroyer. We had to stay below for almost the whole trip. The vibration was terrible. The ship would sway one way then the other. My father said that we were avoiding torpedoes. Once we heard a loud banging as the guns fired very rapidly.

We arrived in Liverpool in mid-September 1943. I do not know the exact date. We were taken to a big shed where people interviewed us. My father had to leave with some important looking people in dark suits. A very nice policeman took me out for tea, then he took me by car to an Aunt in Morecambe where there was so much food I was quite sick. Auntie kept apologizing, saying that there was so little to eat because of the rationing. It was a lot more than we had in Japan.

Francis O'Brien   *Irish-Japanese   Diplomat   Born 1930*

We lived on Kyushu Island, southern Japan, in what was then a small market town of about 20,000 inhabitants called Takeda. My eldest brother was nineteen years older than me and had to join the army. He was killed on a battle field in Okinawa at the age of thirty-two.

Until the start of war we had a nanny and servants and employees, but as the war progressed my father's company had to close since all production facilities in Japan were turned into manufacturing arms and weapons. The domestic help had to be released due to our reduced financial circumstances. Father died of a stroke when I was ten years old. After the war my mother restarted the business but she had been in poor health and died a few months after hearing that her eldest son had been killed.

Up until war started, I had pet chickens and Angora rabbits which I loved feeding and caring for. I also had goldfish in our garden pond that I would feed, but the neighboring cats would catch and eat them. I had a very happy childhood, reading, playing baseball, swimming in the river, fishing, and climbing trees but war changed all that.

I attended school regularly until the war then gradually the school days became less and less as paper and pencils became a luxury. Since all the young men had been recruited into the war, the farmers had no workers so we children had to go and work on the farms. Our teacher would truck us out to large halls of temples or school buildings in the country from whence we would have to go to the various farms to help tread wheat, or plant and harvest rice. To this day I have a scar on one finger caused during scything rice. Generally speaking, we enjoyed living together in these temples or school buildings. As children we were so innocent that it seemed like a picnic outing. We hated the work though. There was one farmer, I recall, whom we all hated because he treated us like slave labor, always urging us to work harder and faster. Otherwise the countryside was peaceful, no noise, no airplanes.

Then when I was eleven years old and I would have been in secondary school, we school children were commandeered to work at the Nakajima Aerospace Company factory on the outskirts of town. Here we had to help in the assembly of airplane parts for the fighter planes. Of course we were a target for American bombings. At one time I was outside the factory when the bombers arrived. There were no shelters so wherever we were we had to lie face down on the ground. During one of these daytime raids I was outside lying face down and I thought I must have been hit because I could feel something very warm against my leg. It turned out that the leg of another lad lying next to me was pressed close against mine. The factory was never hit, but a few hundred yards beyond the factory the bridge was blown up.

Another time the American planes shot at a passenger train in the railway station which was bringing the wounded into our town. There were many civilian casualties from these raids, women and children. They would be trucked in for treatment at the several hospitals in Takeda. We would go and look at them. I don't remember these villagers crying or screaming, just moaning. Usually they would be too exhausted from the journey and their wounds by the time they arrived at the hospitals. The worst sight for me was seeing an old woman with a bullet protruding between muscle and skin in her arm.

Food was in extremely short supply. We were lucky to

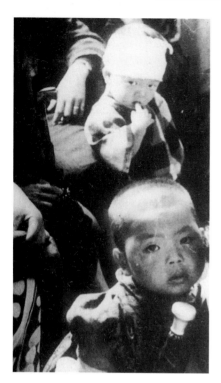

This Japanese child sustained his injuries at Hiroshima. War was no respecter of age – old or young.

live in a provincial town, away from the major cities where many people actually died from starvation. Food was very scarce, just a few potatoes but more often than not only the potato greens in water. Rice, which was our staple food, was now a luxury. We had no tea, no meat, fish, butter or sugar most of the time. We had salt, and occasionally we managed to secure a bit of flour from the black market which was made into dumplings for the salt water soup. At the start of war we managed to barter clothes (silk kimonos) for provisions from the farmers, we also probably ate my pet chickens. Later on there was very little. Spinach and cabbage were another luxury. My family had the good fortune to have a relative, my uncle, who owned a large section of the farm land in our prefecture.* About twice a year my mother and I would go and stay with my uncle for a week or so and then we had more to eat. He would give us provisions to take back to town including rice, and persimmons and plums when they were in season. But most of the time we were hungry.

The war gave me the strength to live. It has made me patient during hard times. Its legacy to my generation is to value the importance of food and not to waste it. To this day I cannot bear to waste food and I am a plate cleaner.

Hiro Soeda   *Japanese   Banker   Born 1931*

Soon after Pearl Harbor, the war in the Netherlands East Indies (now Indonesia) broke out. It was marked by Japanese bombardments on Surabaya, eastern Java, where I was born and lived as a three year old with my parents. My father, a Dutchman, was taken prisoner immediately at the beginning of the war. My mother, who was about to have a baby, took refuge with me from the frequent bomb attacks in the mountainous area of Malang, where she hoped to be safe. My sister, however, was born during air raids and, not long after mom had left with her baby, the doctor's house was hit by bombs and completely destroyed. I remember when we got news of a convoy transport of Dutch prisoners. My mother went and stood along the expected route. When the prisoners went past, she held her newborn baby high up in the air, hoping that dad would notice. [He did]!

Mother had closed off our house in Surabaya, sold some of our belongings, and stored silverware and other valuables, never to see any of it again after the war. Now without income, she made a little money by selling food she had cooked, with teaching, and with small business deals. The business deals were the most profitable. Later, my grandmother sold some of her gold jewelry to keep us going. I remember the day my Belgian grandfather, aged sixty-five, was taken prisoner during a razzia [round up] for Belgians. That was the last time we saw him. After the war we learned he had been starved to death in one of the old man's camps. As a child I could not grasp what was going on. I just stood there in the hall when he was taken away, but I can still feel the agony of the remaining family members, my grandmother, my mother, and my aunt. An hour later we were taken prisoner ourselves, on such short notice that we were unable to prepare what to bring as personal belongings, only what one could carry by hand.

Everything else was left behind. My mother carried my baby sister and I was responsible for my parent's wedding picture, the only family picture that survived the war. I carried my own small bundle of clothes. Ultimately we found ourselves in Kramat camp, a women's and children's camp, in a town area of Batavia [now Jakarta]. We occupied a small storage space which would sleep five people on the floor at sixty-five cm [about two feet] per person. Mosquitoes and cockroaches were a pest, but I liked watching the cicaks, tiny lizards, crawling along the wall and ceiling at night. They could regrow their tail when it was lost and I often wondered how they could do that.

The camp became increasingly overcrowded and was fenced in by gedek [high bamboo fences] through which one could not see what happened on the other side. It was like living in a prison. For us children the world became very limited. The gates were guarded by armed Japanese and we were never allowed to go out of the camp anymore. Only the dead were taken out, for burial, rolled in straw mats. Seven or eight people died every day.

The prison camp period lasted almost three years and to my recollection nothing much happened during that time. For children my age, camp life could be marked by "nothingness." By order of the Japanese authorities education was not allowed, therefore there was no school. No activities either: no clubs, no pets, no music, no radio, no news from fathers or other family members. No books, no paper or coloring pencils for drawing or other art work and no toys. There were no birthday parties or celebrations for Sinterklaas* or Christmas and no religious services for the young. No inoculations against diseases, no dental care, and no medicine for the sick. In general no supplies at all. No new clothes or footwear either.

Food was insufficient, it mainly consisted of rice and soup containing some greens and a daily ration of corn or sweet potato bread. No specials for children like eggs, milk, fruit, or meat, not to speak of sweets or snacks. The food would be prepared at a central kitchen according to supply. Sometimes food was withheld as a punishment for the whole camp. My aunt worked in the kitchen at the distribution of the rice. She had to make sure that all the 3400 people in the camp – up to the very last one queuing – would receive an equal scoop, a very distressing responsibility. Quite often she was blamed for having favorites who would get their rice

pressed a little, thus receiving more than others.

I remember being always hungry, even though my mother gave me extra food from her own rations. The children would search garbage for edible leftovers and so did I. My mother agonized when she found out about this, but would not stop me. She was more sad than mad. I once stole a neighbor's cooked garden snail. It was left unattended and I remember well how it looked: black, shiny, edible, within reach – and irresistible. I quickly grabbed and devoured it. Children also had their secret businesses involving food. I once made a deal whereby I could use a friend's pencil eraser that looked like a magic toy to me for the price of a slice of bread. The problem was how to get a slice of bread? I remember the dilemma I found myself in and the solution – by just nibbling at my own ration, and smuggling it away under my clothes, unnoticed by my mother.

I was sick a couple of times with children's diseases including whooping cough and suffered from nightmares in which a big orangutan would come in through the window to get me, pulling at the skin of my arm which would stretch like elastic, but he never managed to take me along.

What did we do to get through the day? There was roll call twice, "Tenko." The afternoon roll call was in the heat of the day, in scorching sun and one was never sure how long it would last. Children were included and even the youngest had to stand up all the time. When I wanted to sit down, ignorant of the Japanese punishments for the adults who were responsible, I was disciplined "up" by a pull at my hair. My sister, who could hardly stand by herself, was kicked up.

It was very important for the Japanese to demonstrate the proper respect and bow for the Emperor, the Tenno Heika. As prisoners, we were at the lowest position on the human ladder, and we had to make the deepest possible bows. Much effort was spent teaching us, the children, too. Like in a military drill they shouted at us: "Kiotsuke! [Get ready!] Kirei! [Bow!] Naure! [Get up!]"

We played with sand, rainwater, sticks and stones and roamed the different areas of the

A rare photograph of life inside a camp for civilian detainees. Life was much the same in all of them. Here, an American mother cooks the daily meal of corn mush for herself and her children; the strain of their ordeal shows on their faces.

camp with playmates. There were plenty of other children, but because of the always shifting camp population no lasting friendships developed.

Time passed, one grew older and, if lucky, would not die. Sickness and death were all around and I was very much aware of it. I remember how a friend of mine, who looked apparently healthy, died in just a few hours. Of what? I never knew. It happened a couple of times that my little sister would turn blue, seized by convulsions, a frightening condition. What to do? Would she die? My mother certainly worried a lot. I remember her agony and my own feelings of uselessness, being unable to help. One learned to be suspicious and that there was no certainty in life. Nothing. That's what I clearly remember from the camps. Nothing.

Many young children worked in the camps on a variety of jobs. I never did, but my sister must have been one of the youngest. Her job? Cheering up the sick and the old in the camp "hospital." She was paid a spoon of sugar and an extra ration of bread a week.

There was nothing special about this way of life. At the end of the war, barely seven years old, I did not know anything else. Life in prison camp had become the "norm." I was very skinny, clothed in rags, barefooted, with ill-healing wounds on my feet. I had never gone to school. I no longer knew what the word "father" meant, because none of the children had a visible father. In fact, I had no proper recollection of how "white" men like my own father would look. I only knew the Japanese commanders and camp guards, the "Japs," who were armed with guns and bayonets or were swinging their bamboo clubs. In their typical grey-green uniforms and caps they would shout their orders and were quick-hitting.

I have no special memory of how the war ended. According to my mother an airplane flew over one day, waving a red, white, and blue Dutch flag. There was great joy with people crying, laughing, and praying. A live pig was brought in for slaughter. From then on there were no roll calls anymore. We stayed in the camp several more months while nothing much changed in our lives. The food supplies, however, became more generous and our health condition improved somewhat. Outside the camp the situation had become dangerous because of the attacks of Indonesian nationalists on Dutch people. The camps were now protected for safety by English guards and Nepalese Ghurkas. Where could we go?

From this period one event stands out in my memory. An open truck arrived in our camp one day with sailors from a British ship, anchored at Tanjug Priok, the harbor of Batavia, inviting children for a children's party on board their ship. My mother encouraged me to join, but I was very suspicious. How could it be outside the camp, where only the dead bodies went? How could she let me go with these strange looking people, whilst during war transportations she had strapped me close to herself, afraid as she was to be separated from me or even lose me altogether. Now she encouraged me to go and leave the camp without her? What unfamiliar language did these sailors speak? It was neither Dutch, my own language, nor Japanese, nor Bahasa [Indonesian] of which I knew the sounds and understood some words. I could not understand the situation, but joined the party anyway. What a wonderful party it turned out to be!

I remember the truck ride along the wide open spaces of the road to Tanjung Priok, a marshy area at that time. I enjoyed exploring the ship where I could see the engine rooms. The sailors showed cartoons and offered peanut butter sandwiches and chocolate bars for snacks, which I only knew from hearsay, and red-coloured lemonade that looked like. . . poison. I refused to drink it, asking for non-coloured water instead.

At about that time, news of family members came through via the Red Cross. Grandad had died in the old men's camp at Ambarawa. One of my aunts had died. My four uncles and my father had survived. Dad was in a refugee camp in Singapore. After many efforts my mother managed in December 1945 to get boat transportation for the three of us – herself, my sister, and me – to join my father in Singapore. Communications were very difficult because telephone and mail service had not been restored yet. Therefore our arrival was a total surprise to my father, with whom we had a happy family reunion. At last he could embrace his youngest daughter, who was born during air raids, after he had been taken prisoner. It was very joyous. We had so many things to say and didn't know how to say them.

We stayed in Singapore for five months. The Wilhelmina and Irene camps were makeshift camps, where food was distributed through soup kitchens. I was responsible for getting it and hopelessly lost my way the first time. My mother met her former school headmaster and together they set up a school, working wonders with the bits and pieces of knowledge and the variety of students who attended. A blackboard, chalk, slate, and slate pencil were the only instruction materials available. In that makeshift school I finally learned how to read and write.

Nowadays, I feel very negative. About Germans. . . I feel. . . they are not very popular with me. But I can deal with them, I can exchange ideas with them. But not with the Japanese. I lived in Japan but found out they don't know much about the war. They don't learn about it in school. I made friends with Japanese women but found the men – well, horrible. They have a way of ignoring women as if they are air. Perhaps an apology? Yes, perhaps an apology. . .

Beatrix Hilbers-Schoen *Dutch Housewife Aged 3½ – 7*

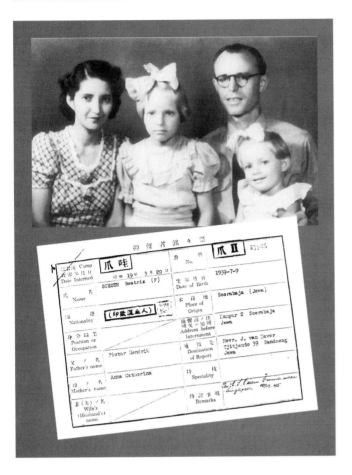

"Time passed, one grew older and, if lucky, one would not die." Beatrix Schoen, aged 7, and her family are reunited after four years of incarceration in separate detainee camps.

As a young Dutch girl born in Java (Netherlands East Indies) I experienced the war years with my mother in a Japanese camp during their occupation. Early in March, 1942, the city of Soerabaja (East Java) in which I lived, was under siege. The Japanese were bombing the town. We could hear the explosions in the distance. My father was a volunteer in the Home Guard and was trying to hold one of the main bridges into town but failed. On Sunday, 8th March, the Japanese Army entered the city. The streets were deserted. Everyone stayed indoors. We all felt something was about to happen that would change our lives forever.

One evening, during the usual blackout, we were finishing dinner when we heard shouting and banging on the door. Our houseboy opened it and a Japanese officer, accompanied by an interpreter, barged into the room. He was shouting and waving his arms. Apparently a light had been visible from the servants' quarters at the back of the house. My father apologized for the oversight, but the officer was not pacified. We were standing together when all of a sudden he swung around to my father with his arm outstretched, ready to hit him. My mother immediately jumped between them. This so unnerved the officer that he lowered his arm, turned around, and left without a word. I burst into tears. My mother looked at my father's chalk white face and said, "I had to do it because I was afraid you might hit him back."

This was my first realization what war and occupation were going to be like. Toward the end of 1942, the first camps were being prepared and bamboo fences were erected around designated streets. The houses were cleared of furniture, except for beds and a few chairs, so that more people could be accommodated. One by one the men were being picked up and sent away to separate camps. My father's firm had been taken over by Japanese businessmen who wore military uniforms. Early one morning after my father had gone off to work, a truck pulled into the driveway. A Japanese officer told my mother that my father had been arrested for sabotage by the Kempeitai [Japanese Gestapo] and that we were going to be interned.

He then gave orders to clear out the entire contents of our house except for my room with its dolls and toys. My mother was in shock. She knew that my father's arrest by the secret police meant his torture. She was on the floor crying, feeling she had lost everything. The house was silent. The servants were stunned and afraid. All the doors were open. I called "Anybody there?" but there was no answer. I didn't know what to do. I hadn't lost anything. All I could think to do was to roller skate through the empty rooms. This of course was not something I was usually permitted to do. The floors of our house were of stone. I still remember the way the iron wheels on my skates echoed through the house.

A few days later we moved across the road into the first camp of our internment. Women and children were separated from the men and those boys older than ten years. Several weeks later we were herded into trucks and taken to the railroad station for transport to another camp. We were shoved into trains with windows blacked out and began a journey to an unknown destination. We eventually arrived in Samarang (Middle Java). The camp was in an abandoned cloister from which the nuns had been expelled.

We stayed in this camp the next nine months. At that point the food supply was adequate, though not abundant. Our first death came soon after we entered the new camp. It was a year old baby boy. He was carried in a small wooden coffin for burial outside the camp. Later on more and more deaths occurred. Soon the supply of wooden coffins was exhausted and bodies had to be carried out in carts pulled by people and placed without cover in graves.

Soon we were transported again, this time to Ambarwa, south of Samarang. By now, the food supply had deteriorated and was insufficient to sustain both adults and growing children. We were sleeping thirty-nine to a room the size of 9 meters by 7 [30 x 23 feet] on raised wooden plank beds, with 45 cm [18 inches] space per person. There were no toilets, just a smelly gutter at the end of a passage. We

THE DOLLS OF AMBARAWA

Like the other children in the prison camp, we had nothing to play with. You were not permitted things like toys. Not officially, at least, so we learned to make our own. I was friendly with another Dutch girl in the camp. Her name was Tommie Prins. She had a little pair of nail scissors and some pencil crayons – just red, yellow and blue. We decided to make our own toys. Paper was rare in the camp but we managed to get hold of the cardboard a carton of cigarettes comes in and from this we made a family of cutout dolls. Mother, father and daughter and then we created a wardrobe for them. We found bits of paper and designed quite an

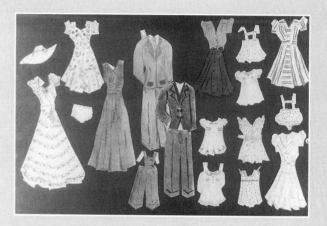

extensive wardrobe with dresses and suits for all occasions, all with matching accessories. Then we cut out the clothes to fit the dolls with little tabs to affix them.

Tommie was the main designer. She was quite good at it. I always thought she might become a fashion designer after the war. Considering she had only three colors to work with, her designs were quite amazing. Tommie was also the one who drew the faces since I wasn't very good at it.

When we played, we'd have conversations with

the dolls. For instance, you might say to the mother doll, "Where are you going tonight? You say you're going shopping? And then to dinner with your husband? And then perhaps to the ball?"

"Very well then, let's dress you in your blue and red striped dress for shopping. You'd look perfect in that. And we'll give you your blue hat with a matching handbag. And while you're out shopping, I'll have the servants lay out a change of clothes for dinner."

Of course, our conversation with the dolls was a reflection of the comfortable colonial life we had once known. But it was the only life we knew and, from the perspective of a prison camp, it seemed very far away, another world.

We were careful to hide our dolls and to play with them in such a way that the guards wouldn't notice. Sometimes we talked our secret language [see page 75] to keep them safe. We managed to protect them all the way through the war. After the liberation we took them with us and now here they are. We survived the prison camp and so did they.

Els Huss-van Ham *Dutch Housewife Born 1932*

were divided into blocks each with our own appointed head who represented us when the Japanese commander summoned her to convey orders or complaints. Occasionally, when we had to be punished for whatever reason he saw fit, we had to stand for hours in the burning midday sun. To stand that long was difficult. Things get blurred, out of focus. You begin nodding but if you fell over you were kicked and beaten until you got up again. Each morning there was roll call. In the evening each woman was detailed for night patrol, just as in a military camp.

It was still possible if you took a chance of going near

the fence to barter with the locals for food. You could get things like eggs. Occasionally someone would be caught and the whole camp might be punished (usually by standing at attention for up to seven hours) as well as the culprit. Offenders were beaten publicly. With fists, the side of a sword, whips. You could be beaten with fists for not bowing deeply enough or for nodding or moving when you were supposed to be at attention.

One of the girls in our room became a lifelong friend and even now we still occasionally talk about our experiences. We developed a secret language, talked about food (especially chocolate). We walked endlessly through the camp to relieve the boredom as we were too young to be put on work details. We had no books, toys, or school lessons. We made paper dolls from a few bits of treasured pieces of paper. [See Box on left]

Sometimes we would sing Dutch children's songs: [sings]:

> Onder Moeder's Paraplui
> Liepen eens twee Kindjes
> Hanneke en Janneke
> Dat waren dikke vrindjes. . .

> [Under mother's umbrella
> Stood two little girls,
> Hanneke and Janneke,
> Who were bosom friends. . .]

Our secret language was so no one could understand us – not that we had much to be secretive about. The idea was to insert the letter "p" between consonant and vowel. We called it the "P" language. If we were speaking the "P" language the first two lines of the song above would look like this:

> Ondeper Mepoedeper's Peparpaplpui
> Lepieppen eens twpee Kepindjes. . .

Since water was rationed, we bathed only when it rained. We'd go right outside away from the long corridors inside the huts. There was another reason I liked bathing outside. I hated to see the older women in the camp when they were naked. They were starving of course and their skin hung down in flaps. I couldn't bear to be with those ugly women with their flesh hanging. Soap had become a forgotten luxury. We never had any but even so, when we were bathing in the rain, we couldn't stop ourselves from making washing gestures.

We had few clothes and toward the end of the war my mother used her secretly saved tea towels to make a pair of shorts for me. Our shoes were wooden Indonesian "clogs" which loudly "clip-clopped, clip-clopped" as we roamed the passageways of the camp.

One day I developed an abscessed tooth. It was a large tooth. A molar. My face became swollen and painful. As there was no medication my mother decided that the tooth had to come out. Someone came forward with a pair of pliers. I was seated on something, then four people held me down. One on each leg, one on each shoulder. My mother was screaming, "Oh, no!" and trying to tell me to be brave. After several jerks, during which I probably passed out for a second, the tooth popped out. It was black with the abscess

hanging from it. Blood gushed down my chin and it is miraculous that I did not die of blood poisoning. I was in great pain for several days and although I was starving, I couldn't eat.

Early in 1945, we were moved to another camp for what turned out to be the last time. With what few belongings we still possessed on our backs, we walked several miles to our new "home." It was the worst of all. But we survived.

At last, on 24 August 1945, everyone was summoned before the camp commandant for "an important announcement." Our guards had been pretty brutal over the past few weeks, perhaps because they felt their power slipping. I was too sick with dysentery to walk so I stayed behind in the barracks with a few other sick people. I hated those barracks. Everything there smelled of death. Every time you woke, somebody was dead. You got used to smells. There weren't any nice smells in that place.

Suddenly, in the distance, I heard singing and, after a few minutes, I realized it was "Wilhelmus," the Dutch national anthem. I began crying. Singing and crying. Somehow, somebody produced a Dutch flag. Hostilities had ended. I learned later that the Commandant had made no mention of atomic bombs nor of the word, "surrender."

For several weeks more food slowly reached our camp. Lord Mountbatten came to the camp one day to see for himself the condition of the women and children and the effects of starvation. The British troops, arriving from Singapore, began to organize a repatriation to our original location of residence before the war. However, the Indonesian freedom movement, who had been armed and encouraged by the Japanese, erupted full blast. When the day came for us to return to our home city of Soerabaja, we were greeted on arrival by jeering young Indonesians armed with spears. "Merdeka [Freedom]!" they shouted. "Merdeka!"

Once again, we were placed in a camp, this time guarded by Indonesian soldiers for "our own protection." Nothing had changed.

Food was scarce and for several weeks we lived in empty houses without electricity. The British Army finally landed troops in Soerabaja and, after heavy fighting against Indonesian "freedom fighters," we were evacuated to Singapore. Several trucks, driven by tough, fierce-looking Ghurkas, arrived to take us to the harbor. As we started to get into the last truck, a woman discovered that two of her children were missing. She called out and, when the children appeared, she discovered that there was no space left in the vehicle. So my mother volunteered to give this woman and her children our space. We crawled out to wait for the next one.

Shortly after the convoy pulled away we heard gunfire down the road. Later we discovered that some of the trucks had come under fire from Indonesian nationalists. Many women and children who had survived years in the horrible camps were killed and wounded just as they were being taken to freedom. Eventually my mother and I were found by the Swiss consul, a friend of the family, and he took us in his official car away from the camp. The car was so cramped that I had to ride on the footboard [running board]. He drove at high speed to the harbor where we were loaded onto an old Japanese troop transport now operated by the British. We arrived in Singapore two days later, truly free at last.

By then we knew my father was alive and my mother managed to get a message to him. He came immediately and we all stood there in shock. "Pappie" and "Mammie" were together again. He was still very thin but by then we had filled out a little. We all just stood there. We couldn't speak or move. At last I jumped up to him. His arms were open. Someone was saying, "All three of us came out of this. . . we're all together again."

Els Huss-van Ham *Dutch   Housewife   Born 1932*

I was eleven and going to school in the morning when I found that an entire main street crossing on my way had been blocked off with a high solid wooden fence. I had to make a detour to get to school. Later on I learned what had happened.

There was a bomb raid the night before. It was cinema time and a cinema specialising in films for young kids (Laurel & Hardy, cowboys and indians, slapstick, etc.) A show was running when the alarm was sounded. Because of the way the cinema was built, the kids could not stay in there during a raid, but had to get to the nearest shelter which was about 100 meters away. As they came out from the cinema, they got as far as the street corner, and a bomb hit in the midst of the crowd. About fifty kids died instantly. It took the cleaning-up crew many days to clean up the place, but you could still see blood marks on the pavement for weeks afterwards. Some garments, mainly caps, were left on one of the street corners to be picked up. I saw one woman pick one up and cry . . . It was her son's.

Borje Kyrklund *Finnish   Aged 7*

Moshe had a small shop in the village. His wife wore a yellowish wig. He delivered groceries to our house and bought things from us. He looked timidly around, bowed many times, his cap held awkwardly in both hands. With his son he lived in a makeshift shed. The boy had black curly hair, a flat nose. I was allowed neither to play with him, nor with other children who, wild and dirty, might carry lice. I longed for friendship but achieved it only in daydreams. I imagined myself, with excitement and clarity, walking with

somebody across an immense plain, understood, sharing confidences.

It was several years later, on the day it was already known that the Germans were going to deport all the Jews to their death, I was with father in the village. Almost stunned, I did not listen to what Moshe was saying to him. His face seemed to be smiling, but from nearby I saw that his skin was shaking and twisting.

To reach our sawmill, it took over an hour to walk through the forest. Foresters lived with their families in wooden houses and, since the outbreak of war, other men had joined them. Allegedly they worked in the sawmill or helped father in other jobs and only father knew who they really were. One day, after this conversation in the village, I saw Moshe's son carrying some timber between the houses in the forest. My father thought that there he would be safe. This lasted for about a month. Then he was killed by a man from the village called Bolek. It was said that he spied for the Germans. Bolek did not get very far. Soon after, he was killed by our men who had seen him shoot the Jewish boy. I went to the spot where Moshe's son died. There I found a small piece of flat bone. I picked it up. There were many similar bones scattered in the bushes near our outbuildings. I had seen farm animals being killed. I had not thought of it as death, and with human beings it was the same.

Once I wanted to have a frog's skeleton. The way to get this was to place a dead frog on an anthill. So I threw stones at a frog for a long time, yet it refused to die. I suffered with it most terribly until, at last, covered with sweat, I ran away.

Magdalena Abakanowicz *Polish   Sculptress   Aged 9*

Sometimes the Germans had raids looking for "Onderdaggers" – the "Submerged People" – who were hiding from the Germans because they hadn't reported for forced labor, for instance, or Jews.

Of the 100,000 Jews living in Holland at the start of the war, perhaps no more than 10,000 survived. People suspected that terrible things were happening to the Jews but there was nothing that could be done without putting your own family at risk. We lived next door to a family named Cohen. We were very friendly with them; the father was a colleague of my father's. One day the whole family just disappeared. They had been taken to Theresienstadt we learned later.

It was strange. All of a sudden they were not there, people we knew very well, but we hardly spoke of them. There were many such things in those days.

Hans Hilbers *Dutch   Director, European Bank for Reconstruction and Recovery   Born 1934*

The metal factory where Jakob Kusmierski worked for up to twelve hours a day, seven days a week. *Insert:* Ghetto money. Money earned by such labor was spent on inadequate rations.

JAKOB MOSES KUSMIERSKI'S WAR

On the 1st September 1939 the war started. On 3rd September, I remember hearing Hitler talking on the radio and on the 5th the Germans came already into Lödz [Poland] and started making and preparing a Ghetto where Jews were to live and work. In April 1940 they were finished and closed the Ghetto. There was barbed wire around it, police on the outside, and Jewish police inside. You couldn't go in or out without permission.

You had to work all day, one or two six-hour shifts. We were paid in Jewish money – Marks – which we used to buy rations though we could never buy enough. The Germans supplied the food which was, of course, very short. You were given two kilos of bread for eight days. This works out to about twenty-five dachas – 250 grams – per person per day. Sometimes in the summer we got potatoes and vegetables. In the winter there were none. Some flour – very little – maybe a kilo for the whole month. We starved. They didn't give us fuel either. We had to burn our furniture, like a cupboard or something, to cook the food. That's why people died. It was starvation and cold: both things are very contributing to people to die, especially in a Polish winter. Many more people died in the winter time. As the war went on rations got shorter and shorter, less and less, and sometimes you had to stand in a long queue to get the ration.

Despite this, we were lucky in that our entire family (my parents, three brothers, and myself) kept together until 1944. We were in the Ghetto, but we were together. I worked in the metal factory at 63 Lagifnizka Street. The factory produced nails for making shoes, special nails. Some sort of metal. We also made parts for the airplanes.

Life was very hard. There were Jewish doctors in the Ghetto but they had little medicine. You just hoped you didn't get sick but with so little food people started not being well. There were no schools, no books or magazines, no toys – maybe an old spinning top, something like that. There was no news of the outside. Some people had secretly some radio. Others said that they could sometimes get a German newspaper. But there was not much news. It was not until after my liberation, after they had thrown the atomic bombs, that I learned that Japan was in the war as well. We had no time or energy to play games. We did not celebrate birthdays; there was nothing to do. Your birthday was just another day. The same with Bar Mitzvah. This, of course, is the day a boy becomes a man. It is very important to us but I never had my Bar Mitzvah. No one in the Ghetto did. There was not time. We worked seven days a week. I never received a present that I can remember. I have no happy memories of my childhood. I don't remember anything that made me laugh.

It was difficult to keep faith. We said our blessings before eating and grace afterwards but on our religious festivals like Passover we still had to work. The same with Saturdays. We couldn't keep Saturday [the Sabbath]. There

Top: A wooden bridge in the Lödz Ghetto carries foot traffic over an "Aryan" street. *Middle:* Children trundling heavy raw material to the Ghetto factories. *Bottom:* The Gehsperre [curfew action] of September 1942. Children under ten and adults over fifty were deported from the Lödz Ghetto to the death camps.

was no religious teaching in the Ghetto, maybe a father or somebody taught you but not organized teaching. Sometimes we sang songs at home, Jewish songs – psalms or songs from the Bible – but nothing organized. We were too tired. One thing that happens when you are starving is that you can't fall asleep. We tried to keep kosher. Sometimes we could get scraps of horsemeat which to us is like the equivalent of pig, an animal with hooves, and forbidden – but we were starving.

The flat we lived in before the war was within the Ghetto so we still had some furniture – a table and chairs at least – so long as we didn't have to burn them to heat or cook. Whatever we had we shared with our relatives in the flat. Until the time we had to go into hiding, we also managed to keep our cherished Shabbat [Sabbath] candlesticks. Once we were forced out of the Ghetto everything was "taken over."

In April 1944 the Russians were near Warsaw so the Germans decided to liquidate the Lödz Ghetto. They were afraid that the Russians would come quickly and liberate the Ghetto. They asked that every factory should give them a list of people whom they should send out first. My two brothers and I. . . we were on the list but my foreman ran immediately to the head office and said they should take me off the list as the eldest and he succeeded. My two brothers were sent away. Of course. . . they were killed. [Weeps].

We were very frightened. We went into hiding in the Ghetto in order not to be taken out. There was a place in the house we were living in – between double doors. It was dark and made it look as if there was nothing there. We were very quiet and the Germans thought the house was empty. They had already written this down in fact. We stayed there for months but survival was very difficult. As we were in hiding, we no longer officially existed and couldn't go for our rations. One of us would go out at night and scrounge whatever was in the fields – very little indeed. Two months later, in August 1944, the Germans came into the Ghetto with a Jewish policeman to look for people who were hiding. This Jewish policeman had told the commandant that we were hiding there. They couldn't see us but the policeman said, "I know where they are." And he did because earlier his sister had been in hiding together with us. She had been promised she would be sent someplace better off, so she had left, but she had told this policeman where we were. So we were captured. We were very frightened. We had an idea of what was in store for us. Notes had been found written on the trains. People suspected the death camps.

They sent my father and mother and little brother and me by all-night train to Auschwitz. We arrived there at five o'clock in the morning and immediately they segregated us. At the segregation my mother grabbed my youngest brother by his hair to hold onto him. My mother and brother were taken to the right. . . straight to the gas chambers. . . [long pause]. . . my father and I went to the left.

We were sent to Block 10 where we were forced to work twelve hours a day on starvation rations. After a few weeks we were sent to eastern Germany to work in a place called Kaltwasser. After two weeks the German officials came back. "There are too many young people here," they said. They wanted to "improve our position," so they said. I didn't believe them and decided not to go, so they asked my father that he should persuade me to go. I gave in and went to be checked together with the others but for some reason the Germans took me out of the queue. They said I was no good for this. I don't know why. I believe those other people went to the gas chambers.

In this camp, one of the German guards gave me every day his portion of bread for a few weeks. He didn't want to talk to me. He just gave it to me like this [gestures] and he even said that I shouldn't work so hard, that I shouldn't run, I should walk to the house. He was actually kind to me. I never knew why. He. . . other people he didn't treat so well. He hit them whenever he could. He made them mad. He would punish them. I never knew his name.

In eastern Germany, it became cold in October. We didn't have warm clothes so at Abfehl [roll call] many people took a blanket, that we had for sleeping, and put it around their bodies. This was Verboten [forbidden]. You were told you shouldn't take the blanket from your bed. One Saturday they wanted to teach us about rules so those that had blankets, they beat them up. Fortunately for me I was wearing my blanket inside my clothes!

When the Russians came near eastern Germany my father and I were taken to Klausenburg in Bavaria. We were there from December 1944 to April 1945. In April the Americans came near to Germany so all the Jews in our camp were put together and counted and on Monday, 16th April, we were put into animal cars to be sent to Dachau. But the Americans came already in their airplanes, shooting at us. They fired on the train each day on Monday, Tuesday, Wednesday, and Thursday. They kept the train from running. The Germans could see we couldn't go by rail so on Thursday, 19th April, they said to us, "Those that can walk, will walk; the ones that can't walk, we will provide transport." So they took my father, who couldn't walk any longer. . . [long pause]. . . they took him and the others by coach to the forest and later on when we were liberated we found out they shot the lot. My father. . . [can't speak]. . .

On Monday, 23rd April, we started walking. At a place near Neuburg von Wald in Bavaria the German soldiers didn't want to go any further. They could see they were surrounded. They left us standing where we were and they packed their baggage. . . and disappeared. I was liberated on the 23rd April by the Americans.

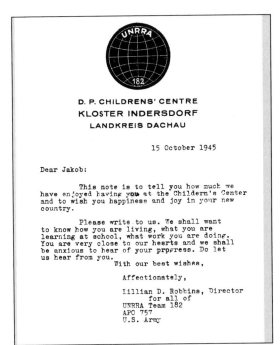

This letter from UNRA* and the clothes he stood in were Jakob Kusmierski's only possessions when he arrived in England in 1945.

After this, the Allied officials took a number of boys and they sent us away to a German church of some sort, near Munich, and there the Jewish UNRA* organized things so that maybe we could go to England. They heard that in England they would allow a few hundred boys under sixteen in. I was among those. Later on, in the middle of June or July, I had a temperature and had to be in the hospital for three weeks. I was worried I would miss transport to England – so I walked out of the hospital. That summer I was sent to England. I arrived with the clothes I was wearing and a letter from one of the children's organizations. I had no other belongings. Nothing belonged to me. Nothing at all. But I remember exactly whatever happened. I can't forget. It's imprinted in my memory. Even today, if I hear German, just the sound of the language, it makes me think me of the Ghetto. My feelings about Germans are not very good [gestures with hand]. Not that I hate them, but I can't be friendly with them. Most of them knew how [the Nazis] treated the Jews and they hadn't protested at all.

The war still affects me in many ways. I'd probably be much healthier, livelier – not depressed and sad. But I have never lost my faith. I always believed some would survive. Maybe I would be one of them.

Jakob Moses Kusmierski, *first-born and only surviving son of Mordechai and Esther Kusmierski, brother of Shmue Kusmierski, Israel Hillel Kusmierski, and Shimson Zeev Kusmierski.*
Al Mekoimom Yovoy'u Vesholoim.
Polish/English "Handbag trade" *Born 1928*

Out-manned and out-gunned, the Danes were unable to resist the German invasion militarily. The Alsung, during which Danes gathered together to sing patriotic songs, was one of their non-violent ways of fighting back. This young girl captures the spirit of Danish resistance.

THEY ALSO SERVE...

It was impossible for Denmark to fight Germany, so our government decided not to resist and they asked us not to fight. At first, people who actively resisted the Germans were branded as criminals by our government. Gradually, however, people began to develop many subtle and non-violent ways of resisting. Perhaps the most powerful of these was the Alsung.

The Alsung was just groups of people coming together to sing Danish songs – not resisting or fighting but not co-operating either when the Germans tried to break the groups up. Sometimes very large groups would come together – up to 150,000 people in one place – all singing. It was beautiful and it was funny. There was nothing the Germans could do about it. Everyone joined in – old people and youngsters as well.

I participated in the Alsung many times during the war. It was our way of fighting back. Mainly it happened in Copenhagen but also in the Jutland and other places in the country. The Alsung spread everywhere. What's surprising is that word about an Alsung was spread from mouth to mouth because of course it was not allowed to announce it publicly. Everybody would agree a certain time and place and then they just somehow came together at the same time and the same place.

We got used to spreading news this way, by word of mouth. There was enormous person to person information going on and we also developed little newspapers all over Denmark during the war. One was called *Information* and it is actually still a newspaper here today but it was started during the war. It was a hand-to-hand newspaper. It was delivered when you passed a person in the street. You took it in passing and then went on because if you were caught with such a newspaper you were taken to the Gestapo HQ, maybe shot. Or sent to a concentration camp.

But about the Alsung, they could do nothing. We sang Danish songs, only Danish national songs. I always remember how intense the singing was – and the feeling it gave you. And there was an irony in many of the songs that the Germans couldn't pick up, lines that would be saying one thing to the Germans and quite another thing to us Danes. For example, there was a line in one of the songs, that could be roughly translated as "Denmark is the best place to stay." It is a long song and this is just the headline of the song. And the Germans would be thinking 'what a charming little folk song' and we would be singing "We could be the best place to be" but meaning that this would only be true when there were no Germans there.

The other thing about the Alsung was that when the Germans tried to break them up, we just ignored them. We just overlooked them. We Danes would speak together but not to the Germans, as if they didn't exist. We just turned our backs to them. That was the worst thing for them. That we couldn't care less about them when they came and tried to interfere with the crowds and push people away. We just gave no reaction like they weren't there. People just stood there singing and ignoring them. The Germans even tried sometimes to put the Danish police onto us. Our police would also try to push us away saying, "It's not allowed to be crowds" because the Germans had made a law that you were not allowed to be more than ten people in a crowd. They were always afraid that our Alsung meetings would be the start of something. But it was just our way of fighting back. Of keeping together as a people.

Last year [1995] there was a big Alsung all over the country. There were bonfires all along the coast of Jutland. You could see from one bonfire to the next. It was to mark fifty years after the end of the war. They say this may be the last time the Alsung is celebrated. I hope not. It was a brave and wonderful thing my country did during the war.

Eyvind Thorsen *Danish Publisher Aged 8*

The Alsung. Parents and children alike shared in this act of national defiance. When ordered by armed guards to disperse, the Danes simply sang all the louder.

More non-violent resistance. In silent protest at the invasion of their country, these Danes wear woollen hats knitted in the form of the red, white, and blue roundels of the R.A.F.

We learned lots of songs in school, for example [Sings in a good, rich tenor] "Jovinessa, Jovinessa,/Prima de Bilase. . ." [Youth, Youth,/Spring of Beauty. . ."] This, of course, was the Fascist Hymn though as far as any of us were concerned, it was just a lively song that we enjoyed singing. Many years after the war, an Italian football [soccer] club was paying a visit to England. The match was held at Stamford Bridge. Probably as a gesture of good will and welcome, the English played this song over the loudspeakers. As far as they were concerned it was just a charming little Italian folk song. The Italians in the crowd went absolutely mad – half of them cheering and the other half booing and jeering. There was a near riot.*

Another song we sang was [Sings] "Alarmi, shell Fascisti. . ." ["Watch out, we are the Fascists/Who order about Communists/For they are frightened to get beaten up. . .]" Everyone used to sing it, even the Communist children, although there weren't many Communists in Bardi – or at least not many who admitted it. At the time we saw nothing odd about a classroom of eight-year-olds singing a song that ended, "We are the Constitution/Our faith is only one faith/We will fight to the last bit of blood. . ."

Tony Sidoli   *British/Italian   Ex-restauranteur, scrap merchant Born 1925*

When my parents had guests, they used to ask my sister and me to sort of perform for them – a dance, a little song. My sister and I used to dread it but on the other hand I suspect we also liked showing off a bit.

Anyway, as one of my party pieces, I had learned the words to "Taps." Not everyone knows there *are* words to it in fact, but there are. [Sings] "Day is done/Gone the sun. . ." and so on. It's a bugle call, of course; short and simple, with only four notes, so even someone as tone deaf as myself could learn it.

At some point in the war, my parents had a bemedalled Marine officer as a house guest and I was duly hauled out to perform. I sang "Taps." Out of shyness I used to look at the floor when I sang. When I finished, I looked up, and was surprised to see tears in his eyes. I thought it was because my singing was so good. It wasn't until much, much later that I understood.

Charles Davis   *American   Retired Lecturer   Aged 9*

Do you remember that song, "Praise the Lord and Pass the Ammunition?" Well, when we heard a doodlebug coming, our teacher made us close our eyes, put our hands over our ears, and sing, "Praise the Lord, and keep his engine running!"

Sylvia Nicholiades   *English   Housewife   Aged 8*

Practical-minded Danes used these white-painted canes to move about during blackouts.

...RATHER LIKE A PRESBYTERIAN MINISTER

Sam Mercer in the uniform of Christ's Hospital School. The school was founded in the sixteenth century by Edward VIth.

The layout of Christ's Hospital School near Horsham in Sussex, is quite distinctive, with four H-shaped buildings arranged around a quadrangle. Its shape made it a superb landmark from the air. On numerous occasions during the war a lone German aircraft would be heard flying low overhead at night. He was in essence a German "Pathfinder." Having located the school, the navigator had simply to check his map and set his compass bearing for London some thirty-five miles distant. To us youngsters it was a bit worrying at first, but we soon became used to it. I often wondered what went through the navigator's mind; thoughts of home? Of his target?

There was a covered passageway in the school nicknamed "the tube" which was used to get from the houses to the refectory during inclement weather. The tube had been sandbagged off to provide some form of shelter from bombs. We also had enormous "Beaver boards" which were held up by toggles over the large windows in the dayroom to provide a blackout during the night.

Christ's Hospital, (which was founded by Edward VIth in 1552), had a curious uniform of long coat, orange stockings, and tailed collars. If you weren't careful with arranging the collar tails, the effect was to look rather like a Presbyterian minister. It took some practice to be dressed properly in this ancient school uniform. Despite this we got used to washing and undressing in total darkness, which became the norm during the war. A result of this has been that throughout my life I have never been inconvenienced in the least by either blackout or power cut.

During the summer of 1944, when I was at home, I would stand on the bridge at Orpington Station watching the doodlebugs go over. Sometimes I would see one pitch over with its engine still firing, while at other times there was just the noise of the engine followed by a sudden silence when it cut off. It was vicariously exciting. I had assumed somehow that I was immortal and that nothing would ever happen to me, particularly since my parents had moved to Orpington from London for safety. It was a bit of a shock when our house was destroyed by a V-1.

Sam Mercer, MBE *English   Civil Engineer   Born 1930*

There was a song I used to like sung by Flannegan and Allen* called, "Run, Rabbit, Run Rabbit, Run, Run, Run." At some point in the war this became transposed into "Run, Adolph, Run Adolph, Run, Run, Run."

Jean Holder   *English   Deputy Head Teacher, retired
Born 1933*

The most popular songs on the radio seemed to be "Mares Eat Oats," and "Three Little Fishes." The Beethoven Fifth Symphony had a special meaning for my father who was a musician before and after the war. He would comment every time he heard it, that "something terrible" would happen.

Tracy Silvester   *American   Real Estate Acquisition   Aged 6*

When I was about six I had to have my tonsils taken out and they used to play a song over and over again – "You are my Sunshine." It was my favourite song for years. I can never hear it without thinking of the war.

Tom Helcke   *Scots   Biochemical Engineer   Aged 8*

The war had a profound influence on me. It could hardly fail to do so when my nursery in the early days of the war was the local Home Guard armoury. Under my bed in the nursery were two astonishingly primitive anti-tank weapons – one called a Blacker Bombard and the other called a Northover Projector. They were actually drainpipes which were allegedly ways of firing grenades at tanks. And there was a box of practice Mills grenades also under my bed.

I remember all the music because we had the Home Guard in Long Preston. There was always something going on like Victory for Troops Day and also the Skipton brass band which played throughout the war. They always played "Colonel Bogey" which of course became the great theme song from "The Bridge on the River Kwai." I remember all the famous songs like the "Sergeant Major Song:" [Sings]: "There was eggs, eggs, eggs,/Jumping about on legs. . .And there was, [Sings]: "We're going to hang out our washing/On the Siegfried Line. . ."

Leo Cooper *English   Publisher/Writer   Aged 12*

One morning, two men from the Soviet embassy paid a visit to our grade school (named for Woodrow Wilson), drumming up support for Uncle Joe [Stalin] and the Russian War Effort. When they reached our third grade classroom, the teacher directed us (as rehearsed) to stand and sing the Russian national anthem, which we had learned through dint of considerable effort from our old but beloved song books.

Anyhow, we dutifully broke out with "God save our little father, the Tzar," or words to that effect. The two Russians looked confused at first, and then horrified. They got quite red in the face, in fact, and the more portly of the two gentlemen rushed over to the school marm, took the song book from her hands, and examined it carefully.

Then, looking somewhat relieved, he said something like, "Very old booook. 1917. *Not* Soviet anthem!"

After that, he attempted to explain to us that things had changed in his country and began describing the boons of the Communist Revolution. We merely thought the fellow was demented, however, since we could understand neither his English nor his fervor. Nevertheless, we all smiled and nodded politely as he prattled on. Our teacher, Miss Johnson, looked decidedly put out and pleased all at the same time, and in my old age I am no longer certain that her decision to teach us "God Save the Tzar" was an innocent act. A couple of weeks after the Russians left town, our class received a thick envelope from the Soviet Embassy in Washington DC, containing thirty barely legible mimeographed copies of the NEW Russian anthem. Miss Johnson let us sing it only once, as if performing some unpleasant duty.

Lee Johnson *American   Archaeologist   Born 1936*

*S**hall I tell you a genuine World War Two joke? Absolutely authentic. I was standing in the playground of Webster School aged about eight when a kid named Tommy Planter came up to me and said, "Hey, do you know why popcorn is so scarce?"*

I said, "No."

So he said, "Because all the kernels are in the Army."

Anonymous *American   Aged "8 or 9"*

At a US school, students have made models to explain what was happening in countries overseas. Here they are holding a peace conference.

I was born in Pontyprith in Wales. My mother, whose name was Jones, was Welsh although she was born in the USA. My father was Italian so I had dual nationality. My father had a wholesale tobacco business which went bust so in the late 1920s he returned to Italy, taking me and my older brother with him. That's why, although I am a British subject, I spent the war and the years just before it growing up in Italy.

In school there was a picture of Mussolini on the wall and one of King Victor Emmanuel III. Every morning and every evening we had to give the Fascist salute to the Italian flag in our classroom. Also to the teacher. At eight years old, none of us were political and had no real idea what this meant. The only thing we knew was that our parents had to have a Fascist party card or they couldn't get work. Up until about 1934 our textbooks were anti-German, a leftover from the First World War. Then, suddenly, one day all our old textbooks were called in and we were given new ones that were not only pro-German but anti-UK and anti-US as well.

During the 1930s, my mother was living in Wales and becoming increasingly concerned about the safety of me and my brother as the war clouds gathered over Italy. In 1939, not too many months before the outbreak of the war, she came over to Italy to take me and my brother back to England with her. My brother didn't want to go, so my mother and I decided to go back together. We got as far as the Italian customs post in Parma only to discover that Mussolini had passed a law stating that no Italian male of fourteen or older could leave the country, in case he was needed for military service. I had just turned fourteen so we were turned back at the border by Italian customs. I still remember my feeling of being trapped and of the injustice of it all. That is why my British mother decided to stay in Italy throughout the war. She wasn't pleased by this. That is also why I, a British-born British subject, eventually found myself serving in the Italian army (from which I deserted twice) and later in the German army (from which I deserted once). The Germans threatened to shoot me if I deserted again. But that's another story.

Tony Sidoli   *British/Italian   Ex-Restauranteur, Scrap Merchant*
Born 1925

Flatbush, Brooklyn, New York. The spring of 1943. A new family appeared in our neighborhood. No one knew when they moved in but everyone knew that men in suits patrolled the neighborhood routinely after they moved in.

Chuck Mueller's dad introduced our family to the Farben family, Dr Carl Farben, Mrs Farben, and "Brother" and "Sister" Farben. We were told that the Farbens left Germany where Dr Farben was chief chemist of a large

chemical company who relocated his family to the US where he hoped to find freedom and peace for his family.

My friend, Courtney McGerraty said his dad, the Brooklyn DA, told him that Dr Farben was helping with the American War Effort. The Muellers said they were "nice people." My Dutch grandma and my dad and mom, both Anglophiles, said, "Watch out! They are very German and they are not like us."

After a few months my sister Ann, my friends Chuck and Courtney, and I knew that Carol ("sister") and Carl ("brother") were just like us. They accompanied us on our weekly raids on the neighbor's Japanese gardener, "Sammy." We learned that only some Germans were bad, but we knew that all Japanese were bad. After all, Sammy was a spy. We knew he had a radio, and we saw him put messages in his lunch box.

Our parents never understood us. After VE Day we found out that the Farbens and the Muellers sent clothes to Germany for homeless families. We asked if we could send some warm clothes to German orphans, and dad turned red and shouted, "We Greeners will continue to send our bundles to Britain," before turning and stomping out of the room. Mother, an English woman to the bone, agreed with dad. Grandma Courtes just muttered to herself and shook her head.

Alan Laurie Greener   *American   8 years old*

Somewhere in the southernmost part of Jaeren [Norway] there is a small rounded point that juts out into the sea. There are no islands, no cliffs, and virtually no trees. On the point there is a rounded mound from where there is a view far to sea and many kilometers inland, as far as the mountains in the south and east. This strategically important place has been a village district for many hundreds of years.

In May 1941, the Germans decided that Haarr would be one of their important posts along the coast of Jaeren. I was five and a half then and the eldest child in the family. I can still see the cars and machinery which rolled over our newly sown fields, though I cannot remember what kind of machinery it was. On the other hand I can remember the number of Norwegians engaged in digging, erecting scaffolding, mixing cement, and moving masses of earth and stones in wheelbarrows. Some were not local people, but other were people from the district who worked for the Germans and whom we called "rats." This word was the first one which told me something about treachery. Many a time my father stood in the sitting room and looked sadly at the destruction of his fields. I heard the grown ups talking about this and that person as being a "rat" and from time to time a tear ran down their faces as they recognised someone they knew.

Norwegian Independence Day. A Norwegian sailor on leave in New York is served by a young Norwegian refugee. New York.

When the "rats" had finished there were five large cannons directed towards the sea on the mound west of our house. There were several bunkers, some close to the house and in the garden, others further off. Some were dug down so deep that you could hardly see them on the surface, others stuck up a little like small spots on one's skin. I learnt the word "siksak" (crisscross), as this was the shape of the trenches. A tower with walls one meter thick was placed north of our garden – later I learnt that it was the command central. There were also spotlights and smaller anti-aircraft artillery. The mound and the four farms on it had been turned into a fortress surrounded by barbed wire. Outside on the shore there were land mines. From time to time mines drifted ashore, and were detonated. When that happened all the windows in the house had to be opened so that they would not be shattered, as the explosion was not more than 150-200 meters away. The children and adults gathered in the cellar when the blast came. Occasionally a window had to be replaced and one or two vases were broken, otherwise there was little damage.

The Germans were everywhere, and we children soon learnt about the military pecking order. The Germans occupied all the four farm houses in the area, and also lived in huts. We had three rooms on the ground floor and had to give them two of these. I learnt my first German words:

"Achtung," "Verboten," and "Schnapps." Schnapps and German parties were to me all one, as there was lots of singing and noise so that my parents had difficulty sleeping.

Gradually the word "German" began to have a bitter taste, and I wanted to do something to these invaders, but never did. None of the adults knew any German before the war, but gradually they learnt some words and the Germans some Norwegian so that they could communicate. They told us that some of these soldiers were also ordinary people who didn't want to go to war.

I can visualise my home surrounded by barbed wire, the Germans singing and marching, and the sound of loud commands. I learnt some of these. One day a troop was practising in the neighbor's yard. I shouted a word which I later learnt meant "join ranks." I was standing against the wall of the house, as I often did, watching, when suddenly in the middle of the exercise I plucked up the courage to shout that one word. It was a wonderful feeling when the whole troop moved, but then I became frightened, as the commanding officer was furious, luckily not at me but at the Germans.

The main road went through our yard, and all the traffic between Stavanger and Egeresund, so we often saw German convoys. We children climbed up onto the water tank next to the road and had an excellent view of the convoy as it wound northwards. It was a strange mixture of marching soldiers, lorries, small cars with officers in, and horses. We were impressed by the beautiful, large and elegant shiny brown horses. We had only seen small pale-brown fjord ponies and smallish darker brown work horses. The four-wheeled wagons drawn by two horses were a wonderful sight. We children watched what passed with a feeling of awe and fear. Here were the conquerors who had occupied our home and our country. We had seen that they behaved exactly as they wanted to and did what they wanted. It was not possible to argue.

War and occupation were part of our everyday childhood. Our games were the games of war. In the sand pit we had stones and blocks of wood which were German tanks, cannons, lorries, and forts. Simple pieces of wood formed in the shape of a cross were English planes bombing our fields.

Only one of the things which the Germans did filled

me with terror and that was when they used the large cannons. I knew they were practising but it was as if those loud powerful blasts pierced my innermost soul and would blow me apart. One kind German soldier realised this and told my parents the day before when they were going to have exercises so I was sent away to some nearby relatives.

None of us children were in doubt that all these fortifications in Haarr were in case of attack or invasion by the English. The words "Englishmen" and "England" had a kind of glory about them. Therefore we thought it reasonable that the Germans had military maneuvers and shooting exercises with the cannons in preparation for the attack. A relative, Ane, who lived on the farm didn't think much of the Germans ability to hit the target with the cannons. The target was on a boat out at sea, and Ane commented, "For the number of times they hit the target I might as well have sat on it."

Special words were attached to these maneuvers: "helmet," "rifle," and "running." We knew whether the soldiers were on exercise by their uniform and equipment. I and my three brothers found out that one stroke on the ship's bell hanging on a pole in the garden was the signal for manning the cannons. One day we managed to lift our little brother up and got him to pull the bell. Then it was the turn of my younger brother, but whilst the other two tried to lift me up, the Germans dashed to their positions. We were frightened and hid, but regained some courage when we saw some grown up faces smiling behind the curtains in the living room.

Lars Haarr *Norwegian   Born 1938*

My father was the officer in charge of our local draft board. My most vivid memories of World War II involve accompanying him down to our local station where the Long Island Railroad, the infamous bane of all commuters, would quietly swoop in on electric power and scoop up my father's latest draftees and deposit them forty-five minutes later near the Army marshalling center in Manhattan. It would be early morning. The Baldwin High School Band would be there in their blue and gold uniforms, John Phillip Sousa music sheets in tow, along with nervous teenage draftees affecting great bravado and tearful mothers, fathers, and siblings, always a few close to collapse. You could sense the fear underlying it all. Maybe as a young undeveloped kid I could sense these things better, or more naturally anyway, not having had much time to develop my life's defences yet.

My father would make a brief, moving speech, quietly reminding everyone why we had to do this terrible thing and more loudly attempting to put into words the community's gratitude to the youngsters standing silently next to their

families, duffel bags at their feet. Then more martial music led by Gene North, Baldwin High's musical conductor for almost forty years. A sergeant always came out from the city on a pre-dawn train and would be quietly standing in the background. The boys understood their new responsibilities and were prepared to meet them – but you never knew!

It all took no more than fifteen or twenty minutes and then the train would slide in almost unnoticed from the east. It would be full of commuters, who by this stage in the war – 1943 or so – knew enough to gaze intently out of the window without much appearing to as the boys scrambled onto a reserved car. From hard experience my father and his colleagues had learned to arrange with the Long Island Railroad and the army for this part of the proceedings to go off with dispatch. I remember to this day, more than half a century later, mothers, fathers, sisters, brothers, grandparents, and friends all trying to say goodbye bravely, maybe even optimistically, and for the most part failing miserably.

There was a lot of resentment and I was occasionally chased home from school – and even roughed up a little if caught – by younger brothers of men my father had drafted. It wasn't until many years later as an adult that it one day dawned on me that without exception the sons he had caused to be drafted were the children of Italian-American and German-American households.

Jim Dougherty *American   Aged 10*

When I was six or seven, we used to spend our holidays at the seaside. We were just down the coast from an important American naval base, but this didn't seem to affect our lives much one way or the other. I used to wake up early every morning and just lie there listening to the sound of the waves coming ashore. I loved the early morning smells of the sea. One morning I got up as usual well before the grown ups and went outside for my early morning patrol up and down the beach. I was permitted to do this provided I didn't go in the water. I was always anxious to see what the sea might have washed up in the night. I certainly got my money's worth this day. For a moment I really couldn't believe what I was seeing.

Our cottage was on a crescent-shaped beach about a mile long. That morning, at the high tide mark, as far as the eye could see, were dead fish. Thousands of them. Tens of thousands, maybe. I've never seen so many fish in one place, before or since. They lay packed side by side like a silvery carpet three or four feet wide and a mile long. All sizes, shapes, and species. It was an extraordinary sight. I began shaking with excitement. My first thought was that maybe I should take some of the fish home to eat but I quickly discovered that, early as I was, every fish on that beach had already been pecked by gulls. The gulls had had a field day but, rather than eat the whole fish, they'd just drilled a neat hole into the fishes' intestines – sometimes three or four holes if it was a big enough fish – and sucked out the insides. I walked along that beach looking for a whole fish. The further I walked, without my at first noticing it, the more my excitement began translating itself into fear. By the time I was halfway down the beach I was just plain scared. I was still the only person on that huge empty beach. Me, and thousands of dead fish. It was eerie. So still and quiet. There was no wind. Even the waves seemed kind of hushed. I don't know what scared me – just a feeling that something was terribly wrong. Like the universe was out of balance. All that death. Suddenly my fear overwhelmed me and I turned and sprinted back down the beach to our cottage. I ran upstairs and woke my parents.

In that annoying way adults had, they didn't understand my excitement – or my fright. They insisted we all have breakfast before we ventured out as a family to see this remarkable sight. By the time we got outside, there were scores of people dotted up and down the beach, standing around in little groups, as incredulous as I had been. By then I had regained my composure. I was a dedicated fisherman and went up and down the beach identifying as many kinds of fish as I could. When I ran out of knowledge I went inside and got my fish book. I still remember my fascination with a very ugly fish my book identified as a deep sea gropian.

I was so interested that I lost all sense of time. It wasn't until that evening in fact that I thought to ask my mother what had killed all those fish. Even at that young age it registered with me that she exchanged glances with my father before she answered.

"There was a storm at sea," she said. "They were killed by a storm."

I accepted this as gospel. It wasn't until I was in my late teens, when I was telling this story to somebody, that it dawned on me that storms at sea didn't kill fish. For the first time distant rumblings and explosions I'd heard offshore that summer and snippets of half-overheard adult conversations with words like "depth charges," "Nazi submarine," and "destroyers" began to make sense.

Charles Davis *American Retired Lecturer Aged 6-7*

In 1942 the Germans began to build a prison camp in Beisfjord [Norway]. Barbed wire, watch towers, and army huts were erected, as well as powerful searchlights. For several years the people in the district were to see the rays from these powerful lights light up the mountainside in the pitch black polar night. We had blackout, and the winter darkness was crushing.

Who was the camp built for? No one knew, but in the course of summer 1942 a long procession of poor Yugoslavian prisoners arrived. They were beaten and maltreated by the German soldiers and Norwegian Young Nazis. All civilian Norwegians were obliged to stay indoors, but there were several who defied those orders and there were terrible stories going round. Even small pitchers had ears then and the grown ups' secret talk even reached our ears. It was incredible that such things could happen.

I remember how dreadful it was for a small boy to see the poor, starved prisoners when they were ordered out to work on the roads. Some of them could hardly stand and even the smaller stones they had to carry seemed like heavy lead. After most of the Yugoslavian prisoners were either killed or deported, the prison camp was filled with Russian prisoners, who were dressed in typical Russian military uniforms. The Russian prisoners seemed to be treated better than the Yugoslavians. They had to do forced labour in Narvik and Beisfjord.

They too were marked by maltreatment and hunger. We young ones exchanged handmade toys of many kinds for food and cod liver oil which we got from home. This barter went on for the most part behind the Germans' backs, but sometimes quite openly. It was during these years that I learnt the meaning of the words "typhoid," "diphtheria," and "dysentery." These were illnesses which flourished at that time due to the dreadful conditions under which the prisoners lived.

It was a great occasion in spring 1945 when the freed Russian prisoners invited the village people to a concert in the army huts. They played, sang and danced for us. God only knows where they got their instruments from. I still remember bits of the melodies and the Russian text.

Rudolf Antonsen *Norwegian Born 1936*

One Sunday, fairly early in the war, we got out of church in Lubbock [Texas] at noon, and we went down to the cafeteria on Broadway, a few blocks from the Santa Fe train depot, hoping to indulge in a large Sunday dinner. However, those

An Italian Prisoner of War is surrounded by curious youngsters in a London park. He takes a brief break from his work of filling in redundant trench shelters. England, 1943.

plans did not work out, for soldiers were busy in front of the cafeteria setting up a water-cooled machine gun! At that time, troops in some US military units still wore puttees* and flat flak helmets, just as they had done in World War I, and as a boy of seven or eight years, I was interested in their attire.

At any rate, the manager of the cafeteria came out to tell the public that we would all have to go somewhere else to eat that day, since the establishment had been temporarily commandeered by the army to feed enemy prisoners – none of whom had ever been seen locally, by anyone.

As we walked back to our old Chevrolet, a column of captive German soldiers shuffled past us through the middle of the street, moving toward the cafeteria under guard. They had been unloaded from a special passenger train which could be seen standing at the depot belching steam, and wore dark olive-grey uniforms and strange peaked caps with cloth bills. To me the prisoners seemed bored and depressed rather than dangerous. And thinking of the situation now, where could one escape to on the barren plains of north Texas? Even for a child, it was easy to tell that the placement of the machine gun, as well as the readiness of the guards, was mainly a show for the public. During the following weeks resentment was often heard over the fact that "filthy Nazis" had been fed good cafeteria food which many a local citizen could ill afford.

Lee Johnson *American Archaeologist Born 1936*

When my father was stationed at Fort Sam Houston, we lived on the post. By that time in the war, there were a fair number of POWs held there. On the bus trip to school we would often see groups of them under guard doing maintenance work along the roads. I remember seeing the strange white lettering on their blue uniform jackets, and wondering what it was like to be a prisoner so far from home and family.

Peter S Marshall *American Aged 9*

On a more somber note, my dad used to take us on occasional drives in our 1941 Plymouth sedan. We had a "C" gas ration sticker on our windshield which meant we couldn't drive very often. But when we could afford it, we would drive down Highway 85-87 to Camp Carson about seven or eight miles away. There, for all passers-by to plainly see, were German Prisoners of War, idly strolling about their compound and looking sadly at us as we drove by. As much as we were taught to hate them, you couldn't help but feel compassion for them.

Andy Thomas *American American President of a British computer software firm Aged 9*

I was born in the war. My early memories are of seeing very sad and lonely men helping the local farmers around my home near Newbury in Berkshire. I realised that these men were Prisoners of War, officers or crew from downed or crashed aircraft. I remember thinking that there was no human difference between the victors and the captured. I believed then as now it is so important to get everyone together after a calamity, and not to punish people such as these POWs, who were as much victims of war as we were. From the sorrow on their faces and their sad bearing I understood their profound longing to be home and this affected me greatly. I was even able to speak to them a little.

Baroness of Winterborne, formerly Emma Nicholson
MP (Liberal Democrat, UK)   English   Aged 3-4

Among my memories from the days of the war are some Russian Prisoners of War, or Russian prisoners as we called them. There were many of them near our town during the war and they had to work on a road close by the house where we lived. They were guarded carefully by German guards with rifles. I remember how they dug and strove in the mud. They were frozen and had poor clothing which was more or less simply rags, and equally poor shoes. It made a deep impression on grown ups and children alike.

We smuggled the prisoners bread when the guards were not looking. They put the food under their clothes and smiled quietly to us. Some days later they were suddenly gone and no one knew where they had been sent. But they had left a small greeting beside the fence where we put the food. It was some beautiful small birds in wood which they had made themselves. They were fastened to a board with threads which could be pulled from underneath so that the birds could peck the board. This was the prisoners' way of showing their gratitude. I kept that present for many years and can never quite forget that experience.

Siv Hanssen   *Norwegian   Aged 7*

The only German I knew was a very nice Prisoner of War called Harry Koch and he used to come and sit at the bottom of our hill to wait for the bus after he'd done his farm work. They'd let him out to do the work and then he was collected and taken back to the Prisoner of War camp near Skipton [Yorkshire] at the end of the day. I used to sit next to him while he waited for the bus to pick him up. He used to say how glad he was not to be doing any fighting and how he'd far rather live in Long Preston, even if it had been blitzed. [For the story of the "Long Preston Blitz," see page 14]. I tried to play cricket with him and taught him how to bowl* but it doesn't seem to have caught on in Germany.

Leo Cooper   *English   Publisher/writer   Aged 12*

Before the war, London buses were red. During the war they suddenly all turned brown. Was that deliberate – camouflage maybe – or did they just run out of paint?

"…something very English." This war-time appeal for "civility and common sense" was remembered by Jean Holder all her life. London.

There were two signs in buses that I've always remembered. One was on the advertising hoardings above the seats. "Kindly pass along the bus,/And so make room for all of us." There was another at bus stops telling you how to flag down a bus. It said, "Face the driver,/Raise your hand,/You will find,/He'll understand."

There we were – in the middle of a war – and London Transport's priority was to make an appeal for civility and common sense. There's always been something very English about those signs to me.

Jean Holder   *English   Retired Deputy Head Teacher*
Born 1933

LITTLE OSCAR MEETS JOHNNY BALLOON

In kindergarten, there was a book entitled *Little Oscar's First Air Raid*. One piece of advice was not to stick one's head out the window to watch; Little Oscar did so and was beaned by a falling bomb, but, with the indestructibility of cartoon characters then and now, he survived to appear on the next page. My mother was appalled that such gruesome fare was being presented to kindergartners, but I couldn't see why at the time. To us, it was like a comic book. No book of cartoons could convey to five-year-olds the danger and the suffering that would ensue from a real air raid.

Civil Defence measures provided games during kindergarten. Two of us, as I recall, got to wear arm bands and see that the others, followed by ourselves, went to sheltered positions, such as under tables, during air raid drills. I was pleased with myself for having decided that the lockers in the classroom were suitable shelters. There was a scrap pile at the school. Eldon Seeley, the other kindergarten air raid warden, made a hit bringing a big metal barrel one day.

James Pringle *American Taxonomist Aged 8*

Hands across the sea. The Special Relationship between Uncle Sam and John Bull is confirmed by these two young fund raisers.

Train journeys in southern England with my mother and sister were rare, but fun while they lasted. My sister was eight and rather precocious. She would announce to a startled compartment, "My name is Joanna Calverley and we live in Esher. We have a dachshund called Fritz and this is my little brother, Brooke."

It broke the ice and in an instant we were sitting on khaki laps. I remember very clearly a soldier reaching up to his suitcase in the luggage rack and showing me a model airplane he had bought for his kids.

You knew the train was nearing a large town because when you looked out of the window you could see barrage balloons on the horizon hovering over it. This reminds me of a book I was given at the time called *Johnny Balloon in America*. It was about a barrage balloon that broke its moorings in England and drifted off to America where it met and fell in love with an American balloon. In this way, small children were reminded of their kinship with allies across the sea; the same thinking perhaps lay behind my wooden toy battleship being named *Stalin*.

Brooke Calverley *English Graphic Designer Aged 5*

I don't remember eating sweets at all during the war. I wasn't that keen on them anyway actually, chocolates and things like that. We had dried egg which we made up into pancakes and fried them. We got it from the Americans. You got these great big containers with aluminium. Later on we got to know this gentleman who happened to be a basket weaver. He was a blind man, and we used to get eggs from him. We weren't supposed to have more than a certain ration but he had free range eggs that he got from his small holding.

I remember seeing bananas after the war and I didn't know what they were. It was directly after the war that we saw bananas, I'm quite sure of it. We didn't have very much cheese and hardly had any butter. I was used to margarine and the bread was grey. You never had white bread in those days. It was grey because it was made from the husks as well. And I didn't like white bread and I've never liked white bread since. I always eat rye bread or black bread.

I remember the first cream I had after the war because we went to Ireland. I went with a Jewish group to Ireland and I never ever remember having cream before and actually I must have eaten a whole of a tub of cream and it was . . . beautiful.

Mike Barnett *English Science Teacher Born 1933*

Left: "Toffees, chocolate creams, humbugs, licorice all-sorts. . ." Sweets were on ration throughout the war.
Below: The magic of a sweet shop window. England.

When I was a kid during the war, I was a Junior Commando. I even had a membership card and a sweatshirt that said "Junior Commando" on it. I was always putting burnt cork on my face and crawling around the garden on my stomach looking for enemy sentries.

One time Captain Commando ordered all us Junior Commandos to eat carrots to improve our night vision. I think we were supposed to be on the lookout for Nazi parachutists or some goddamn thing. Anyway, I ate them and ate them. Even got my mother to buy me carrot juice which was awful but I drank it anyway. Quarts of the stuff. It's a wonder I didn't OD [overdose] on Vitamin A!

George Bailey   *American   Cab driver   Aged "about 9"*

It wasn't exactly that there was a shortage of sweets in Aberystwyth, [west Wales] it's just that you never had enough coupons on your ration card to get as many as you wanted. When you were due for some sweets, you had to scissor the coupons out of your ration book. I think they were pink. Or orange maybe. I used to stand at the window of the sweet shop looking in on row after

row of sweets in big narrow bottles with screw on lids: toffees, chocolate creams, humbugs, licorice all-sorts. . . the, uh, the ones that changed color as you sucked them. . . aniseed balls, that's it. . . bull's eyes, sherbets. . . I could go on and on. The sweet shop window was a kind of magical place.

I bought sweets four ounces at a time – or two ounces if I didn't have much money that day. I'd pick sweets from all the different bottles and they'd be poured together into an old fashioned pan balance – iron weights on one side, sweets on the other. As the jars came open there'd be the most wonderful smell. I think sweets smelled differently in those days. Then the owner would take the pan off the scale and pour the sweets into a square paper bag. He'd hold the edges of the bag like this, then flip it over once or twice to seal it, then hand it to me.

Martin Ambler   *Welsh   Teacher   Aged 6-7*

I am not sure the war greatly affected us as a family. Like most of our neighbors, we had a "Victory Garden" and gas rationing curtailed family vacations. It also led to car pools for swimming lessons, church, etc. In our case, my sister and I were the only Presbyterians in an Episcopalian neighborhood with the result that we switched denominations for the duration. After the war, much to my parents' consternation, we refused to go back to the less colorful Presbyterian service or to leave our friends.

One of the games we played on the way to church was to see how many service flags one could spot in the windows of houses we passed. Gold stars counted double.

R C Elwood   *American   Aged 8*

Children in uniform. *Clockwise from above left.* a) US schoolchildren in this picture were asked, "Who wants to be a junior Commando?" b) "Sergeant" Vincento Biscardo and Elena Cimballi. Italy. After Vincento's family was killed, he was adopted by US soldiers. c) Doodlebug watchers on the alert in Kent, England. 1944. d) Hitler awards the Iron Cross, second class to a twelve year old youth who had fought in his name. Weeks later, Hitler was dead. Germany. March, 1945. e) Hitler Youth help the German War Effort by shoe-making.

THE WAR IN STRAW'S POINT, NEW HAMPSHIRE

In summer we used to stay at Straw's Point on the New Hampshire coast. Because of the nearness to Portsmouth Naval Base, parts of the coast were taken for defence and coastal guns. We were allowed to remain in our house but during the early part of the war the Point was defended by a detachment of perhaps twenty US Army soldiers who stayed in the Coast Guard station behind the Point and immediately dug defensive positions on their ocean perimeter. During the summer, the five to seven-year-olds like myself who lived on the Point would have a good time playing army games with the soldiers. We would often get instruction in Army tactics from soldiers who had probably just finished basic training themselves. I remember one of these soldiers solemnly telling enthralled children to "maintain frontal fire while using part of your force to encircle and attack from the rear." Pretty heady stuff if you were a small child.

Eventually, a watch tower was built at Straw's Point. There were silhouettes inside of German and Japanese aircraft. We kids were permitted inside and we dutifully memorized all the aircraft types. Sometimes, as a drill, the volunteers on duty in the tower would call Grenier Field near Manchester and summon a flight of P-47s, I think they were, for a mock sighting of an enemy ship or submarine. These aircraft would come in as low over Straw's Point as they could – actually below the level of the flagpole – so as not to be spotted I suppose in case there was a real enemy out there. I can't tell you how exciting it was as they skimmed over the roofs of the houses, their engines roaring. In a funny way it made me happy because I felt we needed all the help we could get.

About seven miles offshore, are the Isles of Shoals, a string of low-lying, rocky islands. One of them was designated as a bombing range and sometimes we could see the planes dropping bombs on it, and the flashes of the explosion. It's only very recently that it was decided that the island was safe enough to be returned to public ownership.

Once, there was a large oil slick washed up on the beach, and local rumor had it that a Nazi submarine had been sunk just offshore. We never knew for sure that this was true but I have a vague memory that after the war a submarine which had gone down somewhere in the shipping approaches to Portsmouth had to be moved or blown up.

There was a woman in her eighties who lived on the Point. Everyone called her Aunt Carrie Meigs – and I suppose she was a typical New Englander of her time. Her house backed right onto the ocean, above a stretch of the coast known officially and unofficially as "Pebbly Beach."

Aunt Carrie was very patriotic and was always urging us kids to be alert. The Enemy Was Everywhere, she said. As an example she told us about a sinister thing that had happened to her. She had been sitting outside, rocking on her porch, when a car had pulled up and stopped. Three men got out, Aunt Carrie told us. She knew instinctively that one was an Italian, one was a German, and one was a Japanese. The men asked Aunt Carrie for directions to Pebbly Beach. Aunt Carrie said that she "remained calm," and pointed out the way to the beach past her house. As soon as the men had gone, she rushed inside and reported them to the Coast Guard. Even to a six or seven-year-old as I was by then this seemed a bit far-fetched but, as we found out later, Aunt Carrie's calls to the Coast Guard were real enough. And frequent enough. I suppose they must have livened up many an otherwise tedious watch for the young Coast Guardsmen on duty. So far as I know, on this particular occasion the Coast Guard didn't send anyone to investigate Aunt Carrie's reports about dangerous enemy aliens on Pebbly Beach.

The much-decorated Malcolm Swenson, aged six.

When the war in the Pacific ended, all we children formed a parade and marched around the Point shouting, banging pots and pans, and generally making as much noise as possible. As a joke, we ran up a war trophy Japanese flag on the flagpole in front of Aunt Carrie's. As far as I know, this was the only Japanese flag raised on the American mainland during the war. We all thought it would be a good joke on the grown ups. Unfortunately, it was Aunt Carrie who spotted it first. Within minutes of the Rising Sun being hoisted over Straw's Point, Aunt Carrie's daughter, clearly acting on orders, came storming outside, hauled down the flag, and gave us all a stern talking to.

Malcolm Swenson   *American   President, Swenson Stone Consultancy   Born 1937*

During the war, we spent a summer on the New England coast. My father had a little eight millimeter movie camera and early in the war he was taking holiday pictures of us kids playing on the sand.

At that moment, a Navy patrol blimp chanced to fly overhead and on an impulse my father aimed his camera at it for a few seconds. A Coast Guardsman, who was patrolling up and down the beach with a rifle over his shoulder, saw what my father had done and came over and impounded the camera!

It was totally ludicrous, of course. What on earth did he think my father was going to do with a film of a blimp? ("Mein Gott, Adolph. Look at ziss!") My father eventually got his camera and film back of course – plus a lecture on national security – but "Our Father the Spy" became something of a family joke.

Charles Davis   *American   Retired Lecturer   Aged 12*

I remember getting a new picture book featuring vehicles from around the world, and being shocked that a picture of a jinricksha* was the first illustration. Mrs Rand said some very nice things about the Japanese people, and how they must not be associated only with the war. She had a great collection of seed and nursery catalogues, one or more of which illustrated a plant called the "Gold-banded Lily of Japan," which I thought was marvelous. Despite my reaction to the picture of the jinricksha, I was horrified when Mrs Rand told me that the Munseys had ripped out their plant of this wonderful species because of its association with Japan.

James Pringle   *American   Taxonomist   Aged 8*

One night there were 600 Russian planes over Helsinki, dropping their bombs. They got a direct hit on the Soviet legation. Nobody put out the fire and it was, of course, unoccupied at the time. However, as part of the peace treaty, Finland had to build a brand new luxurious Soviet Embassy, about ten times as big.

Still, at the time, we thought it was worth a good fire!

Borje Kyrklund   *Finnish   Aged 7*

The youngest soldier (messenger) in the Finnish army, Juhani Utkin, salutes his commanding officer. Like many other Finns, Juhani had been driven from his Karelian homeland., never to return. Finland, 1941.

Off to one side of our main living rooms was a smaller sort of parlor which contained a huge radio set on legs that placed it quite high off the floor. Members of the family would gather around it in the evening to listen to the news and programs like "Jack Benny"* and "Fred Allen."*

I was allowed to lie on my back in front of the radio, with my head sticking under the bottom. Sometimes dust would fall in my eyes, making me think it was electricity somehow leaking from the radio.

Next to the radio was a small rather ornate sofa where my Gram would take her afternoon nap and listen to soap operas like "Ma Perkins" and "Stella Dallas." I would be bundled off for my afternoon nap as part of an unvarying routine. But one warm spring day, time seemed to come to a stop. No one sent me to bed and as the afternoon wore on more and more people gathered around the radio listening to

Roosevelt was a hero to Americans who looked to their President for strong leadership. Most children of this generation had known no other President. USA.

PRESIDENT ROOSEVELT'S HONOR GUARD

My brother Denis is two years younger than I am, and someone gave him a huge campaign button with a picture of Franklin Delano Roosevelt on it. By huge, I mean the size of a pie tin. My brother Denis wore that button every day of the 1944 election campaign.

When we heard that President Roosevelt had died, Denis went upstairs and found the campaign button. The four of us – my sisters Maureen and Eileen, as well as Denis and I – went into our backyard at 76 Dawes Avenue and dug a grave.

After a brief respectful ceremony in which we paid our last respects, we buried the President of the United States.

John Murphy   *American Lawyer   Aged 9*

John, Maureen, Dennis, and Eileen Murphy buried President Roosevelt in their garden. Connecticut, USA. 1944.

the news. Everyone was crying. Neighbors came and I heard people talking about FDR. I knew who they meant. He was our President, our Commander and Chief forever. I did not understand what death meant. Even to this day the memories blur together in my mind – the death of Roosevelt and the death of Gram, who went to the hospital and never came back. I was too young to comprehend that war was a place where people went, many of whom would never come back. And the spaces they left in our lives were never really filled.

James O'Shea Wade *American   Publisher   Aged 4*

Americans pronounce the name Roosevelt in two ways. Some say "Rose-velt" and some say "Rews-velt." I was quite young when I overheard Pete, our handyman, saying to my father "President Rews-velt is dead."

My family pronounced it "Rose-velt" so this different pronunciation kind of stuck in my mind I guess and, well, you know how kids' minds work. The next time we had a show and tell in school I stood up and solemnly announced to the class, "President Rooster is dead."

Anonymous *American   Retired Lecturer   Aged 8*

During World War II, I lived, with my parents and my younger sister, in upstate New York at the Saratoga Battlefield, a National Historic Park on the Hudson River. One afternoon, as usual, I walked the several miles home from school. My parents and sister were in town, shopping, so I built a fire in the kitchen stove to dry my boots and listened to my favorite programs on the radio. Suddenly, it may have been in the middle of "Jack Armstrong" or "Sky King,"* an announcer broke in with an important news report. President Roosevelt had died! When I informed my parents on their arrival back home, they didn't believe it – until it was confirmed on the evening news broadcast.

Wayne L Hamilton *American   Park Ranger   Aged 9*

I had been riding my bicycle beside the large stone retaining wall in front of my house, when I heard that President Roosevelt had died. All of my father's brothers and sisters came to our home (he was the middle of seven) and stood around, talking quietly.

My parents, Aunt Sarah, and Aunt Anne and her husband were seated around the dining room table. Aunt Anne was crying. I remember her saying, "What will become of the Jews without FDR? He has been our best friend."

Interestingly, although my family lost relatives in the Holocaust, these aunts and uncles had all been born in the United States. They were Roosevelt supporters and felt that

Roosevelt would protect them. It wasn't until years later that we heard that, for political reasons, Roosevelt had turned back a boatload of Jews who had sought refuge in America.†

Maxine Weintraub *American   Insurance agent/ Management, retired   Aged 10*

†[In 1939 the German steamship, St Louis, loaded with 1,000 German Jews, was successively refused permission to disembark its passengers in Cuba, the USA, and Canada. Forced to return to Europe, three quarters of these refugees perished in the Holocaust].

When I heard – actually overheard – of the death of President Roosevelt, I was an eight-year-old and I was hanging out at my Dad's store, probably after school. Roosevelt had been President as long as I could remember and, to me, in a funny way he was America. I had never thought about life after Roosevelt and was a little surprised to find that, despite the news, business was still going on in the store. Still, it was reassuring to know that our way of life appeared to be continuing much as before.

I knew the news was momentous and I could see that not everyone coming into the store had heard it. More excited than saddened, I wandered the aisles of the store giddily accosting customers: "Do you know that President Roosevelt's dead?"

There was a strange pleasure in being the source for what was adult information of tremendous impact. I could hardly stifle my glee. But then, suddenly, my father appeared. "Have some respect," he said. "No one wants to hear such things from a child." He had tears in his eyes and an expression that told me that I

President Harry Truman, who succeeded Roosevelt, buys the first "Buddy Poppy." Americans wondered, "What course would Truman follow?" USA. 1945.

had somehow trespassed into the adult world. I slunk off to the stockroom and stayed there until it was time to go home.

Arnold Goldstein *American   Retailer   Aged 8*

ADULTS TOO COULD FEEL LEFT IN THE DARK . . .

At eight years old I was, in most respects, too young to understand what it all meant when Franklin D Roosevelt died on 12th April 1945. It was a somber time for the country, and a dark time, literally, for me. I had the measles and was isolated from my brother (nearly seven) and sister (four months) in a sick room where the shades were pulled and the lights were dim lest the glare cause me discomfort. There was no TV, but Mother had provided a radio to relieve some of my boredom. Two days later I distinctly remember listening, engrossed, as the funeral procession through Washington DC was narrated over the radio. It was 14th April, my brother's birthday. He was given a party that I could not attend, and I listened to Roosevelt's funeral on the radio. It was eerie to be listening, to be alone, and I picked up on expressions of anxiety during the broadcast: Roosevelt's leadership in the War Effort had been strong; what course would Truman follow? Might the plans for ending the war be stalled? As a youngster of eight I did not understand these questions of adult concern, but I was learning how adults too could feel left in the dark and not always understand.

Victory in Europe came less than a month later. Less than a month after that, on 30th May 1945, my dad, a B-25 bomber pilot with the Marines, died with four others of his crew while on a strafing mission over Mindanao Island in the Philippines.

For the next five years things went downhill for us; Mother drank too much and did not cope well as a single parent. A move to Illinois was made for a new start, but the toll on Mother mentally and physically had been too much. She had a breakdown and went out at night, abandoning us three kids in a Chicago hotel room. Seeing us coming and going alone through the hotel lobby throughout the day, the manager, Abe Weiss, stopped us one evening. Piecing our story together, he assisted in making arrangements for us to go live with aunts and uncles in New York. Until he died several years afterwards, he stayed in touch. He remains in my memory as a person who did understand, and understanding led him to reach out to us, and care.

My father had gone to Dartmouth and, as the son of a Dartmouth graduate killed in the war, I was awarded a Hopkins War Memorial Scholarship, providing four years' tuition, board, and room. There were many Hopkins Scholars at Dartmouth in those years. We were given a lot, and much of who we are today comes out of our Dartmouth experience, yet I suspect that to a man we Hopkins Scholars would have chucked it all to have grown up with our fathers.

Dale Sarles *American Episcopal priest Aged 8*

Top: Dale Sarles' father, a Marine pilot. *Inset:* Dale Sarles' mother. *Above:* A wartime portrait of Dale Sarles (left) with his brother and sister, Allan and Sandra.

I remember feeling very, very scared. Perhaps because the war was so frightening, the voice of the President on the radio became a reassuring sound, a promise of safety and Franklin Delano Roosevelt became my first and finest hero. I remember the day he died quite clearly. I heard it on the radio at a neighbor's house and ran home calling for my mother, crying inconsolably. I grieved for him as deeply and sincerely as a child that age would grieve for a loved uncle or grandfather. And I remember that day and its grief much more clearly than I remember the day the war ended and the celebrations that followed.

Helen Simmons *American Editor Born 1939*

I remember rationing, though it caused me little grief. Once I needed winter boots, and my mother found a pair for me while on a short visit to Montreal where US citizens could buy them without a ration coupon. She brought them home (I think she actually smuggled them into the country) and they fit me perfectly. In the spirit of the time, though, mother then took out a ration coupon for shoes, tore it up, and threw it in the cook stove.

There were occasionally calls for people to gather resources for the War Effort. The people at my father's office kept the tinfoil from their chewing gum (it really was tin in those days) and rolled it into a ball. Every now and then, the ball was turned in somewhere. As my contribution, I used to help gather ripe milkweed pods. There was a bad infestation of this weed on the Battlefield, so family and friends would go out and fill burlap bags with the pods. We were told the fiber, called Kapok, was used to stuff life vests.

Wayne Hamilton   *American   Geologist, retired   Born 1936*

We collected milkweed pods and were told they were used for parachutes.

Peter Bennett   *American   Financier   Born 1935*

When I was in about the second grade, our school Principal, Mr Altman, said the Government needed milkweed pods for the war. As many as we could pick. I think he said they used them to make life preservers. Anyway, the Government would pay us a nickel a bushel and Mr Altman said he'd match that with a nickel of his own.

My sister and I went out with a basket in the fields around our house and picked and picked. Night after night after school. We'd come home half-frozen and covered with burrs and mud. After a week or so, we took our milkweed pods into school. We thought we had about a ton, our fortunes made. As it turned out, we had three quarters of a bushel. But Mr Altman gave us a dime anyway.

Steve Jordan   *American   Businessman   Aged 7*

We used to gather milkweed pods to help the War Effort. Our school was a collecting center. I handed in my sackful and asked one of my teachers why we were gathering them. "They use them to make life preservers," I was told. A few days after that, I was watching some milkweed seeds drifting on the wind. Some of them settled on the surface of a pond. They sank.

Robert Maine   *American   Retired language teacher Born 1933*

During the war, my Aunt Katie used to eat lard sandwiches. Then, as now, lard came in thick slabs so she'd just cut off a slice and mush it down between two pieces of bread. She never put anything on it either. I squirm even now to think of lard sandwiches but nutritionists should note that she lived a full, vigorous life and died at the age of eighty-three!

I remember going to the cinema and Churchill appeared in one of the newsreels. Everyone began booing and hissing. In that part of Socialist Wales, Churchill wasn't a hero; he was the man who sent the troops into Tonypandy* during the General Strike.

We lived in Gilwern, a small village in west Wales. There were troops from India stationed nearby. They were cavalry and looked very exotic with their turbans. I was fascinated by them. Once I was standing at the gate of our house – the Poplars, it was called – with the Indian cavalry riding past on the road. I still remember looking up at them. One of the riders stopped and, smiling, bent down as if to pick me up. I began crying and ran off. I think it was because he was the first brown man I'd ever seen.

Huw Williams   *Welsh   Education consultant   Aged 6-7*

When the American Army arrived, we ran out to greet them. The soldiers were smiling and handing out chocolate and gum. I was especially excited to see that some of the soldiers had black skin, the first I'd ever seen. I thought the black soldiers were the friendliest and I still feel that way. I remember being disgusted when I heard one of the adults saying, "Why didn't they wash first?"

Margot Hamilton   *German, naturalized American   Business Manager, retired   Born 1936*

We knew the war was over when the American troops marched into town. I was standing by the road, wearing my new Hitler Youth cap that I'd just got the day before (you could join at age ten), when a big black US soldier came up to me. I was scared to death. We'd heard all the propaganda that blacks ate children. He chatted with me, but I couldn't understand a word, and then he took my cap, twisted off the metal Swastika medallion, and stomped it into the ground. Then he gave me a Hershey bar.

I was sorry to lose my medallion – I think now it probably would have brought twenty cigarettes on the black market. That's what we lived on for the next four years: trading this for that for something else.

I didn't eat the Hershey bar right away. I took it home and asked my mother if she thought it was poisoned. She didn't seem to think so, so I tasted one edge of it and when nothing happened I ate the whole thing.

Erwin Perrot   *German   Electrical Engineer   Born 1934*

PART SIX

ON THE HOME FRONT

Me, Bobby Johnson, Donald Sage, and Ronnie Ruwet waited until dark, then we put Mr Opperman under surveillance. Never mind that he owned a family drugstore on Main Street in Torrington [Connecticut], never mind that his daughter Jane was my sister's best friend – the fact was that Mr Opperman had a German name, and that was all we needed. We were working for the FBI.

Sure enough, as we watched from the woods, a light went on inside the house. Right then and there we all knew – Mr Opperman was sending signals to German submarines waiting offshore on Long Island Sound.

Never mind that Long Island Sound was seventy miles away. Never mind that there were hills and mountains in between. It didn't matter. We were working for the FBI and Mr Opperman was a spy.

John Murphy   *American   Lawyer   Aged 7*

In 1942 I was a second grader. Brothers and fathers of my friends were leaving for "the service" and those of us at home were being exhorted on all sides to contribute to the War Effort. I badly wanted to do my share. My opportunity came when the Principal of our grammar school announced a scrap metal drive to collect material to be recycled for the war industry.

I had noticed a stack of pipes and metal parts piled in the cellar of our two-family house. Over a period of days and with great effort I carried the pieces to school. I was pleased to be cited by the Principal for my unusually large contribution but decided to remain mute a few days later when the landlord stormed about the property angrily demanding to know what had become of the parts he had stored for the purpose of upgrading the building's heating system.

He never solved the mystery.

Arnold Goldstein   *American   Retailer   Age 7*

Recycled as planes, ships, and tanks, scrap metal was a precious commodity during the war. Collecting scrap was an important contribution by children of all nations. Butte, Montana. 1942.

One thing that was different about those days was the patriotism that people had then that they don't have now. In those days everyone did what they had to to help the War Effort. We lived near an air base and my grandfather often invited soldiers (it wasn't the Air Force then) back to our house for a meal. He'd meet them anywhere – in a store, at a bus stop, and invite them back. We always had soldier guests for holidays like Thanksgiving or Christmas.

We are a Polish family and maintained many of the traditions from the old country so some of our guests – who sat down expecting turkey probably – were a bit surprised when they found straw stuffed under the table cloth and they were fed things like pirogis and cabbage. They all seemed to enjoy it though!

Although I was very young, I did my bit for the War Effort by picking up bits of metal everywhere l could find them. I went to Saint Casimir School and they organized metal drives all the time. I remember dropping my bits of metal on a big pile near St Joseph's on Lowell Street.

Stan Lencki   *American   Professional Golfer   Born 1938*

One of the first things that I can remember about my childhood in West Hampstead [London], was the time just after World War II had been declared. Hitler hadn't started his bombing raids yet and we lived in an air of expectation. Twenty-one years is not a long time between wars and many of the older people lived in fear of a repeat of the last one; limbless men were still hobbling around as a reminder to us younger ones that it wasn't just another game. Stories of the horrors of the trenches in France were on most men's lips and of course there were the men who panted and wheezed as they walked a few steps, their eyes showing that they should have been dead long ago, chests heaving as they fought for breath – the gas victims. It was because of this last horror that the population of England would be provided with gas masks before the Germans had us all wheezing and panting. No agreement had yet been signed between the two sides so it was a real and horrific possibility.

After much publicity my parents, with me and my two brothers, arrived at the library in Westbere Road (destroyed by a fire bomb in 1940). A long queue had formed so we waited our turn to be ticked off on the local register; another wait while the WVS* volunteers tried, sometimes in vain, to put a mask over the head of a terrified child, or squeeze a baby into the red 'Mickey Mouse' ones, as if it was some sort of game. Children were slapped, threatened, and blackmailed, parents appealing that the family was being "shown up." In all the din the WVS ladies did their best.

When our turn came it was no better. I was given a black, S for Small, mask which I ripped off immediately, complaining that I couldn't breathe, which I couldn't. My brother John did the same saying that he couldn't see, because the thing immediately steamed up. We both decided there and then that it would be better to be gassed than spend the war blinded and asphyxiated. We were quickly ushered out onto the pavement, cardboard boxes slung around our necks with string. These boxes were to become symbolic of the children of the 1940s.

Some time later, having become familiar with our black masks, we enjoyed frightening the girls walking along the dark corridors of Beckford School. We put on our coats back to front, and our masks and I don't blame them for the screams and tears which sometimes greeted our bravura performances.

This silly game came to an abrupt end when we were caught red-handed by the Headmaster. A friend and myself were marched into his study for a caning "as an example to all the other idiots who think gas masks are things to play around with." Making us wait by the side of his desk, he filled a large ledger with a very scratchy pen – the only sound in the study apart from the ticking clock and his heavy breathing. Terrifying stories of canes with iron rods through the middle, and hands that were cut to pieces, rushed through my head. A look at my friend's tight-lipped and pale face told me I was not the only one to be scared. The Headmaster tortured us like this for what seemed hours, then he closed the book with a thump, sprang to his feet, put the book on a shelf, and disappeared into a small back room where we soon heard the swishing of a cane as he warmed up. Out he came, twitching the bamboo, striking his thigh and calf to get a good sadistic noise.

"You first, Bowler," he snapped. As he gripped my wrist the cane was already on the way down. Before I really knew what was happening there was a thwack, then the pain and the numbness, and I'm sure I saw him smile. Before he could get another one in I snatched my hand away from his grasp.

"Do that again and you'll get six where it hurts most," he snapped. I submitted to the other three blows with screwed-up face, shoving my burning hands under my armpits as soon as I could. It seemed the only place for them to go. I watched as my friend submitted his hands to that terrible swishing sound and then the thwack.

After the Headmaster had finished, tears started to pour down my friends's face without his really crying. "Here, if you are going to cry, cry in that," said the Head, pushing a wastepaper tin towards him with his foot, "we don't want you flooding us all out."

As soon as we could we rushed to the boys' toilet and poured cold water on our flaming hands.

Teachers weren't very friendly in those days.

Norman Bowler   *English   Actor   Aged 8*

We moved to London, perhaps surprisingly, in the winter of 1942-43. My earliest memory, probably, is of the shelter at the bottom of the stairwell. Here we played "Bears," crawling around on the scratchy mattress, each trying to growl the loudest. The shelter seemed enormous and I was amazed years later

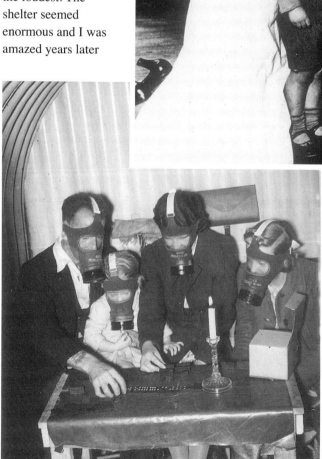

when I was shown the metal sheet that roofed it; it was only the size of a double bed. We also used to play with our gas masks a lot. I was delighted that the one with the floppy yellow Donald Duck beak was mine. My older brother had Mickey Mouse with dusty black rubber ears, while my younger brother's was only a green box, the size of a doll, with a transparent lid, though it did have a fascinating handle which made wheezy noises when you pushed and pulled it.

Helen Fletcher   *English*
Schoolmistress   Aged 3

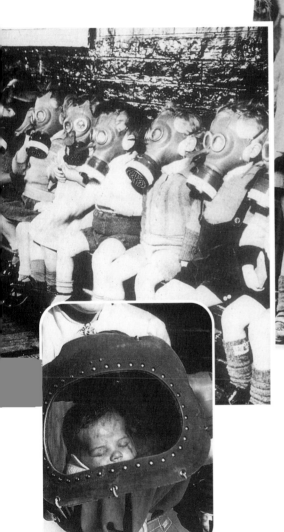

*O*ne note of warning: little boys should not attempt to convert their gas masks to diving helmets by tearing off the canister and attaching a long garden hose to the opening. These do not make functional diving helmets and can cause death by drowning!

Bob McCorriston   *American   Retired Personnel Executive   Age 7*

*Y*ou never forget gas masks – the smell of them, that feeling of terror as you pulled them on. They were claustrophobic. Adult gas masks didn't bother me. It was the special masks designed for children that used to frighten me. The one I had was designed to look like Mickey Mouse. It had round staring circles for eyes and a nose like a leaf that flapped around in front.

There was a totally enclosed model designed for babies. I was put into one of these and stuck in a local shop window to convince mothers how safe and comfortable they were. Apparently I screamed so unremittingly that I was quickly removed from it and the shop window.

Brooke Calverley   *English   Designer   Aged 4*

I am a Swiss citizen but I grew up in Alexandria in Egypt where my father owned a hotel. We were very close to the war, right at the heart of it, but we didn't really experience it. I always had enough to eat. I was never frightened. I remember that Alexandria was always filled with soldiers. Mainly British but also Australian (which is how I learned "Waltzing Matilda"), Free French, the Foreign Legion. At that time, Egypt was a British possession and many of the officers stayed in our hotel.

The only part of the war that directly involved me was when the Italians used to come and bomb the harbour. Frankly, they weren't very good and often missed so, although our house was well out in the suburbs, we used to

Top: Nurse Eileen Fitzgerald helps children from a London nursery school with their gas mask practice. *Above right:* Gas masks cannot disguise the droopy socks of these English boys. *Inset:* A gas mask for babies. "I screamed so unremittingly that I was quickly removed from it!"
Below left: Propaganda photographs such as this portrayed playing dominoes in gas masks in an Anderson shelter as just an everyday part of life. England. 1940.

go down into the cellar when the Italians were bombing.

As Swiss, we were neutral but my German governess was of course pro-German. She used to ask our Sudanese chauffeur to drive past a German Prisoner of War camp nearby where she'd get out and throw cigarettes over the wire to the prisoners. Eventually, the British interned her as a German national. My father was well connected with the British officials and officers and got her released but I don't think she ever changed her sympathies.

At one point in the war I heard all the radios saying, "Rommel is coming. Rommel is coming." My parents were very worried about this, particularly about the time between when the British troops would have to leave the city and the Germans would arrive. Everybody feared that there would be chaos.

Rommel kept getting closer, but in the end my parents needn't have worried. Rommel got as far as El Alamein, eighty kilometers [fifty miles] from Alexandria, but he was stopped there by General Montgomery. I can still remember listening to the sounds of that battle – the cannons, the bombs. I was glad when the radios said, "Rommel isn't coming any more."

That's what I mean when I say we were in the middle of the war but not in it.

Bernard Baehler   *Swiss   Investment Banker   Aged 3-9*

I knew when El Alamein occurred that we would win the war. Don't ask me how I knew, but I did. I went to the Gaumont cinema in Wednesbury to see the film which was quickly issued, *Desert Victory*. I had never seen anything like the flashes of the artillery barrage. I thought that if our armies can fight like the 8th Army, we had got to win. Of course I didn't understand anything about film editing then, but I was right anyway.

Earlier, in the car park of that very cinema, a German Heinkel III-K, was put on display after it was shot down. A number of these wrecks were towed around on long RAF trailers to maintain civilian morale. A lot of boys, including myself, bought cheap aircraft recognition books, which showed in silhouette almost all of the planes of the warring nations. Some of us became experts at spotting, we could also spot the different marks of the various planes and knew the difference between a Spitfire MK1 and a Mark 111E. We knew all the German planes, Messerschmitts, Heinkels, Focke-Wulf, The Junkers Ju 88, The Dornier 215 (the Flying Pencil) and any you care to mention. Then later the Americans culminating in the Mustangs and B27s or Flying Fortresses. I think that we were more excited than afraid. If you grew up in the Black Country you were used to noise.

My Aunt Lou (Mother's sister) gave me a copy of Odham's, *Britain's Wonderful Fighting Forces* for Christmas

1943, I was then 11, with hundreds of photographs, detailed plans, and diagrams. I was in seventh heaven.

John Bradley   *English   Aged "about ten"*

During the war in the park they had a plane, a German plane, which had been brought down and you could go into the cockpit for a few pence (which they gave to the War Effort) and also they had a great big wooden sort of thing outside and you could knock a nail into Hitler's coffin. That plane started off as complete but when all the children had got onto it they pulled off little bits of the fuselage and after a few weeks all the fabric had been torn off in their efforts.

There were the [barrage] balloons all the time. I saw those, and we had air raids, sirens. But in the country you didn't have any raids. You could hear the planes going over sometimes but you didn't hear the actual bombs falling. They were a long way away.

Mike Barnett   *English   Science Teacher   Born 1933*

One of the shopowners in our village, Mr [Jones], was rumored to be making a lot of money from selling food on the black market. My mother was always very nervous when we went into the shop. There was a kind of tension between her and Mr [Jones] that I picked up even at that age [six]. When we came out of the shop she always seemed angry and resentful. I never understood why. It was just one of those mysterious things grown ups did from time to time. Looking back, and from things that were hinted at later, I think it may have had something to do with my family refusing to buy food on the black market.

Huw Williams   *Welsh   Education consultant   Aged 6*

They came at night, in 1943, drunk. They bashed at the door. Mother rushed to open it. One opened it to everybody. She did not make it. They began to fire. A bullet tore her right elbow. It severed her arm from the shoulder, wounded her left hand. The capable, wise hand suddenly became a piece of meat, separate. I looked at it with amazement. I had seen dead bodies, but they somehow had always preserved their completeness in front of others.

We had to wait until the morning to go by carriage to the small town where there was a doctor. My mother survived in spite of a terrible loss of blood and excruciating pain. When she returned from the hospital, maimed, I attempted to replace for her the hand she had lost. I never left her alone. It was thought at the time that I would become a nurse.

Magdalena Abakanowicz   *Polish   Sculptress   Aged 12*

THE WAR IN CYPRUS

I grew up in Cyprus which at that time was a British Crown colony. Bloody Italian planes used to come over from Rhodes to bomb us. Rhodes was an Italian colony at that time. My village, Katydata, was near Nicosia aerodrome so we'd hear the Italian planes coming and the British planes would go up to meet them and the sirens would go and the guns and we'd all head for the shelter. The British had dug shelters for each village. Later, bloody German planes came too sometimes. We could tell by the different noise they made.

We were terrified in the shelters until the planes went away. Children screaming and crying. Adults at each end of the shelter wouldn't let you out. We'd wait for maybe an hour or two. The shelter was dug straight into the clay. Six or seven feet deep. And it smelled. Not a good earth smell like when it rains. Even today when I smell that smell of dug-up clay I am back in that shelter. I remember what it was like to be a frightened little boy. I think war is bloody terrible. We should never have wars. Never. Never. Never.

I saw lots of dogfights. Planes on fire, falling out of the sky. One of the pilots who fought against the Germans was a Greek. He flew a Spitfire. He was a brilliant pilot. Everybody loved him. He was kind of my hero. He was from Crete I think. I'll tell you one thing; the Germans were bloody good pilots. You could tell that from watching them. Once a German pilot parachuted out. People from the village he landed near shot him. They said he was trying to pull out a pistol to shoot them but who knows the truth? It may even have happened elsewhere. This was not a thing I saw myself. I heard about it in my village. The grown ups talking. Everyone said it was so but you don't know the truth. Not today. Not ever.

On Cyprus, during the war, we didn't have to go to school until we were seven so us boys used to play lots of baseball and football and hunt sparrows with our catapults [slingshots]. We never had enough to eat. We were lucky if we ate once a day. Official ration was four slices of bread a day. I never tasted a sweet until after the war. If we hadn't lived on Cyprus we'd have starved. Four months every year we could eat melons and watermelons. In winter, asparagus maybe. We had oranges, grapes, apples, figs, tomatoes, cucumbers, cabbages, but even so there never seemed to be enough. We lived near the Klareos River – the biggest river in Cyprus – so we'd catch and eat crabs and eels. Millions of them. Millions and millions. Today there are no crabs or eels on Cyprus.

Cyprus was still British then. The British troops stationed to defend our village were Iraqis. And the British troops defending the next village were Palestinians. Cyprus was also defended by British troops from India and Nepal. Times change!

There was a woman we used to hear on the radio. Sophia Vempo. She used to sing on the front lines for the Greek army. We loved her songs and as a young boy I learned many of them. I used to sing one when I was four or five. It's about Mussolini. We'd sing it in Greek and English. [Sings].

Κοροιδο Μουσολινι
Κανενασ δεν θα μεινει...

[Koroitho Mousolini
Kanenas then tha meni...]

Here. I'll translate for you: [Voice grows progressively louder with each line].

Make fun of Mussolini!
We're going to finish you off!
You and all your army!
We'll fight wherever we see you!
Anywhere we see sons of Italian blood!
We'll hit 'em hard!
Anything you throw at us!
We'll throw right back
And hit 'em hard!!!

[Long pause]. Of course, things are better between Italy and Cyprus now.

Andrew Joanides   *Cypriot   Garage Owner   Born 1938*

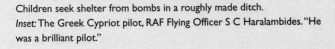

Children seek shelter from bombs in a roughly made ditch.
Inset: The Greek Cypriot pilot, RAF Flying Officer S C Haralambides. "He was a brilliant pilot."

DOLLE DINSDAG

By September 1944 the Allies had managed to liberate the whole south of Holland. They had reached the big rivers, the Rhine and other rivers south of Rotterdam, so that people were speculating that if they continued to advance at the same pace they would be in the Hague within a day. Rumours spread northwards in little increments of fifteen kilometers. In Amsterdam people were saying that the Allies were already in Haarlem; in Haarlem that they were approaching Leiden; in Leiden that they were in The Hague; [laughter] in The Hague that the Allies had liberated Delft; in Delft that they were in Rotterdam; in Rotterdam that they were coming into Dordrecht; and in Dordrecht that they were in Moerdijk, which is probably where they really were. Moerdijk is on the bank of the big river – the Rhine – that cuts through Holland from east to west. It separates the country into two parts, the northern part from the southern part.

People just went crazy. They seemed to forget that they were in the middle of a German Occupation. On Tuesday, 5th September 1944, everybody came out into the streets waiting for the Allies to arrive. They lined the major roads they thought the Allies would come along. They were quite openly cheering. We went to the centre of Leiden, Breestrasse, and waited with the others. People began putting out Dutch flags that they had hidden, and they were celebrating. But of course nothing happened. The progress of the Allies stagnated. We were actually liberated in May 1945. So everybody just took their flags home and hid them again. It was really crazy. "Dolle Dinsdag" they called it – Crazy Tuesday. In fact, that's what it's been called in Holland ever since.

The Germans were very nervous and also the Dutch collaborators. (There was a Dutch Nazi Party, NSP, National Socialist Union or something like that; they were also nervous and started to leave the west part of the country. They wanted to escape as quickly as possible to Germany or further away). The Germans didn't want to provoke anybody, I think, so on Dolle Dinsdag there was no violence. They were nervous themselves and there were some troop movements because probably they were better informed than we were, but they were also not certain whether the advance could be stopped. But afterwards they didn't get much better of course. I'm not saying they took revenge but I think that some people who exposed themselves that day later got caught. I was very disappointed afterwards because the worst was still to come for that part of the country.

Hans Hilbers *Dutch   Director, European Bank for Reconstruction and Recovery   Born 1934*

"The Allies will be here soon." Waving Dutch and British flags, and carrying flowers, Dutch citizens await their liberators. As it turned out, they would have to wait another seven months. Ryswikseplein, Amsterdam. 5 September 1944.

My parents had decided to keep us with them in London during the war. My father was in the Home Guard because he was a refrigeration engineer and was needed to fit out vans to collect whole blood supplies for the injured. In 1943 our flat in West Hampstead was bombed and my parents decided that my brother (eight months) and myself (two and a half years) should go and stay with our respective grandparents in Scotland (Aberdeenshire) and Cumberland.

We were to board a train at King's Cross station. My parents queued for hours for the tickets and had to leave the queue several times and dash to the underground shelter when the sirens sounded. Then they'd have to start all over again in the queue.

I have no distinct memory of it, just the atmosphere.

The sound and smell of steam trains, their piercing whistles, and the acrid smell. The repeated sirens and the crush and the feeling of panic around us. For many years I could not go into a train station without the same panic engulfing me – though I never quite understood why. It wasn't until British Rail went diesel that I was able to go into train stations with a degree of comfort.

Jean Helcke   *English   Community Nurse   Aged 30 months*

I remember an episode that says something about the dark side of American society during the war years. In the early 1940s, my brother and I were often taken to my grandfather's farm near Wilson [Texas] for long stays. In rural areas there was always plenty of meat, fowl, butter, lard, and other foods that could not always be had in the town of Lubbock, even if one had the proper ration coupons to buy them.

But I particularly remember the time my brother and I arrived at the farm just as my twenty-year-old auntie returned from college for a visit home. Aunt Marjory was all in tears as she stepped off the bus from Lubbock and, as a matter of fact, was angrier and more bitter than I had ever seen her. It seems that her bus had stopped in the countryside to take on passengers waiting in a queue at the edge of a cotton field. The white Texan bus driver haughtily had ordered a black Army sergeant among those trying to board, to step back to the end of the queue and remain in the last place until the white passengers had all taken their seats.

As there were not enough empty seats to accommodate everyone, the driver had rudely slammed the bus door in the face of the black soldier, leaving him with his duffle bag at the edge of the highway. As the bus sped onward, Aunt Marjory got ever more incensed at this treatment of a US Army serviceman – one who was a sergeant, at that! In the Texas of the 1940s, some white people were considerably less racist than others.

Lee Johnson   *American   Archaeologist   Born 1936*

In the second grade, Raymond Ormsby was the only Negro (that's what African-Americans were called back then). Raymond was also the best artist. His father was a sergeant in the Army Air Corps and Raymond drew a picture in Miss Jefferson's class that was so good she hung it on the blackboard.

It showed Raymond's father flying a plane that was dropping bombs on Nazi Germany.

The drawing has stayed in my mind all these years because it was the first time I'd ever seen a war hero whose face was drawn in with a brown crayon.

John Murphy   *American   Lawyer   Born 1936*

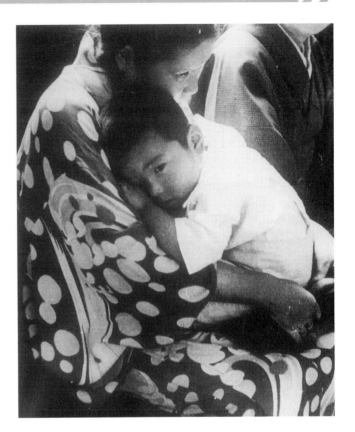

A mother's love and concern for the safety of her children was universal. Japan, 1945.

Since the beginning of the war, I had seen little of my father who was heading up an experimental plant to synthesize oil from coal using a technology imported from Germany. He spent much of his time in Omuta, a coal mining town on the island of Kyushu, that was an outgrowth of rich coal mines. By the fourth year of the war, my father knew that defeat of Japan was a matter of time and he decided to bring all of us from Tokyo to Omuta so that the whole family could be in one place when the end came.

One spring night in 1945, as my mother, three sisters, and myself were preparing for the journey, we heard the long lazy wailing of an air raid warning siren, followed not long after by the shorter, more urgent, blasts of the air raid siren. My mother herded us into a tunnel we used as our air raid shelter that connected our basement to a nearby street. I had no idea how long we were there in that damp clammy tunnel, but at long last we were allowed back into the house. We immediately went upstairs and out onto a balcony that looked toward downtown Tokyo. I have never seen a view like that before or since; as much of the horizon as we could see from our hillside house, more than 180 degrees of vista, was ablaze. The distinct outline of the Diet building was clearly silhouetted in its midst. This marked the first incendiary bombing of Tokyo. Two days later we left for Omuta.

Shortly after we moved there, Omuta became a regular target for B-29s. During raids we often went to my father's plant and into a deep underground shelter which connected to some of the old abandoned coal mine shafts. Other times, we simply hid in the bamboo woods that surrounded our house. One evening in June 1945, a major part of the downtown area was flattened by a blanket incendiary bombing. This time I did not see the town in flames as I had in Tokyo. What I saw this time was the aftermath at very close range. The school we went to, the train station, the retail stores along main street, houses, shrines, temples, they were all reduced to pile after pile of blackened lumber and ashes. The distant view of burning Tokyo had been like a dream, even beautiful as an erupting volcano might be beautiful from the safety of a distance. This was not beautiful. This was disaster. This was war.

As I went downtown the morning of the bombing, I saw people shifting through still smoldering remains of houses in the hope of finding some of their possessions; anything worth saving. Strangely, I do not recall ever seeing corpses or people looking for their loved ones. Nor did I see despair in their faces. The average Japanese still believed in ultimate victory and were prepared to accept the loss of their houses and possessions with stoic endurance.

Mamoru Mitsui   *Born Japanese, naturalized citizen of the United States of America   Architect   Age 7*

There was no leather for shoes and we would grow out of our shoes and so there were no shoes and the climate is not suitable to go barefoot so we got real Dutch wooden shoes.

Dutch children greet their liberators with an impromptu concert beaten out on the Allied food tins they've emptied. Bare feet and wooden shoes testify to the hardships suffered by the Dutch. Amsterdam, 1944.

The last year and a half of the war I walked with wooden shoes. You get used to them. You kicked them off before you went into the house. They were warm, particularly if you lined them with newspapers. The wooden shoes made a noise in the streets but there were not too many. I would say that it was the children mainly who would wear them. I also saw quite a lot of wooden sandals – sort of a shoe, not a 100% wooden shoe – with a linen top and a wooden sole. In the summer my sisters also had sandals. They made a great clatter.

Hans Hilbers   *Dutch   Director, European Bank for Reconstruction and Recovery   Born 1934*

My memories of World War II are happy ones; no struggles and in fact most enjoyable. This may well have been due to the fact that I had a very protective mother who probably shielded me from the horrors that war inevitably presents. My father had TB and was more often than not away from home recuperating in a sanatorium in the mountains.

In 1943 my mother was pregnant with my younger brother. I remember that in the evenings when the sirens sounded my mother would pack a little suitcase, take me by the hand, and rush across the local square to the Rifugio [Air Raid Shelter]. I always had a wonderful time there, because there would be many children and we would play and chatter together for many hours. We often had to sleep underground but all that was an adventure for me. Being an only child at that time meant that on these occasions I could be with my peers. I do not recall being alarmed by the sirens. In fact I thought they sounded beautiful because for me they announced playtime with many other children.

One day, when I was about four or five years old, I was walking in the Corso Ferruci where we lived [in Turin] and was fascinated to see a house, three houses away from ours, blazing away from a direct bomb hit. I watched as mattresses and other belongings were being thrown out of the windows and I laughed at the wonder of it all. I still remember being scolded by an old woman for laughing at what I know now was a serious and sad matter. The only German soldiers I remember were those that occasionally walked down our street. Everybody would be frightened but I didn't mind them as they always smiled at me.

Wilma Corradi   *Italian   Former actress   Born 1937*

We *must often have retreated from London to my grandparents rambling rectory in Essex, where various aunts were staying for the duration of the war. Here I remember a newly-acquired American uncle chiefly for his bear-hug. Like most English people of our background, my family*

An American GI helps British children put up Christmas decorations. As Helen Fletcher (below) discovered, a common language can sometimes disguise cultural differences. England, 1942.

---

tended to avoid close physical contact. I can still remember panicking as I was lifted and pinned against his rough khaki battle-jacket and bristly chin, engulfed in the unfamiliar smell of American cigarettes. It was quite terrifying.

Helen Fletcher   *English   Schoolmistress   Aged 3½*

My father was drafted into the Navy so, because my mother had to work, my sister and I were sent to boarding school. I went to St Vincent de Paul and my sister went to the Presentation of Mary Convent. Being a Catholic school there was a lot of praying for our soldiers and sailors. There was Mass every morning, and we would always have prayers. I don't think I was too creative in my prayers. Probably just Hail Marys or something along that line. We prayed in a vague kind of way for the soldier's lives. That's all. I don't remember being too specific about anything.

Our school was very close to a military air field. When an airplane took off, it would fly over the school so you couldn't hear anything. The nuns devised a system so that while the planes were going over everything came to silence. During that time was when we were supposed to say our prayers for the soldiers and for the war.

Gerald Durette   *American   Photographer and Store Owner Born 1936*

I *was the youngest of seven children and we lived in a small village, called Settefrati, halfway between Rome and Naples and very near to Monte Cassino. An area where there were many caves.*

One day my father said to my mother, "Pack everything. We have to move. The Germans are coming." So everything we could carry including my mother's trousseau trunk (containing all her best linen sheets, pillow cases, and towels) was taken to the caves which were about ten minutes walk away from Settefrati. All the villagers did the same. We would stay in the caves for several days, even months, and periodically, when the coast was clear, we would return to the village. The Germans would come into the village to find young men who had avoided joining the army, which included one of my brothers. They would even come to the caves and I remember the torches they had on their helmets which shone as they searched the caves.

I used to enjoy these sojourns in the caves because there were twenty or thirty families there and we children had fun together. I do remember one occasion when we had to leave the caves because a bombing raid was directed at the caves. But we might as well have stayed there because the caves were so deep and solid that direct hits did not make them collapse. Anyway, I remember my brother taking me under one arm and my sister under the other arm and running to a cave further away. I asked him, "Are we going to die?" and he just said, "Stai zitta!" ["Shut-up!"]

We used to play all sorts of games at those times. Some games were played with numbered stones; another game was a type of Bingo using numbered pieces of cardboard. We always played for buttons and I used to get mine by cutting the buttons off my father's shirts. He never scolded me. We had plenty of food because we grew all our own vegetables and we owned olive trees and had a vineyard. We even grew wheat. We had a goat so we had milk. Also because of the war all the sheep were ranging far and wide amongst the hills, ownerless, so we would just catch one for our needs. Eggs were obtained through a barter system as were other small luxuries, but there was very little salt.

My mother would bake white loaves from wheat using wild yeast – sour dough. She would also use corn meal and this bread we called 'red' bread. It did not taste as good as the white bread so we would always eat it first. I recall that my mother would bake a bread doll for me once a week, which I would play with until she baked the next one and then I would eat the first one. As there was not much money, she would sometimes make me a doll from sticks that she fashioned into a doll with rags.

The bombing raids usually came at night and we would hurry to the caves, where we had left our blankets and cooking utensils. Mother rarely forgot to bring matches. On occasions when she did forget, she would take two stones

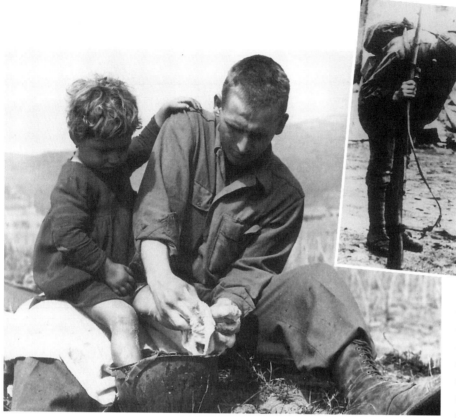

another. We younger children would be taught by the nuns in the church and that is where I learned to read and write. There was no school for the secondary school children.

The Fascistas would pay us one or two lira to collect shrapnel for recycling. The adults encouraged us children to do this because money was very scarce. We loved this job and would pick up anything. One day I picked up a hand grenade and was astonished when all the adults screamed at me. My brother took it out of my hands and we were all warned never, ever, to pick them up.

Father would often play cards with the other men in the village pub and when he won he would come home with his pockets full of sweets or biscuits or sometimes even a kilo of spaghetti. I would always search his pockets for sweets which was a special treat. But often he came home with empty pockets.

There was no tea or coffee except for a type of ersatz coffee and camomile tea. If I had a cold or tonsillitis, mother would make a brew from dried apples, prunes and grapes which would simmer for ages in a pot on the stove and then give me the liquid to drink. This would be my medicine. A special treat was being given the stewed fruit to eat later.

Teresa Tamburro *Italian Housekeeper Born 1937*

An American soldier washes the feet of an Italian child in his helmet. Italy, 1944. *Inset:* Velodya Lukin, aged ten, talks to a Red Army soldier. Forced to flee his home, the boy has frostbitten feet. Russian front, 1944.

and strike them together until she produced a spark to light the fire for cooking. There was also plenty of water because of the many wells in the area.

I remember one man being so frightened that he went down a well and couldn't get up again. He was there several days until he was rescued by a villager who was looking for straw for his horse and heard the poor man shout.

When I was about six years old the Fascistas came and looked for the women in order to take their gold wedding rings, gold chains, and bracelets. My mother was very upset at having to relinquish her wedding ring. Later on the Fascistas also took all the trunks containing the linen, which was another source of grief for the women in our village; particularly as new born babes were always swaddled in these fine linen towels. Nothing else would do. There were many times when I would see villagers bleeding from wounds. On these occasions my mother would tear a strip off her petticoat and order the injured person to pee on it and whilst it was still warm she would bandage the wound. The wounds always healed and did not become infected.

We went to church regularly, even sometimes during the week. If we were in the caves then the priests would come to us. When one church got bombed we would attend at

My father sent my mother, my sisters, and myself from Hong Kong to Manila where he thought we would be safe because, he said, the Americans owned the Philippines and that was that. Shortly after we arrived, the Japanese captured Manila and in due course we were interned in a camp called Los Banos.

One or two memories stand out. I suppose the first was, one day somewhere in the middle of it, the Japanese released us all for one day to go out and collect food from the surrounding countryside and that was seized by everybody. The Japanese knew we couldn't escape anywhere. We were too weak and wouldn't know where to go anyway. We all set off and almost everybody collected bananas, papayas, guavas, mangoes, you name it, all the soft fruit which grew in profusion outside the wire. But my mother, bless her socks, said, "We'll go and dig up ginger roots," which we duly did and, of course, in her wisdom, the ginger roots lasted three months and the bananas lasted three days. I have had a love for ginger ever since and indeed only last week I was in China and bought in memory of my mother a large ginger root.

The other one was a rather more curious story perhaps. I remember listening to a radio transmission by Alistair Cook recently, where an old and rich man had come up to Alistair and said to him, "Your father knew me when I was aged nine and was an orphan." And Alistair said, "Oh yes, tell me more," and this rich old man said, "Your father discovered that as an orphan I had never been given a present in my life. What do you think he gave me?" And Alistair said "I haven't the faintest idea; what do you give a child who has never had a present?" And so the man said, "Well, actually he gave me a candle, which was a particularly significant thing, and I enormously appreciated it."

And I remembered in a flash that the only present that I've given to anybody was a present to my mother of a tin, a cigarette tin. In those days cigarettes came hermetically sealed in tins in order to keep the water condensation out of them. I gave her a tin of cigarette ends [butts] for her birthday. It had taken me a complete year to collect them, one at a time. She was, at the time, a smoker totally devoid of cigarettes and this was of course a treasure of countless price. People managed to buy cigarettes in the camp by selling whatever jewelry they had or using whatever money they brought in with them. Every cigarette was smoked to the absolute infinite butt because it was so precious in those days; one didn't get much out of a dropping. I don't recollect having a great deal of competition for the cigarette ends, mind you, but I always made sure I was there pretty sharpish, scooping them up.

What I remember most about the camp is being eternally hungry. Whereas we started off by being fed moderately well, by the end of the war our total ration was a small wineglass full of unhusked rice each day. It first of all had to be husked, which I remember being an absolute pain and a most awful labour and then duly soaked and cooked over open fires to the best of our very limited ability because by then we had no central kitchens, then mixing in whatever weeds, grass, or leaves we could find around the camp and that was our ration for the day. So we were intensely hungry and I recollect that well. Other than roll call most of the rest of the day is rather a blur. My mother records that towards the end we were an absolute pain because we wouldn't even play because we were so lethargic through lack of food and just bickered, all day and every day. Food and preoccupation with food and preparing and everything else to do with food and at the end husking this damned rice. Of course unhusked rice kills you. I also recollect being beastly enough when queuing for food, because I had to ensure that I got everybody's food for them. But then I made sure that my meal lasted last so that my sisters would be envious of me as I ate the last scrap.

Major General Sir James Templer *English Army, retired Born 1937*

*I*n France, parsnips, or "panais," were root vegetables traditionally used only to feed farm animals. During the Second World War, however, the Germans did not like them and they were plentiful, so I remember my Mama cooking them every which way – boiled, braised, roasted, in stews, out of stews. By the age of fourteen, I could not bear the sight of parsnips.

Albert Roux *French Chef and food writer Aged 9-14*

A French boy presents a bottle of his family's treasured wine to an American soldier as his jeep moves through Carentan in Normandy. France, June 1944.

We never had any sweets in the war. We ate cocoa, sugar, and dried milk in a little screw of paper. We considered ourselves very lucky when we had "Sticky Lice" to suck. This was a piece of licorice root which we chewed and sucked to a pulp and was rated a great treat. Our local sweet shop was called Dawson's. One Sunday morning they took sweets off ration, the first time ever in my lifetime. And people just seemed to go mad. Within a hour, or maybe two, the shop was empty. It seemed ages before we saw sweets again.

Beryl Stephenson   *English   School mistress   Aged 7*

Almost 20,000,000 Russians died in the war, many of them children. This boy and his cat were amongst the lucky survivors – for the moment. Russian Front, 1944.

The winter of 1942, during the Continuation War,* was the hardest in Helsinki. The food was very short, no potatoes, no butter, very little bread and milk and it was a cold winter. In '42 we ate the minimum. We had bread but very little for breakfast. Sometimes we had a little butter, no coffee, no tea, but hot water and a little milk. Sometimes we just had hot water. We didn't have coffee but we had a malt-coffee made from roots – Korvikee, we called it. Sometimes it was mixed with buttercup roots and also sugar beet. Sometimes all we had for breakfast that year was hot water with some milk, or Korvikee. And then there was also tea from the birch tree, the dried leaves from the birch. It didn't taste so good but it was the only possibility. It was supposed to be healthy but it wasn't good. It's all we had until two or three years after the war when we got ration coupons for real coffee and tea which we used until 1952. Even today some people my age still make tea out of birch leaves; it is supposed to be healthy but not for me. Saccharin is one of the very typical tastes from the war time. Not sugar but saccharin, so much that it was too sweet.

The main thing we ate was curry with fish. We ate a lot of fish. A fish something like a herring that came from the Gulf of Finland. We might have fish for lunch perhaps. In 1942 you couldn't get potatoes so we ate a lot of turnips. "Lanto" they are called in Finnish. And in the evening maybe a little bread and Korvikee or tea.

Later in the war, we began to get lots of potatoes. They had to gather them all at once because they couldn't dig them out after the ground was frozen. Every family was given some to last over the winter time. There was no refrigeration but, since the winter was 30-40 degrees below zero, there was no problem. We had them stored in our house, a roomful of potatoes. We couldn't eat them all at once so when spring came they started sprouting and rotting. We were hungry and starved but rotting potatoes are no use and we had to throw them away. That's one of the things I remember very strongly from the war. The smell of rotting potatoes.

That's one of the things that they managed to keep going during the war – garbage collection. Not that there was much to collect since people ate everything. They came in trucks that had big boilers and ran on steam. Raetontto, that's what they were called. They used to burn wood. Only the army had gasoline. Public transport – trams and the railway ran on wood and coal, because we have so much wood.

Every week we saw films. It was the only possibility to relax besides the radio. Films were very important to us. Mainly we saw German films and later in the war American films. Most of the German news was full of propaganda but the films were not so. We saw "Munchhaüsen," the first colour film made by the Germans. We had very good comedies. Heinz Frumann was a very famous film star and Ilse Werner. We also had American stars – Olivia de Haviland, Errol Flynn, Rita Hayward, Clark Gable, Greta Garbo. All the American films. You never forget them. I can still see that film. . .Vivien Leigh and Robert Taylor. . . "Waterloo Bridge," that's it. 1940.

And also during the war I saw "Lumikki ja seitsemän kääpiötä." "Snow White and the Seven Dwarfs" you'd call it. [Laughs]. I still remember their names, their faces. Ujo [Bashful]. . .Viisas [Doc], the wise one. . . Jörö [Grumpy]. . . Nuhanenä [Sneezy] with his red nose. . . You'd sit there in the dark and watch the films and then go outside to the war. Bombing. Rationing. Being frightened or hungry. But you weren't resentful. And it didn't seem strange. It was magic. That's something maybe people today have lost. How magic films were then.

Vesa Lyytikäinen   *Finnish   Housewife   Born 1929*

Probably the most exciting experience I had when I was a boy. . . I think it was when I was in the third form at elementary school, so I was nine or ten then. They raffled a Walt Disney train set. It had everything on it. It had a Mickey Mouse, a Donald Duck, and all the rest of them. It was in tin plate. I know it's tin plate now, but I didn't know that then. The tickets were a penny a time and I won it.

I kept my train set for several years but unfortunately it got broken up by somebody else. It couldn't have been by me – I loved it too much. It was a proper train set. The Mickey Mouse was an actual figure. He was the driver of the train. Goofy was the coal man and there was at least one other Disney character who was probably the guard. There must have been at least four carriages and there were the rails to run along. It was wind-up, clockwork. There wasn't electric then.

Mike Barnett   *English   Science teacher   Born 1933*

We always had plenty of food and even toilet paper, which my father would acquire through the black market. I also remember that we received American food parcels and this food was very different to what we normally ate. The packaging was different and the food was in tins, like butter which came in a bronze color tin. We also had rice bread, which I think was from the Americans. It was very heavy as it was unyeasted. We had tinned compressed meat that came in square cans with rounded corners which opened with a little key. We also drank sweet tinned milk rather like today's Carnation milk. Sometimes the parcels contained cake.

I remember chewing gum, which was very big and you could blow bubbles with it. I would add a bit more to it every day until I could not contain it in my mouth and at night I kept it in sugar to retain its flavor.

Wilma Corradi   *Italian   Former actress   Born 1937*

Late in the war I saw a terrible thing. I saw a plane. . . an American plane. . . you know, one of those ones with two. . . two tails, you know like this [Gestures] . . . P-38? OK. I saw a P-38 attacking a bridge across a river. There was a German flak position nearby. The pilot dived down on the bridge, dropped his bomb, and missed. Not too far away, a farmer was plowing his field with a pair of horses. The fighter plane looped around and dived on the horses with his machine guns firing. When the farmer saw what was happening, he ran and hid under the arches of the bridge. The plane made a second pass, killed the horses, and flew off. The farmer emerged from under the bridge, went over to his two horses, and stood looking sadly down on them. At that moment the plane came back again from a different direction. This time the farmer was killed.

Tony Sidoli   *British/Italian   Ex-Restauranteur, Scrap Merchant   Born 1925*

In the last years of the war, my mother, my sisters, and I walked down a tree-lined country lane to the nearby town of Flöhte to buy new coats for Easter. I can't remember any kind of store so I'm not sure if the coats were new, or just new to us. At any rate, this was a special treat, and we felt very dressed-up in our new green coats. It didn't occur to us that green coats look like uniforms. On our way home I heard the sound of a plane coming low. It swooped down and started shooting at us, so my mother threw us into a ditch and herself on top. I think my feeling was that so long as my mother was there, we'd be safe. Our new coats were dirty when we got home. I think I was more upset by this than I was being strafed by a plane.

Margot Hamilton   *German, naturalized American   Business Manager, retired   Born 1936*

Margot Hamilton and her mother and sister crouched in this ditch in their new green coats while being strafed by an Allied plane. Germany, 1945.

FINLAND CAN'T BE FAR AWAY

Juha Lehtiranta with his mother and
brother. Finland, 1940.

During the Winter War* in 1940, when the Russians were threatening to invade, the authorities sent children from Helsinki to Sweden and other northern countries like Denmark and Norway. Denmark had already been invaded so Finns preferred their children to be in Denmark under German occupation rather than face the Russians. Altogether 70,000 Finnish children were sent abroad. I was sent to Sweden.

On my arrival, I had a very thorough medical examination that went on for several days because there was a lot of TB in Finland at that time. Eventually, I was sent north, to the Swedish island of Sollerön – about two miles off the coast in the Siljan Sea [Lake]. The village was inhabited by about 200 people, mostly farmers. The houses seemed very prosperous and tidy to us after Finland. I was lodged with a farm family called the Andersons – Anna and Anders. At first I spoke no Swedish but slowly I learned it. Or at least I thought I was learning it. What I didn't realize until much later was that the people on Sollerön speak a special language which even other Swedes can't understand! I think it's the original Viking language, that they had in the late 800s when the Vikings left the Continent. It's totally different – like Welsh for an Englishman – you can't understand a word. If a Swede wants to say, "How would it be?" he would say, "Hut skulle det vara?" On Sollerön they would say, "Ur-edde-su-ve?" So I grew up on the island thinking I could speak Swedish – not a language that only a few hundred people could understand.

In Sweden, on the island, they had local folk music which I liked very much. They had mostly violins, and one accordion. In the mid-summer there was a party on the island, near the church. There was a huge tree with streamers and flags and then there was dancing and folk dancing and so on. Anna Anderson, the farmer's wife, had a Swedish folk dress which she wore on special occasions like that.

I got on well with the Swedish children. It was countryside and we went swimming and skiing; we had a lot of good times. There was no playground but the village streets. They had bicycles. Two of my brothers, Jouko and Jouni, were with me on the island and the three of us used to play together a lot. We were out all the time and there was a small wood in the neighborhood and we used to go there to collect wood. We played games like hiding and of course we played soldiers. In school, partly because of language, partly because I'd missed so much time, I was put back into first class. We had wood-carving lessons and I was busy carving some machine guns and pistols and rifles to play with at home. I accidentally cut my finger off when I was carving one day. Later, I learned to carve boats and to make useful things like the wooden pins that were part of the hay rakes they used on the island.

There was another Finnish boy on the island named Pentti Limmonen. Early in our stay he was very homesick and I was homesick too. We missed our parents. We missed. . . Finland. We decided we didn't like it here on the island any more and he said to me, "Enough. We must go back to Finland." So I said, "OK." We didn't have any food or plans or any idea really of where Finland was – or how far [about 350 miles and on the other side of the Baltic]. Pentti said, "Finland can't be far away." It was winter and the lake was frozen so we just put on our skis and started off for Finland. We didn't get far, only about 300 meters, before the Andersons discovered we were leaving and came to fetch us back. I think maybe they knew by the way we had said goodbye that we were up to something. Later, Pentti became a boxer in Finland; he became a professional boxing champion – a lightweight I think he was.

In Sweden the war didn't affect me at all. I remember Sven, the Anderson's son. He was crazy to build model aircraft and he used to listen on the radio every evening to hear the news about the war. I remember him cursing the Russians when they made progress and, of course, finally beat us, in Finland. We never heard planes passing overhead. Apart from the radio, the war was far away.

Then, in 1941, I went back to Finland and the war was suddenly very real. I remember vividly how the planes came overhead to bombard and all the firing from the Finnish artillery a couple of kilometers away. In the night you could see the flames and the ammunition and the planes bombing on Helsinki. We stayed about twelve kilometers from the centre of the town and we had to run for shelter in the cellar of a wooden two storey house, which of course was no shelter at all. One bomb fell less than a kilometer away and I was very frightened. When there was school, I had to go, but I had been taught a different curriculum in Sweden so I was put back into first class.

In Finland we had a small garden with some potatoes growing and carrots, cabbages, and beets. My mother used to make soup from it. There were bread and meat and milk coupons. Of course everything was poorer and the meals were poorer. In Sweden we had proper meals but in Finland it was mainly soup I remember.

Eventually, in 1942, I was sent back to the island. I was put back into first class again because of what I'd missed. There were two Finnish girls on the island, Leila and Lilja Finnberg. Our father knew their father. We didn't see the girls often but I can remember seeing them at Anna Anderson's Sunday School. After the war, we returned to Finland and years after that our fathers met up and the families became friendly again. My brother Jouni married Lilja. And in 1956 I married Leila. Later in the 1960s, we went back to Sollerön with our two daughters to visit my step-parents, the Andersons. We have been there a few times since.

Juha Lehtiranta   *Finnish   Shipping Coordinator, retired   Born 1935*

In early August 1945, my mother was taking my younger sister, Tamiko, and me to a farm house we had rented to prepare it for family use in case of emergency.

On the way, we were crossing a narrow valley on foot, when suddenly we heard the sound of an unfamiliar airplane engine. By now we could identify the distinctive drone of a B-29 from miles away, but this was a much sharper sound of a smaller and faster aircraft. The next instant, a single engine fighter-bomber with gleaming silver wings and fuselage appeared at one end of the valley. As we ran, I heard a series of sounds, "fiew-fiew-fiew, bhut-bhut-bhut." As I looked back to see where the
sound was coming from, I saw the face of an American pilot through the cockpit dome as he flashed past us. Much later I realized that the strange sound I heard was made by the bullets whizzing by us and burying themselves in the wet rice field in the valley.

Looking back at the experience of war, it was to me a very abstract affair in that we never sensed the presence of the enemy. You didn't feel there were human beings behind distant aircraft and unseen bombs. Seeing the face of a pilot on this occasion, however, made the war as personal as it ever became.

Mamoru Mitsui   *Born Japanese, naturalized citizen of the United States of America   Architect   Age 7*

Lappish brothers on the evacuees' hard road, but still happy. As the Germans retreatd from Russia across Finnish Lapland, children were moved to places of safety. September, 1944.

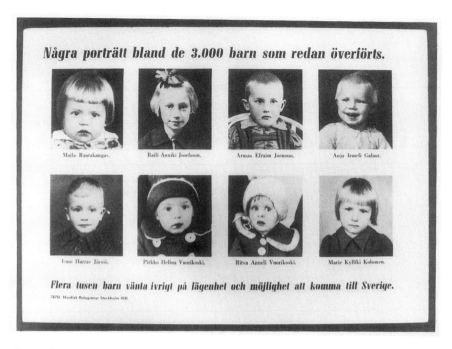

Några porträtt bland de 3.000 barn som redan överförts.

Maila Rantakangas.   Raili Anniki Joselsson.   Armas Efraim Joensuu.   Anja Irmeli Galası.

Ismo Harras Järvio.   Pirkko Helina Vuorikoski.   Ritva Anneli Vuorikoski.   Marie Kylliki Kohonen.

Flera tusen barn vänta ivrigt på lägenhet och möjlighet att komma till Sverige.

Finnish children evacuated to Sweden in 1939-40. There were more children than homes immediately available for them, so advertisements like this appeared in Swedish magazines and newspapers to persuade people to take the children into their homes.

On 9th April 1940 Narvik [Norway] was attacked by the Germans. During the battles many thousands of people had to flee from the town. Many of them came to Beisfjord, a steep mountainous fjord near Narvik. There were about forty of us in the cellar of our house when Beisfjord was set on fire by the British warship Warspite. *Luckily we were not hit, but our neighbor's house was and twelve people were killed. We had to escape further into the district. I remember that my mother carried me in a blanket, and the screaming and crying women frightened me.*

Many people sought shelter in caves in the mountains. My father carried me up the mountainside but as the sky was full of planes, and projectiles of many kinds were flying around in the air, we had to seek shelter behind a stone where I lay underneath my father. I didn't feel as if we were there for long, but apparently it lasted several hours.

In 1942 all the radios in our village and district were collected by the Germans, and as they had occupied our house for some time and had broken our gramophone – maybe because it was a 'His Master's Voice' product! – there was little music during my childhood. All the same, I can clearly see marching and singing German soldiers, sometimes wearing gas masks.

I started school in 1943 at the age of seven. We went to school every other day and had four classes in the same room with one row for each class. During the last year of the war the Germans occupied our school for several months and we had little teaching. Lack of teaching was one of the prices we youngsters had to pay.

One of the things which was typical of the war years was the shortage of things. Clothes and shoes could not be bought, and there was a shortage of food both quantitatively and qualitatively. Everyone had to take part in picking wild berries and potatoes to ensure winter supplies. The bus service which took work people to and from Narvik had a gas generator fired by alder wood, because there was no petrol. On the steepest hills all the men had to get out and push so the journey took one hour. Today, it takes fifteen minutes!

The special conditions under which I grew up have of course marked me for life. Even as a grown up I have several phobias which are probably a result of my childhood experiences. I feel really sorry for the millions of children who are the victims of the horrors of war.

Rudolf Antonsen *Norwegian Aged 4-7*

I was evacuated from my home in the East End of London – a nightmare that began in a station master's house on the side of a track in Devon somewhere. The village I was taken to was called Butterley, although I hated it so much I've never even looked it up on a map. We were lined up and I can remember the, I suppose it was some kind of waiting room, on the platform, and we were lined up, several of us, maybe fifteen or twenty, and a really horrible old farmer came in with a really nasty, mangy dog and he pointed to five of us and we were then lead away by him and taken to his home and then began a period of great pain, is the best way of describing it.

There was always the feeling that in some way it was one's own fault and I think that that's part of the difficulty, perhaps, of recalling, that if one hadn't got something wrong it wouldn't have worked out like this. I can't explain it, but it was always one's own fault. And then of course the beatings started. They were a particularly kinky family who, when one of the kids had a birthday, would begin the day by giving the child a beating. Sunday lunch would be followed by beatings in front of everyone, where a child would be pulled away from the table and trousers taken down and given a beating.

I think now they were instinctively cruel. My memory of them filtered through the rationalism of an adult, tells me that they were a very backward people and I think that in all probability, life in rural districts was extremely backward at times. There was a joy, I remember, in the nine o'clock news at night, or in the morning news saying that London had been badly blitzed the night before. It was a joy because that had been happening to London. It was a kind of ignorance born of isolation, I suppose, and poverty. I guess we were taken in for the five bob [shillings] a week they got for us.

A Ministry of Health poster urging London children to leave the city. For many children evacuation has left memories of ill-treatment and misery. England, 1940.

The food must have been very poor, because we all developed impetigo and malnutrition, but it took a very long time for anyone to notice the fact that we were in that state. Five of us slept in one double bed and of course, I didn't see my parents for a very, very long time and time just seemed to pass. Very little in the way of schooling. I don't remember much about schooling there at all but I can remember Christmas presents arriving. A parcel arriving from home and I can remember the presents spread out on the landing like board games and toys and things, spread out on the landing outside our bedroom, but I don't remember any kind of joy being attached to it. The presents were attractive but I don't remember having possession of them and I don't remember the Christmas itself because there was just extreme cruelty in the house.

Bernard Cohen *English   Artist, Director of Slade School of Fine Art, UCL   Born 1933*

I will always remember Christmas 1940. I was a young child and my brother was a baby at the time and he was teething. So off I went with my father to deliver Christmas presents to our relatives in Cheshire, while Mum stayed home with the baby.

On our return, as we neared Manchester, the whole sky was bright red; the Blitz had begun, so we had to take shelter for the night. The following morning we made our way past heaps of rubble, where people's homes had stood. Smoke still filled the air. Happily our house was still intact apart from a few broken windows. Some of our neighbors were less lucky. As we were a close knit 'Coronation Street'* type of community, we decided to put out all our food, toys, and clothes so that everyone could share our Christmas. On Christmas Day our house was packed with people, and someone brought an accordion. The piano was wheeled out, and we all had a good old knees up.

Even to this day, people still talk about that wonderful Christmas. Perhaps it was because it caught the true meaning of Christmas – caring and sharing with those less fortunate than yourself.

Elsie Hughes *English   Housewife   Aged 7*

After one and a half years all the civilians were evacuated from the fort at Haarr. We had to move everything, animals and equipment, and put our things in different places spread all over the village district. Being driven from our home is something I shall always remember. I can still see we three children and three grown ups, my mother carrying the youngest on her back and holding my younger brother by the hand.

Father Christmas, wearing his steel helmet, weathers the Blitz to deliver the goods. London. December, 1940.
Inset: An evacuee blows his Christmas trumpet. Shenfield, England. 1940.

and sweetmeats called Toroni, which were very chewy and hard but very tasty and a special treat. She also baked animal shaped biscuits. We did not have a Christmas tree but we drank our own wine and ate delicious dry cod fried in batter. Mother knew all the local herbs and would gather them from the pavements in the village for her cooking.

Teresa Tamburro   *Italian   Housekeeper   Born 1937*

We didn't have any contact with the British, but the Americans were accepted relatively quickly by the people. I think the people saw them more as liberators than as the enemy. Maybe they handled it well psychologically. They helped a lot. They did a lot for the children. They took us on excursions and gave us lots to eat. People were happy to have peace and were busy surviving. I think the feelings were similar toward the British and French in the areas where they were. It was easier for the Americans because their country was not affected by what the German Army had done in the beginning.

We children thought everything from America was great – films, ice cream, Coca-Cola, cars. My father installed a kitchen for some Americans and that Christmas Eve one of the colonels came to our house and brought toys for me, and ice cream, ham, and white bread. They gave me a big metal building crane that worked, and it was my favorite toy for a whole year.

Not many toys had been available during the war; my father built me toy airplanes and a little spotlight just like the real ones the military used.

Erwin Perrot   *German   Electrical Engineer   Born 1934*

We had enough food on the farm but I remember how the grown ups compensated for the lack of other goods. They made their own potato flour. Burnt peas served as coffee, and tobacco plants were grown in the garden and dried in the barn before being smoked. Somehow or other my mother managed to save enough rice for us to have rice porridge every Christmas – a traditional Norwegian Christmas dish – and in the circumstances a real feast!

Lars Haarr   *Norwegian   Born 1938*

Despite the war, Christmas Eve in our little village [in Italy] was a family occasion. Mother would knit long socks for father which would be used as Christmas stockings. We were never given toys, but each sock would have in it: one orange, one apple, one piece of coal, a few walnuts and hazelnuts and one piece of cake. Mother would bake a Christmas cake

My father was arrested on 2nd October 1941 and my mother two hours later. The door bell rang and fifteen men stormed into the house and asked for my parents. They dragged the duvet off my parents. There were so many of them because they had been informed that my father was a dangerous member of the Resistance. My mother was arrested as a hostage. Even though it is fifty years ago it still fills me with fear.

In the beginning we did not know where she was but the jungle telegraph managed to find out that she was in Bergen District jail. Later, she told us that she spent the whole of the first night sitting up as she thought it would only last for some few hours. In fact it lasted three months. When she was called in for interrogation she had to walk right through the centre of town from the prison with two Germans on either side of her – a degrading experience.

We managed to get up a correspondence with her. When we were allowed to visit her with coffee etc, we had two thermos flasks, one of them had a cork, but in the other we rolled up paper to function as a cork and inside the paper we wrote small messages to each other. Every evening at 7 p.m. we stood outside the prison and saw her at the window, although she had to climb up to see out. My mother was never the same after that experience. At last she came home and we could live a somewhat normal life. In 1942 her salary was stopped and we had little to live off, but other good Norwegians helped us from time to time, and at Christmas there was a little money in our post box Kr. 37.50 [$5.75]. It doesn't sound like much today but it saved that Christmas for us.

Svanhild Stein Sohr
*Norwegian   Business Woman
Born 1924*

finding a cafe. Some were open, but there was no water! Finally we found a rather battered milk bar, which had milk but no food. Luckily I had with me a large box of chocolates which had been sent from Ireland, and which I had collected the previous afternoon. So our lunch consisted of cold malted milk and 'Black Magic!'

Sometimes when I smell the Christmas turkey in the oven, I recall that festive meal! We were together – we had reason to celebrate!

Marie Moran   *English   Housewife   Aged 13*

Left: The magic of Christmas in Germany. Father is safely home on leave. For a moment, the war is far away. Germany, 21 December 1944. *Below:* Captain Carpenter of the US Army offers a French orphan marbles from under the tree. Christmas in France, 1944.

It was the time of the Manchester blitz and one night, just before 24 December, from a shelter on a hill some miles away, I had watched the blazing city, heart sick with the knowledge that somewhere amidst the dreadful conflagration were all my loved ones.

When morning came I set out to find them. A bus took me as far as the outer suburbs, but could go no further. From there I walked for miles, picking my way over broken glass, smouldering rubble, and hose-pipes. The streets were packed with people either driven from their homes or trying to get to work. Among all these crowds I suddenly came upon three of my sisters. They had spent the night in a shelter, but assumed that the rest of the family were safe.

Since they had eaten nothing since tea-time the previous day, we made our way to the city in the hope of

PART SEVEN

TOWARD THE LIGHT

**Russian children in front of their bombed-out home.
Belorussia, ca. 1942.**

I don't remember quite how I felt about the Germans. They were bombing us and we weren't very fond of them, I suppose, but that's as far as it went. Oh, yes. I just remembered something. We used to call them "Nasty Nazis."

Jean Holder   *Retired Deputy Head Teacher   English Born 1933*

My mother had a serving tray. It was kind of an oval shape, black, with a flower painting on it with a little gold trim. It was probably about seven by fourteen or so. My parents would serve drinks on it. On the back of the tray it said, "Made in Japan." My folks must have been talking about the Nazis and Japanese and different things because when I was about ten my sister and I took the tray downstairs without anybody knowing and threw it in the garbage.

My mother was pretty upset with us for doing that, because it was a nice tray, but we were never punished. My mother had a great sense of humor. She understood what we were doing but I know that she was hurt because it was probably a wedding gift or something along that line. She never told us what it was but I think she was hurt.

Gerald Durette   *American   Photographer / Store Owner Born 1936*

My hometown paper was pretty far to the right even for a staunch Republican like my father. It often made him angry when he read it, particularly the editorial page, but it was the only paper that reported local news so we always subscribed. One evening during the war he threw the paper down on the floor with a thump. It was folded on the letters page.

He was so angry he was all but spluttering. "Can you believe that some idiot wants to chop down all the Japanese cherry trees in Washington?"

Charles Davis   *American   Retired   Lecturer   Aged 7*

When the anti-aircraft guns behind our house hit a plane and the pilots parachuted out, we boys would run to see where they landed. But the only one we ever found was dead. His chute hadn't opened. Where he hit made a hole in the ground like a bomb. He was such a young man, not much older than most of us, and suddenly I felt sorry for him. That's amazing how a strong feeling of hate can change from one moment to another in a human. I was young and was shocked at this moment when I realized that this terrible bomber pilot looked like my brother or friends. At this moment you get a completely different view about things .

I was sure the pilot and I could have played together as friends and we never would have a reason to be enemies.

Erwin Perrot   *German   Electrical Engineer   Born 1934*

When the newspaper in Amarillo, Texas announced that a trainload of German prisoners would be passing through town on the Santa Fe railroad, a large crowd gathered at the train station. We all stood very quietly staring at the prisoners and they, equally quiet, stared back. It was amazing to me that they looked like our own young men. I felt confused. I knew they were our enemies, but they didn't look so hateful.

Betty Eberhart   *American   Psychotherapist   Aged 14*

Early in the war, we had prisoners of war as labor for our family's commercial truck farm. We had French and Russian prisoners who lived with my grandparents. They were all good people. We could see that they were people just like us. One of the Russians – Alex – used to take me riding on the bicycle; my grandparents would let us go everywhere together and no one worried about it. That was in 1940-41.

Erwin Perrot   *German   Electrical Engineer   Born 1934*

An Army Air Corps glider base was opened just outside of Lubbock, [Texas], at the site of the municipal airport, and we used to go out to watch the men training to pilot the gliders and the C-47 transport planes that pulled them. It was fascinating to see the planes towing and then releasing one or more gliders, while cruising at low and high altitudes. One day a C-47 crashed during take-off. We heard about it from a friend who was an Air Corps private at the base, and I went out with pa to inspect the site. Although military police had the crash area roped off, we could see the burned earth, the bits of metal and twisted propellers, the fire trucks, and the stains where the bodies had lain. It was exciting to me and horrible, all at the same time. Although I was just a lad, that day I finally realized that war was something real and deadly.

Lee Johnson   *American   Archaeologist   Born 1936*

About twenty children on our street played together. One thing we liked to do as Frankfurt and the towns around us were bombed by the Allies was collect the bombs that didn't explode. A lot of them hit soft ground. The kids took them to a little stream behind the town and threw them at the rocks in the water until they exploded. If we threw enough of them in, the water would really start boiling. Some of the bombs would bounce off the rocks and back onto shore. Some of them were incendiary bombs which start to emit sparkling fire when they hit – then you could run, when the sparks started flying.

Some of the bombs were phosphorous bombs; water just made them burn more. The phosphorus ones were really bad. If you brushed cold phosphorus spots that were on a wall they started burning again. Some of the boys would throw the phosphorus bombs, but I never was that dumb. A pair of my friends burned their faces and hands – they still have the scars. Those bombs were so heavy you could hardly pick them up. If one exploded in your hand, it would blow your hand off or worse.

We also collected the splinters from the anti-aircraft fire that was shot at the planes when they came over. The splinters were about a thumb long and 1 to 2 centimetres thick. We children sometimes helped carry the grenades to the anti-aircraft guns – there was a battery of twenty-four anti-aircraft guns directly behind our house in Neu-Isenburg, about a five minute walk away. They were the famous 8.8 guns. They were wonderful – precision cannon – they were the most feared. We'd carry the shells over in the afternoon, and the next morning the streets would be covered with the shell splinters. I had some really good collections. My mother always found them and threw them away, but I'd just start collecting again. The boy with the largest and best collection of shell splinters was the hero.

Erwin Perrot   *German   Electrical Engineer   Born 1934*

At the bottom of the hill there was a brewery, because it always smelled of hops. We would play against the brewery wall after school. We played marbles. . . we played matchsticks. We used to collect matchsticks from the road and hold them between our first finger and the thumb and we used to push them against each other. Just like with conkers,* it used to be a "oner" or a "twoer".* The matchsticks stood up between our first finger and thumb and we pushed them against each other so that they would break. Going to school in the morning we used to look in the gutter all along the road for matchsticks. Swan* sticks were very good, you didn't get many of those, but they were very good matches in those days, quite thick.

Left: A helpful youth hangs out washing for the girls at a rest center for people who have been bombed out of their homes. Mile End, London. October 1940.

Center: Finnish girls playing mother on a bomb site. Helsinki, 1942.

Above right: Determined children can find a place to play anywhere – including this bombed-out ruin. England, 1940.

In elementary school, the classes were in the region of forty-two to forty-six in a class. You didn't have any problem with discipline. Children were very, very good. We never seemed to have noise. We always seemed to work. The day was divided almost equally into

different lessons. You always had your mental arithmetic, spelling test. You usually had a writing lesson, so that you were writing copy plate writing. We used pens with nibs, we had inkwells, and we used to have a composition and we had arithmetic and we used to have reading lessons each day. We must have had games, and of course there wasn't grass. It was all tarmac like it is here now. That was in the country. There wasn't any grass to play football or anything like that.

Mike Barnett   *English   Science Teacher   Born 1933*

In school we played a lot of games. One we called Völkerball. It was played with a medicine ball. We threw the ball at each other. If the person caught the ball, it became his turn to throw it; if it hit him and then the ground, he was out of the game for that round. We played another game bouncing a soft rubber ball against the wall and then against parts of our bodies. We had a chant for it, and our actions with the ball would follow the chant. "Ober, Unter, Gabel, Löfeel, Messer, Kopf, Arm, Knie, Fuss!" ["Over, under, fork, spoon, knife, head, arm, knee, foot"]. Then you had to catch

the ball at the end. If you got all the way through the chant without dropping the ball, and then succeeded in catching it at the end, you could stay in the game for your next turn. There were usually three or four – or more – kids involved. Skipping rope and hop scotch were very popular, but l don't remember any rhymes that went with it.

Like children everywhere, given half a chance, we could find enjoyment anywhere. One of the favorite sports of me and my friends was to ride our bicycles down into bomb craters and up the other side.

Margot Hamilton   *German, naturalized American   Business Manager, retired   Born 1936*

My neighborhood friends and I fought the war in our backyards and in vacant lots. We manufactured our own weapons using coping saws, jack-knives, sandpaper, and pine. Our imagination at this age was phenomenal. We even designed airplane cockpits from 10-penny nail barrels. We had a barn with a loft. This made a wonderful command post and sometimes we used it as a C-47, "parachuting" out of the loft doors onto freshly spaded "enemy" soil eight feet below.

One summer we decided that we needed camouflage suits so we could be less conspicuous in our "patrols." Each of us was left to his own resources to come up with the critical clothing. While the other troops engaged their mothers as "supply sergeants" (using green dye), I decided to make my own out of a pair of old pyjamas. I hand-painted these with dark green, oil-based paint. Unfortunately, I had to go into action before my new camouflage suit was dry. There wasn't anything else to do but don it and go into battle. I still cringe when I think of the wet paint sticking to my skin. Our first mission was to cross a rag-weed filled vacant lot, crawling on our bellies.

I obviously survived but not without getting a permanent dose of hay fever when near rag-weed even to this day. That Christmas, my mom gave me a soldier uniform and plastic helmet she procured out of the Montgomery Ward catalog.

Andy Thomas *American   Vice President of a British Software Firm   Aged 5-9*

One of our favorite pastimes was playing soldier. My Dad sent us a footlocker filled with all kinds of military clothes, leggings, cartridge cases, etc. My brother and I would march around wearing all of this stuff, and were quite the envy of our friends.

Dorothy Tuttle Frye *American   Archivist   Born 1935*

We had a game we always used to play in the blackouts. I *suppose we shouldn't have done it but I can't think what difference it would have made. We lived on an estate and the roads on the estate were constructed of concrete so we'd throw pieces of iron on it which created great sparks. And because of the blackout you could see the sparks. We used to do it again and again. It was like having fireworks, watching the sparks. they were the only fireworks we had for things like Guy Fawkes night. Sometimes we had a devil of a job getting the piece of iron again because of course we couldn't see it.*

Tom Helcke *Scots   Biochemical Engineer   Aged 8*

It was a very hard winter. We had this moat in front of the house and we used to go skating there. I remember in the winter, there were some people skating, but as a child my

Nine-year-old Bobby Swanson in uniform as acting Corporal and mascot for the US Coast Artillery Detachment Newport, VA. USA. October, 1942.

mother would say, "Why don't you go skating?"

"Oh it's too cold," I would reply.

I probably didn't have the energy and because of lack of food you feel colder. The house was unheated too. We only had a little stove on which my mother cooked and we would stand around warming our hands. I remember I didn't like to go out and go skating.

Hans Hilbers *Dutch Director, European Bank for Reconstruction and Recovery Born 1934*

*T**he Saratoga Battlefield is a National Historical Park in upstate New York. My father was in the National Park Service. He was appointed Superintendent of the Battlefield and our family moved to Saratoga from the Grand Canyon. At one point in the war, the US military held maneuvers there. A tank ran up and down a dirt road along the fence line while a small aircraft practised bombing it with sacks of flour. We all noticed the irony of this taking place just where the American Revolutionary Army defeated the British nearly 200 years earlier, at a time when the British Army was supported by German mercenaries.*

Wayne Hamilton *American   Geologist, retired   Born 1936*

We subscribed to the usual American magazines – *Life, Saturday Evening Post, Reader's Digest, Collier's, National Geographic*. In one of them, I'm pretty sure it was the Geographic, I came across a picture of an old man weeping, his face buried in his hands. The caption said something about him having lost his dog in a bombing raid. For some reason, this upset me terribly. I cried about it for days. Whenever I saw that magazine lying around in the living room, without even picking it up I'd burst into tears.

No one knew why at first but eventually my parents dragged it out of me. They had always encouraged me to read so, rather than forbidding the magazines to me, my mother used to censor them, sealing off the parts about the war with five or six paper clips.

That was when I was about five. By the time I was six, the bits under the paper clips were the parts I read first.

John Lane *American   History Lecturer   Aged 5*

My father was a businessman and a knowledgeable seaman from his former days as a young man with the English Merchant Marine. He would occasionally set ships' compasses for the Honolulu Harbor Master when requested to do so. He was asked to join the Merchant Marine as the first officer on the Permanent, *the only ship taking civilian passengers during the war years to the US mainland from Hawaii. The ship returned to Hawaii to rebuild the military bases and to work in the shipyards at Pearl Harbor. In order for my father to become First Officer, he had to take examinations in navigation, Morse code, etc. To assist my father in relearning Morse code, my mother learned it and she would sit across a table from my father at night and they would carry on a conversation of the day's happenings via Morse code.*

Robert M. Chapman *American Businessman Age 10*

†[How was your day, dear?]

I grew up in the village of Dorney near Windsor. One day, at age two or three, when I was playing in the garden, a number of soldiers marched in. They must have been on an exercise of some sort because they started shooting through the fence (blanks, I suppose). I remember running terrified, into the kitchen, and hiding under the table. To this day, I am neurotic about loud bangs. When I go to the cinema with my daughters and there are loud noises, they have to reach out and hang on to me. I hate noisy fireworks to this day.

Caroline (née Cholmondeley) Woollett *English Social Worker Born 1940*

I was born in 1940, so my view of the war was from the curious perspective of someone looking mostly at the bottom halves of adults. I soon learned that the legs clad in khaki belonged to soldiers.

James O'Shea Wade *American Publisher Aged 5*

My earliest memory of World War II was around the age of four when our house in the country shook from the impact of a bomb that had dropped nearby in a field. I was sitting on my potty at the time and leapt off in bewilderment!

Countess Hanna Jankovich-Besan *Hungarian Therapist Aged 4*

As if the reality surrounding them weren't enough, boys play war in the remains of their London neighborhood. England, 1943.

WHO'S THIS MAN?

We heard that the Americans had landed on Luzon and were approaching our internment camp from the south. The camp held about 2,000 people, mostly Americans, and information reached the camp that we were all due to be executed. Two men escaped and made contact with the Americans, who in the space of two days laid on a combined air assault by parachute, amphibious assault by DUKWs* across the lake in front of the camp, and land assault by local guerrillas.

This gloriously succeeded. The first we heard was the firing from the guerrillas. I remember the chaos of the battle, in which we spent our entire time under the bed, deposited there sharply by my mother; then, the subsequent bewilderment as to what to do next, culminating in being told to go to the main gate where we would be removed and that we were only to take one suitcase with us; and, finally, my returning because of my determination not to be separated from my cash, which can have been no more than Japanese funny money but it was clearly very important to me. My mother took with her a silver milk jug which she had kept throughout the war and, very sadly, left behind her entire war diary which was completely illegally kept throughout the war.

The Yanks were in a terrible hurry to get us out of the camp. What we didn't know was that there was a Japanese division about ten miles down the road, far too close for comfort. They started shelling the camp with artillery and because we didn't know what to do and wouldn't leave, or some of us wouldn't leave, the Americans set fire to the palm frond roofs of the camp in order to smoke us out. An amateur film was taken of the whole thing which I saw a few years ago. Absolutely fascinating because there were the parachutes coming down, there were the airplanes and the view from the airplanes, there was the camp burning, there were the DUKWs arriving, and us being loaded on; it was quite eerie to see the whole performance. We were put into the DUKWs and taken across the lake. Halfway across we were machine-gunned from ashore by Japanese gunners and our machine-gunners shot back. I remember our machine-gunner being hit in the leg and the spent shells coming down in the well of this DUKW one of which hit the back of my sister's neck who promptly cried, "I'm shot and I'm dead."

We got to the far side of the lake. We had with us our last tin of bully beef. We had received only one Red Cross parcel in the 3½ years we were interned by the Japanese and of course this one parcel was enormously precious to us. This one tin would normally have lasted the four of us for at least two weeks but to celebrate we consumed it all in one enormous meal, by our standards, and were promptly sick. I remember that vividly, the anticipation of the meal and then

Suitcases stuffed with comic books, Jenny, Hazel, and James Templer arrive at Euston station in London after three and a half years of internment in Los Banos Camp, Manila. May, 1945

the dismay of being sick was really too much. After that, we were taken to a nearby civilian prison where the Americans had set up a reception for us and food. Milk was the first thing we were offered. I drank it and was again promptly sick and I have never drunk milk to this day.

After some weeks, we were shipped across the Pacific in an American freighter battened down because the war was still going on and I remember fighting for the air vents below decks and eventually persuading one of the sailors to let me up on deck against all orders. We arrived in Los Angeles and were put on a train to Halifax, a trip that took a week. We stopped frequently and at each halt the three of us leapt out and bought comics and read them till the next station. We reached Halifax with a pile of comics four feet high and I never saw America or Canada at all. And then we went across the Atlantic and arrived back in England and I was promptly put into a prep school by my mother. My father returned about a year later and appeared at my prep school and I said to my mother, Who's this man?" having not seen him for over five years. That I suppose is my recollection of the war.

Major General Sir James Templer   *English   Army, retired   Aged 6-9*

I remember the day I lost my country. It was April 1942. We Japanese-Americans were taken from our homes in Seattle to Puyallup [Washington] fairgrounds ten miles away. Our family's few possessions were placed in storage, but never returned. We were assigned one room in a hastily built barracks – one room per family. We were immediately ordered to fill sacks with excelsior hay. These were our mattresses, which we set on iron cots. The huts were so unfinished that I could see daylight through the knotholes.

It was the end of the world. I didn't know what was going to happen to us. I didn't want to go out the door. At the time I wasn't aware of my good fortune. I did not have to sleep in a horse stall as some did. I had grown up in an Asian area of Seattle but, even so, as reality sank in, I was shocked to find myself among a sea of faces that looked like relatives, so many I could not count. I had never seen so many Japanese in one place before. I quickly learned the meaning of such words as "barracks," "latrine," "mess hall," "community shower," "diarrhea."

In spite of it all, I realized how much easier it was for me. I was young; I wasn't pregnant; I wasn't a mother; I wasn't elderly. My heart went out to pregnant women who had not choice but to use community showers. The camp population was composed mainly of the very young and the elderly. What was so threatening about them to America? The old were past their prime. The young were still too young for serious political views.

Then the army recruiters came. They asked the young men to volunteer, to fight for their country and to prove their loyalty to America – the country that placed them in prison camps. Lo and behold, volunteers came forward without hesitation. The young men were willing to give their lives to Uncle Sam. But not all went willingly. There were those who we called "no-no boys" who felt that an injustice had been done. They refused to join until full citizenship rights had been restored to them. This, too, took courage. These young men were sent to a federal penitentiary as draft dodgers. They served two years in prison.

I didn't understand what I'd done. I was a native born American citizen. I'd lived all my life in America. Japan considered me an enemy, and I never considered Japan as

About to be interned as a dangerous alien, this Japanese-American child looks apprehensively into the future. USA, 1942.

my country. What had I done wrong? What was my crime? Who do I pledge allegiance to now? I can't forget that feeling of total rejection, the feeling of not belonging, the feeling of complete emptiness. Growing up in Seattle, I'd never encountered racism before. But after Pearl Harbor, anti-Japanese feeling ran so high that Chinese-Americans began wearing pins saying, "I am Chinese."

After six months at Puyallup, we went on a long train journey to a "relocation center" in Minidoka, Idaho. The camp was a sagebrush dustbowl. The air made your skin go dry and your hair brittle. The sand choked you. Our family, like others, lived in a room sixteen feet by twenty. Many people grew ill. Some died. What I mainly remember was the boredom. White friends came to visit the internees sometimes. I would see them touch through the wire fence. One camp guard expressed anger about the internment. He was quickly reassigned. Eventually we had school of sorts in the camp; we even played sports and had a newspaper, but young people were so bored that we volunteered to work in the mess hall just to have something to do. Some learned how to knit.

Time dragged. Through the partitions you could hear couples arguing, babies crying. At night, sleepless, I would listen to the coyotes howl.

Sylvia Kobayashi   *American   Public Relations Consultant*

My father, Kristian Stein, was a member of the Resistance. He was captured and taken to the Gestapo house. After a month we were allowed to visit him there. It was obvious that he had been subjected to hard interrogations. Later he was sent to Ulven and then to Germany in 1942 where he died on 16th July 1943. We were not allowed to say goodbye to him, and have never had an official explanation of what happened to him. We have just read about it in books that have been written about him.

There is one dream I cannot forget. It was a short time after the peace. In the dream I was in town with my grandmother. In Strandgatan my father was standing outside

Nic Nicolaysen's. We asked him why he didn't come home, and he told us that he could not do so because he had no heart, but we should give his greetings to everyone. It seemed so real that I often think of it.

One of the things I react to today is that nobody here in Norway has thought of us and all the traumatic experiences which we have had to deal with ourselves. Today it is so fashionable with psychologists, etc. Of course, we could talk to the other war veterans, but they have enough problems of their own.

Svanhild Stein Sohr *Norwegian   Business Woman*
Born 1924

Toward the end of the war I have a vivid memory, and I guess it shaped my view of mankind and my function as an artist ever since. My mother took me to the cinema one day and they were showing the first films released from the concentration camps and what does a child of eleven or twelve make of that? These days, of course, children see these kinds of things everyday on television, but you didn't then. It was a society that even through the war had certain things prescribed and certain ways of behaving and looking and censoring and so forth. And, of course, everything during the war had been censored anyway and then all could be made into propaganda and suddenly you saw these face images.

*On the bus going back my mother was carrying on about the foul Nazis and I said to her, this sounds terribly precocious, "Surely the thing is that it was **people** that did it, which means that **we** did it," and actually being given a slap by her for saying it.*

It's funny because, as one gets older you may have found this too, I am sure you have, you realize that your earliest, most innocent perceptions were correct and that your parents were most often wrong because their judgments no longer were innocent. I think that that remark I made has probably colored the rest of my life because the next thing of course was the news that we had blasted the hell out of hundreds and thousands of Japanese. [Hiroshima and Nagasaki]. The next thing was that one was standing in line for the army to fight in Korea, not that many years later it seems. In terms of lifetime it wasn't that many years later.

Bernard Cohen *English   Artist, Director of Slade School of Fine Art, UCL   Born 1933*

*T*he thing I remember most about the war was the loneliness I felt as a child when my mother began to work in the defense factory. She worked second shift which meant that she went to work about the time I was coming home from school. I spent time at the homes of friends, but much of the time I was alone. My brother Don was off with his friends, and there was no one else to look after us much of the time. I went to a lot of movies on the weekends, often by myself. I still suffer from this loneliness, I think, even though I later married and had a family. But this early experience did help me become self-reliant.

One vivid memory I have of those years was how much I worried that my father or brother would be killed in the fighting. We saw a lot of war movies which didn't help much. Every night I would say prayers for them, and I remember that when I prayed for my brother I always envisioned him standing up high on the ship while gunfire and bombs exploded around him. My family didn't go to church, but I did, and I never told anyone how hard I was praying for these men in my family.

Dorothy Tuttle Frye *American   Archivist   Born 1935*

*M*y mother was worried all the time. At one point in the war, my father was sent abroad – to Africa – and she didn't hear from him for three months. Her hair started going grey at that time. She was so worried, because she didn't know where he was. One minute he was at home, he'd come back on leave, the next, he went back to wherever he was at the time and then we found out later on he had been sent up to Scotland and then on a convoy to Africa. We never heard from him for months. All I knew was that there was a war on and that I wanted my father home. When a letter arrived my mother actually began crying with relief. After that, then we began to get postcards. He used to write about what he was doing, but he couldn't write very much obviously, because he was in the campaigns. I had a mother who was marvelous to me. She was a wonderful mother. And I was brought up by her. In fact when my father came back, I think I resented him coming back almost. He came back in early 1945. . . March I think, so I was already twelve then. My mother was very sweet; she coped marvelously. I think women did.

Mike Barnett *English   Science Teacher   Born 1933*

I often wondered why the adults always spoke in whispers and there was this pervading air of secrecy. I couldn't understand this as I was unaware of what war was all about. Of course, later on, during the Civil War, 1943-1945, people were being hanged in the streets, but somehow I never came across such sights although my parents did. I recall hearing from time to time when I should have been asleep in my bed, grandmother relating stories about so-and-so (a female Fascist) being captured and having her hair shaved off by the partisans. Another time I overheard conversations about a friend of my mother's, who had been a Prisoner of War of the British, having been maltreated to the extent that he had been deprived of water and had to drink his own urine. But I never really understood these things. Nor for that matter, when at the age of eight, my father left my mother and did not come back again.

Wilma Corradi   *Italian   Former actress   Born 1937*

As far as meat and things were concerned, my mother always used to give us her ration. I don't recall being undernourished because my mother was like that.

Looking back on it now, I was conscious of the great stress and strain which the adults around us were under. I often think of what people went through so that I can be here today. That's why I publish the books I do. To remind people. I'm a military publisher because the influence of the war on me in those days was so profound that I took a continuing interest in what it was all about afterwards. And then, of course, I was in the Army myself later and I saw the Army actually working. The British Army is a marvelous organization. Adaptable and flexible. And I've always done my best to keep it in the minds of people almost as an act of gratitude for my existence. Sounds rather pompous. But it's true. That's all I've got to say.

Leo Cooper   *English   Publisher/writer   Aged 12*

FRONTLINE IN THE FLORENTINE HILLS

My family had been evacuated from our house in the south of Florence to the other side of the river Arno, in a three floor high villa of friends. In the first days of August 1944, the front line drew very close, and the Germans decided to set up a defence line at the base of the Florentine hills, which passed right through the villa we were staying in.

Like in a dream, I remember being in bed and my mother bent over me shaking me and saying, "Marchino, come on, come on. Wake up because we must leave."

I glanced towards my grandmother who was standing there with a brown, velvet bag in her hand which, in that period, was always ready with a few essential things: a few belongings, a little food. While my mother was dressing me, I kept my eyes fixed on that bag and my grandmother's hands which were adding to it other things. For the first time in my life, I felt the perception of fear, of dismay. The atmosphere and the behaviour of the people who surrounded me were full of fear and I could feel it.

Marco Banti, aged four, holds a souvenir left behind by the British when they used the villa behind him as a headquarters. Florence, 1944.

We entered the courtyard of the villa and stood beneath the beautiful arched arcade, which ran along a side of the house. There were my uncles, also refugees in this enormous house. My aunt held my cousin in her arms, only eight months old at that time. The crying of the little one is the most alive "sound" of the whole story. In the middle of the courtyard stood a massive figure wearing a helmet, holding something in his hands, pointed towards us. He was wearing a short pair of boots with a cylindrical object protruding from one of them. A dark figure, a silhouette. My fear became terror and I hid behind my mother.

At the last moment, the Germans abandoned the idea of occupying the villa. They withdrew somewhere and we stayed on. The front line passed by one night in a very quiet manner. We woke up free.

Marco Banti   *Italian   Publisher   Aged "nearly 4"*

On 18th April 1942, there was an air raid on Tokyo. The first one. It was so unexpected that nobody thought to run to a shelter in spite of all the air raid drills we were supposed to have had. I was in my upstairs room alone, having just finished lunch. The house we lived in at that time was situated on a south-facing slope of a hill overlooking downtown Tokyo. Standing there in my own room, I saw what appeared to me to be a large seaplane fly by the window, dead level with my eye, and not more than a hundred yards or so away.

Many years later, sometime in the 1970s, I went to the Smithsonian Air and Space Museum for the first time and walked into the room where World War Two aircraft and photographs were displayed. As I strolled through the room, I involuntarily froze in front of a picture of an airplane. There was the exact side view of the "seaplane" that was so vividly burnt into my memory; only the seaplane turned out to be a B-25, the Mitchell Bomber, which had a rounded front end below the cockpit, making it look like a seaplane to a glancing view. What I had seen that day was part of the famous Doolittle raid* on Tokyo.

A Mitchell B-25 medium bomber of the type flown by Jimmy Doolittle on his famous raid against Tokyo in 1942. From this perspective, the aircraft's hull suggests the "seaplane" mistakenly identified by Mamoru Mitsui.

Mamoru Mitsui   *Born Japanese, naturalized citizen of the United States of America   Architect   Age 7*

I was in the first year of Junior High when some planes flew over our school at an extremely low level and it took minutes before we all realized that it was American invading air planes. The Doolittle raid flew at extremely low altitudes so that the radars could not detect them as they invaded our air for the first time.

Doolittle dropped a couple of bombs but the physical damage was negligible. The shock which the people had was tremendous, much greater than the damage caused by these bombs. It was only after Doolittle flew away from Tokyo that the siren sounded the invasion by the enemy and everybody got excited and ran into the shelters. The psychological impact was tremendous and the government imposed a lot of restrictions and from then on Tokyo was almost under a

quasi-curfew situation twenty-four hours a day. Perhaps it gave the government the opportunity to tighten controls and restrictions on the citizens. Until the very last moment we were fed by government slogans like, "Kill more Yankees, kill more Britons," and, "We must fight until our last bit of blood has been exhausted," and, "Each citizen must kill at least one Yankee and at least one John Bull."

Before the end of the war we were told by the then Japanese military government that Americans were all devils, and to bring about peace in Japan as well as the entire Asia we would have to fight against those devils and demons – (that was the image given to us). After the war, everybody was scared that now the devils were coming over. But they were not devils at all, but other humans, speaking in English, and believing in another religion, Christianity, which made us feel a little bit at ease but we had to start to learn a lot of things which were totally contradictory or opposite to what we were brought up with.

Masachika Onodera   *Japanese   Executive Secretary, the Britain-Japan Society; Financial consultant   Born 1930*

We lived near the German barracks in the Hague. For this reason, the Allies bombed us almost from the beginning. The raids weren't very accurate and they always managed to hit civilian houses as well. One night our house was in the middle of a series of bombs. We had a lot of damage. That was actually the most terrifying part of the Occupation; that you were never safe from this type of raid. Never a day or night passed by without an alarm.

In 1942, already the Allies started to bomb Germany. They usually flew over during the night and I remember that we could always distinguish the engine sounds. We knew exactly as children whether they were German planes or Allied planes. It was interesting that we felt quite secure when the planes were German because we knew they wouldn't bomb us [being occupied]. We felt less secure, when the sound was our Allies, high up and far away.

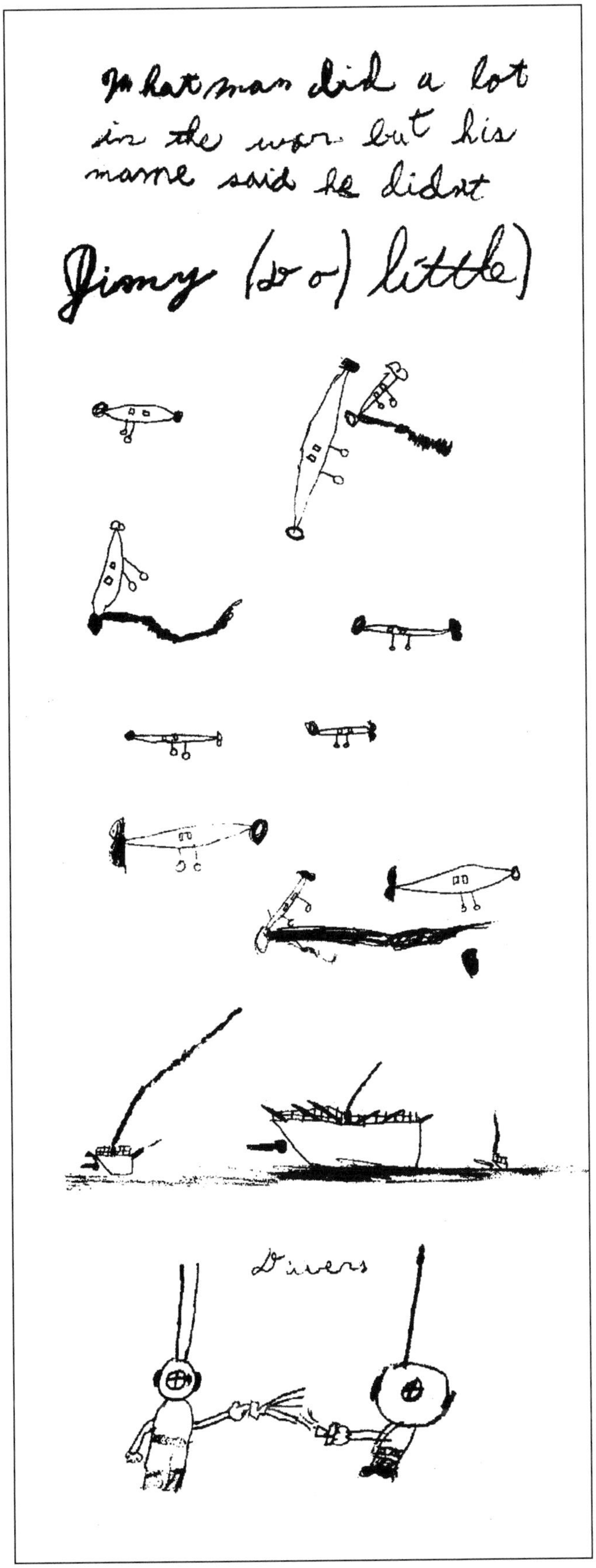

What man did a lot in the war but his name said he didn't

Jimy (do o) little)

Divers

Authentic children's joke and drawings preserved from World War II.
USA, 1943.

One memory I still have vividly. I like it very much. One fall day late in the war, the bombers, that used to fly over at night, now also flew over during the day so you could actually see them. I remember once or twice that they flew over to bomb German cities and the sky was filled with Allied planes. We had a good view of the sky where we lived, and there were thousands of planes in the sky.

At the same time the Germans could do nothing about it because they had no fighters any more. The Allies flew a little bit too high for the usual anti-aircraft guns but you could see there were little puffs. It didn't bother the Allies at all and the noise was very heavy. Of course there was another reason we liked that because we said, "Now if this goes on like this, they will have to surrender and the war will be over soon." There were enormous numbers of planes – big Flying Fortresses and the big Lancaster planes. Unbelievable. It was a sign of the victory, that during the daytime thousands of planes would fly to Germany and it was a very impressive sight, which I remember very, very well, and you will never see it again in your life. At least, I hope not!! Everybody ran out into the streets, my sisters, I think also my parents. We were happy to see this, of course. We didn't realise the suffering that was coming to civilian Germany, but they had it coming to them we thought at the time. It was fantastic.

There was no cheering or anything. I think we were talking among ourselves. You still had to be careful how to express yourself because there was a part of the Dutch population that were with the Nazis, not a big percentage, maybe five percent, and we always had to be careful. They didn't accept signs of German defeat.

Hans Hilbers *Dutch   Director, European Bank for Reconstruction and Recovery   Born 1934*

You could hear the bombs coming; they make a terrible whistling noise and you think, oh God, don't let them fall on me. There was the noise of the planes getting nearer and one bomb exploding after the other, getting nearer and nearer to you. We went to the basement but hardly got in before a bomb blew out the basement door. My heart really stood still. That's when you think "I've got to get out!" Then we went to the attic and threw the bombs out. It's a funny situation. You try to save your house, knowing the next bomb may be an aerial mine that could kill you. When the bombers moved on, we looked out and the whole sky was red. You feel so helpless and that is an awful feeling. Strategic planners may believe such a bombing demoralizes a society, but I can tell you the opposite is the case.

Erwin Perrot *German   Electrical Engineer   Born 1934*

In sixth grade, my friends and I were too young to go out with boys, but not too young to flirt. We lived near Fort Devens, and called each other whenever there was a convoy of army trucks. I'd quickly brush my hair and wish that I were old enough to wear lipstick. My friends and I would then rush to the roadside to watch the long lines of khaki-colored trucks with canvas tops as they passed. Inside the trucks, seated on benches which ran the length of the trucks, were handsome young soldiers who called to us and waved back. It was very exciting.

Shirley Upton *American   Retailer   Aged 12*

I remember falling in love with the best man at my baby-sitter's wedding. Her sailor fiancé and his ship-mate came home on leave for the big day and a few more. My cousin and I were flower girls with long satiny dresses and flower crowns. My feeling of being special was indeed enhanced when that good looking sailor danced with me at the reception, gave me his address, and asked me to write to him. I know we wrote back and forth several times and he even sent me a necklace of south sea island shells, mailed in a metal can instead of a package. Then he didn't answer any more and I never did find out if he came home or not.

Joan Perry Morris *American   Administrator, Florida Department of State   Aged 6-10*

When Pearl Harbor was attacked, I was just four. I do not remember the war years as depressing. Our windows were

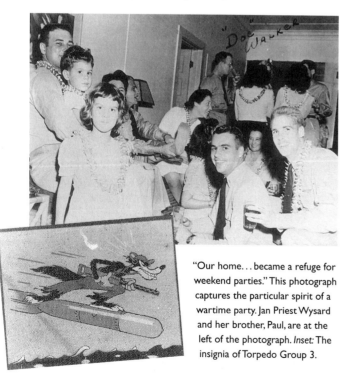

"Our home... became a refuge for weekend parties." This photograph captures the particular spirit of a wartime party. Jan Priest Wysard and her brother, Paul, are at the left of the photograph. *Inset:* The insignia of Torpedo Group 3.

all painted black, but we kept a number of animals and a lovely vegetable garden. Every day, two young Japanese girls, wrapped in colorful kimonos and wearing slippers, would appear at our house to clean, cook and take care of my brother and me. They were like older sisters, only fifteen or sixteen years of age.

Our home, as well as many others, became a refuge for weekend parties. There was much drinking, eating, dancing, singing – and poker. The many young and handsome men from Torpedo Group 3 and Squadrons VF 3 and VC 3 became part of an extended family. When they were prevented from visiting, the only way to let us know was to dive at the house and put on a short aerial show before waving their wings in sad goodbye and heading away.

I did manage, at seven, to fall in love with a flyer named Manoch. He *promised* he would marry me when I grew up, which he said would take many years. At the end of the war, he wrote to say that he was lonely and was going to marry a very nice young lady. My heart was broken and I never saw him again. Like so many other survivors, he never returned to Hawaii. They all said it would be too painful.

Jan Priest Wysard *American   Aged 4-7*

The day the war ended we drove up the main street amidst a surging, cheering crowd. My nine-year-old brother kept screaming, "Yippee! We won the war. Yippee...yippee! We won...."

At thirteen I found this embarrassing and hoped that I wouldn't run into friends. Later, we walked down the street, my brother still screaming, "Yippee! We won!"

My parents walked closely on either side of me afraid that I'd be kissed by a drunken sailor who approached me – and every other girl who walked by. I felt over-protected and wished that I could be kissed by the drunken sailor.

Penelope Upton *American   Psychotherapist   Aged 13*

My brother was home on leave from the Air Force and about to be married. We were waiting for relatives to get off the train in Biddeford [Maine]. Then this soldier swung off the train: tall; blond; handsome; really spiffy and alert; eye-catching; curly hair.

I asked my sister who he was and she was surprised I didn't recognize him. "That's Benny Tito," she said. His family was well-known to my family. Friends even. Same religion. Same country of origin (Albania). My family always visited his family on Holy Days: Christmas, Easter, New Year's, and Name days. I couldn't believe that this was Benny Tito all pressed in his summer uniform and looking like a movie star.

"Tall; blond; handsome, really spiffy and alert" Benny Tito in his army uniform. USA.

I was fourteen years old. I said to my sister, "Oh, my God! Do I want to go out with that guy!" I had a big crush on him from day one. He was so handsome in his uniform. I knew immediately in the back of my head that I wanted to marry him.

Five years later, I did marry him. And now, three children, seven grandchildren, and forty-seven years later, I still have a crush on him.

Dhimitra Vangel Tito *Albanian American   Owner, Colonial Pharmacy and Julia's Gift Shop   Aged 14*

In those days before Doctor Salk, we had polio epidemics just about every year. Each summer a few children would die and a few others be left paralyzed. The summer I was eight, a girl I knew at school who was the same age as my sister, died of polio. Her name was Sally. I was very upset by this.

Sally and my sister had just graduated from grammar school and though there wasn't much film about during the war, most families had managed to beg or borrow some to take photos of their children's graduation. After Sally died, her parents asked all the other parents for any photos they might have with pictures of Sally in them. My parents had a few pictures of Sally and of course gave them to her parents.

It seemed strange for someone to die of natural causes in the middle of a war. It shocked me. Up until then, I'd thought dying was something that grown ups did.

Charles Davis *American   Retired Lecturer   Aged 8*

We collected "war cards" like they collect sports personalities today but the war cards had pictures of planes, ships, generals, battles, etc., on them. I think we got most of the cards with chewing gum at Mike Lyons' Variety Store.

We played endlessly with the cards, holding competitions of different kinds. Whoever won the game, won the cards. One game was to throw the cards for distance with a skimming motion for either distance or accuracy. We called this "scaling." Another game was called "flipping." This was done by holding the two long edges of the card between the thumb and the other fingers, and either spinning it down side-over-side or dropping it from waist height. The cards would land either picture side up or on the reverse which had writing on it that described the picture. I think we called them "heads" and "tails" depending on which way they landed. Your opponent then had to get more heads or tails then you. As boys will, many of my classmates practice this quite intently, and it was not unusual for the most skilful to be able to land eighteen or nineteen heads or tails out of twenty throws. Some boys built up huge collections of cards.

The challenge to a contest was "I'll scale ya," or, "I'll match ya." Interestingly, I don't remember simply trading the cards like they do nowadays. All exchanges were on the results of these games. We played scaling and flipping right up until the end of school in June 1945. During the summer vacation peace was declared and after our return in September I can't remember that we ever played cards again.

Fred C. Hart *American   Born 1937*

New England is famous for its white clapboard churches. At one time almost every village had one. Their steeples were made not out of wood but out of metal. During the war, almost every church donated its metal steeple to the War Effort. That's why even to this day you'll see little village churches all over New England with missing steeples.

Lloyd Jameson *American   Aged "tennish"*

I've always been curious about something. Maybe you can tell me the answer. When I was very young, Lucky Strike cigarettes used to come in a green packet. As I recall, they had the red circle in the middle like now, but the white part of the label was a kind of dark green.

Then suddenly one day the green disappeared. It was as quick as that and very noticeable when you saw displays of Luckies on shelves and things. What had once been green was now white. I don't know why, but I was fascinated by this. I didn't smoke of course. Just one of those things that sticks in your mind.

Shortly after that, and still during the war, I remember hearing on the radio the phrase "Lucky Strike green has gone to War." It was part of an advertising campaign. Apparently they needed the green dye for something to do with the war though I never knew what.*

John Lane *American   History Lecturer   Aged 6*

We had an old 1940 Mercury which, because of gas and tire rationing, we used very carefully and very sparingly. By 1944 or 45, it badly need a coat of paint. Unfortunately, the only color paint available to civilians was the same paint available to the services – olive drab. For that reason, my family drove around in a kind of pseudo-staff car for the rest of the war.

Malcolm Swenson *American   President, Swenson Stone Consultants   Aged 4*

I was the smallest kid on the block. When we played War, I was always the German.

Eben Charles *American   Businessman   Aged 13*

I could never understand if my parents were talking about Berlin, Georgia, or Berwyn, Pennsylvania.

Pete Paxson *American   President, Alphabet Graphics, Inc. Born 1938*

Vic Reis returned from the war without any hands. The first time I saw him was at St Francis church on Sunday morning. He was walking up the aisle with his head bowed on his way back from communion.
 I stared.
 He was praying by putting his hooks together.

John Murphy *American   Lawyer   Aged 9*

Funny, but one of the things that always brings the war back to me is the smell of brick dust. Like when I pass a demolition site. Or not too long ago when we had some builders in our house take down a wall. It made me think again of the war – people I knew, things that happened, some good, some bad.

Tom Helcke *Scots   Biochemical Engineer   Aged 8*

The one smell I most associate with the war is bacon. We didn't get it often and when we did it was home-cured and smelt different from normal bacon. It was black market bacon.

Leo Cooper *English   Publisher/writer   Aged 12*

Sights and sounds don't bring back memories. I think none of us today thinks much of the war. It's past, and we want to look forward. But there is some food I still enjoy because it was a treat when I was a child – potato pancakes, Schmalzbrot, pea soup in big pots like the Red Cross used to serve. I still can taste it if I close my eyes and think about it – amazing.

Erwin Perrot *German   Electrical Engineer   Born 1934*

I remember the end of the war very clearly. I was at a baseball game with my father watching our local team, the Manchester, NH Yankees, playing, I think, the Nashua, NH Dodgers. During about the fifth or sixth inning a man came over the loudspeaker and said, "We thought you'd like to know. . . we've just heard. . . the Japanese have surrendered. World War II is over!" And everybody stood up and cheered and cheered, louder even than for a double play. The players from both sides ran out onto the infield and began jumping around, cheering, yelling, and hugging each other.

 This was so long ago that one of the first baseman – I'm not sure which side he was on – had one of those gloves that looked like a scorpion's claw. Like a lot of the players during the war, he was also getting on a bit in years to the extent that he had a distinct middle-aged spread. Even so, he ran and cavorted around the infield with the others, whooping and shouting, waving his claw in the air, and jumping up and down in a series of puffy, unathletic leaps. Everyone was laughing and cheering though I'm sure part of the laughter must have been at the antics of the first baseman. After about a minute, everybody stopped cheering. The players returned to their positions. A few people left but most of the crowd sat down and went silent, and everybody got down to the serious business of a baseball game.

 I wanted to stay but my father dragged me away. When I began whining he said, I've always remembered his exact words, he said, "Come on. You can see a baseball game anytime, but you'll only see a war end once in your lifetime."

Charles Perkins *American   Publisher   Aged 8*

A first baseman's mitt of the "scorpion's claw" variety. At one time, all first basemen used gloves that looked like this. (Photo, courtesy of Mike Ross).

Dried egg was a highly colored yellow powder and it tasted foul! **Beryl Stephenson** *English*

I don't remember too much about food except that there was never enough. We were allowed two sweets a day. I liked powdered mashed potatoes. I liked dried eggs. I liked all the wrong things. **Leo Cooper** *English*

When I was a boy I loved eggs but of course they were just about the first food that disappeared in the war. You couldn't get them anywhere. All we had were powdered eggs which were OK for things like omelettes and scrambled eggs. But they weren't eggs! I don't know why but the one food I really missed was eggs.

Toward the end of the war, when I got old enough, I enlisted in the Navy. To my disappointment, the Navy also fed us powdered eggs but shortly after basic training they shipped me to Egypt. As soon as I could I went ashore and I ate seven fried eggs. **Tony Williams** *English Bookseller Aged 13*

I remember powdered eggs all right. Very bright yellow. We used to make them into scrambled eggs or very flat omelettes. They didn't rise because they didn't contain egg whites. I thought they tasted all right. If you made cakes the cakes turned out yellower too.

The Americans used to send the eggs to us. I know this because there used to be a Stars and Stripes on each tin. **Jean Holder** *English.*

I liked dried eggs very much. A great treat. I don't remember exactly when real eggs became available again but I'd have carried on eating dried eggs after the war if I could have. You mixed them with water and fried them. They came out as a kind of eggy-tasting pancake.

The only time I've had dried eggs since the war was when I was working in Afghanistan in 1971. I encountered some members of the Himalayan Mountain Club who were climbing in the Hindu Kush. My eyes must have lighted up when I saw they had dried eggs with them. I talked them out of some and. . . well. . . a lot of tastes had intervened over the years, I guess. Your palette changes. The eggs were OK but I wished that they had had more taste to them. I felt like I should have covered them with chili! **Huw Williams** *Welsh Education Consultant Aged 6*

I spent a lot of time as a boy huddling under the roof of a Morrison shelter in our dining room, so I suppose it was quite natural to me and my sister to play under tables a lot. When we were under the kitchen table, my mother and a lodger would be cooking, and to keep us quiet they would hand down presents of powdered egg wrapped in small packets of paper.

People will tell you a lot of funny things about powdered egg. Personally, I found it delicious – but only as a dry powder. Make it into anything else and it tasted disgusting. If you gave me a tin of powdered egg today, I would eat it. **Brooke Calverley** *English Designer Aged 5*

As far as I know, I was the only person in England who actually liked the taste of powdered eggs. Don't ask me why. Most people hated them. I wouldn't mind trying them again sometime. **Brian Conneler** *English*

We used to dilute egg powder with milk and dip bread in it and fry it and call it French toast. But real eggs were scarce and on ration. Mainly, we had powdered egg. I suppose we didn't have much else. You never forget the taste of powdered eggs. Some people get quite sentimental about it in fact. Because of my job [with a food ingredient manufacturer], people occasionally come up to me and say, "Can you get me some egg powder like we used to get during the war?" And of course I can and do. But they never ask twice. **Tom Helcke** *Scots*

Editor: Mr Conneler, in our previous interview [above] you mentioned that during the war you actually enjoyed the taste of powdered eggs as a child.

BC: Yes.

Ed: And that you'd like to taste them again sometime.

BC: Yes.

Ed: A few weeks ago, I got you a tin of powdered eggs which, I understand, your wife prepared for you.

BC: Yes.

Ed: Would you like me to get you some more?

BC: No, thank you.

PART EIGHT

NACH DEM KRIEG

The King Thanks the Nation

This message from the King to the nation was issued from Buckingham Palace when peace had been established again:—

The time of anxiety is past, and we have been able today to offer our thanks to the Almighty for His mercy in sparing us the horrors of war.

I would like now to thank the men and women of this country for their calm resolve during these critical days, and for the readiness with which they responded to the different calls made upon them.

After the magnificent efforts of the Prime Minister in the cause of peace, i is my fervent hope that a new era of friendship and prosperity may be dawning among the peoples of the world.

George R.I.

A newsboy brings momentous news.

Inset: **A message from the King.**

My younger sister, Christel, was born in Essen during an air raid. I don't remember the noise of the bombing, or being scared, but I do remember the blackout curtains being in place. I felt interested in what was going on more than anything else. I remember standing at the table watching my new sister get her eyes washed out.

"How did the baby get here?" my other sister, Erika, asked my grandmother.

"It came down a ladder. The angels brought it," said my grandmother.

"But I thought the stork brought babies," was Erika's reply.

After the heavy raids on Essen began, my father became concerned and moved us to an apartment in a rural area near Braunschweig where we would be safe. When we returned to Essen after the surrender, we found the bombed-out remains of our apartment building. A few family possessions were dug out of the rubble. When I visited Braunschweig this year for the first time in over forty years, the same siren went off. It was just for a small apartment fire, but I still hate that sound.

My sisters and I were often sent out to look for food, particularly nach dem Krieg [after the war]. Nach dem Krieg was much tougher than during the war. We would go into the potato fields after harvest and bring back the leftovers. Sometimes we'd sneak over a fence and find coal to bring home to give some heat in winter. At night, since our apartment had no bedroom, my sisters and I walked to a relative's house, where we'd sleep in an unheated attic under down comforters. On winter mornings, we'd wake up to find our snug cocoons covered in hoar frost. Our mother hung the wash out in the attic of another apartment and in winter we had to be careful not to bump the frozen sheets or they'd break. We kept a chicken in our basement in a coal bin, feeding it scraps. We could rely on the hen to give us five eggs a week. What a treat for Sunday! . . . until a hungry weasel found the hen.

Braunschweig is where I started school, but school wasn't exactly safe either. Sometimes the air raid siren would blow, and we would have to go into the musty basement of the school until the bomb attack was over. In the basement during raids we sometimes continued classes, sometimes played games, sometimes sang. We sang a lot in those days. In school, at home with the family. They were mostly folk songs. I don't remember any patriotic songs except "Deutschland, Deutschland, über Alles," which we heard often. One of my favorite folk songs was (and still is):

> Es dunkelt schon in der Heide.
> Nach Hause lasst uns gehn.
> Wir haben das Korn geschnitten
> Mit unser blanken Schwert.

> [It's already growing dark in the heather.
> Let's go back home.
> We have cut the grain
> With our sharp sword].

I live in the United States now with my American husband but this song still pops into my head when I think of the war and of Germany. It makes me think of my sisters with whom I sang it. When I was about ten or eleven, my father took us kids on a bike tour into an area where there was a lot of Heide (heather) blooming. We went there to pick blueberries and to camp out one night. Perhaps that's why I like the song so much.

After the war, my aunt in Canada used to send packages. It was chocolate for us and precious coffee for our parents. I still remember the taste of those chocolate drops. We used to eat them one at a time; just a few each evening. When it was time for my sister to go to high school, my father sent a letter to his sister in Canada with a tracing of her foot superimposed over the writing. There were shoes – of the right size! – in the next package.

Margot Hamilton *German, naturalized American Business Manager, retired Born 1936*

Towards the end of the war it was obvious that the situation for the Germans was getting worse. I can remember the endless rows of German soldiers and horses which drew out of Larvik and other towns in southern Norway after Finland had capitulated and the Germans had to withdraw. Many bridges and factories were blown up or set on fire. The many fires were part of everyday entertainment for the boys in the street.

There were often air raid warnings and we went into the cellar at night. Once when we got down there grandmother was already sitting there clutching her handbag – a rather comic situation. Finally peace came. I remember the Nazis being arrested and taken to jail on lorries. School children were directed to walk in processions among other things to greet the English general, Thorne.

Eigil *Norwegian Born 1936*

I'm quite sure I never hated the Germans or the Japanese. I felt a bit uneasy with Japanese for a few years after the war (not that there were many where I lived), but that was mainly because of a couple of films I saw.

One was called *Beasts Of The East*, an unbelievably bad film filled with cruel caricatures of Japanese – all glasses and buck teeth – jabbering away while they did nasty things to the heroine and the obligatory plucky little guy named Joe from Brooklyn. It was the crudest kind of propaganda imaginable but it made an impression on me all the same. Do you think the Japanese had the same kind of films?

The other film had all the Japanese soldiers disguising themselves as *trees*. I suppose this was to emphasize the sneaky way they fought. All through the film American soldiers kept getting shot by trees. No, honest. [*Laughs*]. I remember one scene where a whole bunch of trees came charging across a clearing at an American machine gun nest. Even at that age I thought it was about the funniest thing I'd ever seen. I just collapsed on the floor of the theatre clutching my sides I was laughing so hard. Can you imagine a film so bad that it was laughed to scorn by a ten year old? I'd give a lot to see that scene again. [*Laughs*]. Please believe me, I have nothing but respect for the Japanese, but for years after the war, whenever I saw a Japanese male, it was very hard not to think of him disguised as a tree!

Mike Taylor *American   Ophthalmologist   Aged 10*

When the Japanese surrendered, the celebrations were never to be forgotten. My mother took me downtown with her to join the crowds of people. Joy radiated from their faces, and over and over I heard my mother tell people, "Now my boy will be coming home." Many people had also been drinking, I recall, and when one very large lady passed out in the street, everyone laughed and someone covered her with an American flag.

When the war ended, so did the good jobs for my mother. She was given a small pin with the inscription, "Manhattan Project" and it was then that she learned that she had actually worked on some part of the atomic bomb. I still have that pin. My father returned from the war looking fit and handsome in his marine uniform, and I was so proud of him when he came to my school to see me that I nearly burst with joy. I had not seen him for several years. My older brother returned several months after the war, and married his high school sweetheart within a couple of weeks. They will celebrate their 50th anniversary next spring.

Dorothy Tuttle Frye *American   Archivist   Born 1935*

A few years ago, I became closely acquainted with a senior German diplomat. He was twelve years old when the war ended, living in what became the Federal Republic. Once while we were hiking, having taken a short break, we each began to eat an apple. He consumed the entire fruit – pips, stem, and core, top to bottom. I must have given him an odd look as I threw my core away. He said that in the first terrible winter of 1945-46, all he and his family had to eat were potatoes and apples. Nothing was wasted. To this day he eats the entire apple.

Michael G. Wygant *American   State Department, retired   Born 1936*

My uncle, John Brown, had the same name I do. He was a small farmer and exempt from the draft, but he enlisted in the Army anyway. It was the end of the Depression in the US and I think he may have wanted to get a bit of extra cash together. Because of his exemption he didn't have to stay in for the duration and he was discharged from the Army in the last year of the war.

He returned to his farm. The name of the place, although it's not on any map, is Peaceful Valley. Everyone who lives there calls it that and that was the name of my uncle's farm – Peaceful Valley Farm. He used the money he'd saved from the Army to buy a caterpillar tractor, the first one most of us had seen. Up to then most tractors were John Deere tractors with big wheels at the back, and little

ones at the front. My uncle used the tractor around the farm but also hired it out on a day basis for things like logging work.

Peaceful Valley is heavily wooded and everyone is constantly cutting back brush. Because of the danger of forest fires you couldn't burn the brush where it was cut. Instead, everyone hauled it to an old, disused field on my Uncle's farm down by what we called Brown's Corner. Then we'd burn the brush either in the winter or after a long spell of rain. By mid-summer 1945, the brush pile was the biggest it had ever been – eight feet high maybe and fifty yards long.

One day in August we got two pieces of news. The first was that the Japanese had surrendered and the war was over. The second was that my Uncle, John Brown, had been

doing some logging work that day and his new tractor had overturned and killed him.

We buried him in the field where the brush pile was. Someone got special permission from the Town to burn the brush pile and that's what we did. In his memory. We did it at dusk. It was a huge fire. Very intense. The grown ups stood around in groups talking quietly; the side of them nearest the fire was colored orange. The younger kids, too young to understand why we were burning the brush, were excited, shouting and dancing around down near the fire. We older kids sat together at the higher end of the field where he'd been buried, trying to remember. At the far end of the field was a stone wall, then the forest, and above that the shoulder of the south mountain. Years later, I built my house within ten yards of the spot where I was sitting that day. I remember sitting there in the dark feeling glad about the end of the war and sad about my uncle, all mixed together. And that's how I remember the end of the war.

John Brown   *American   Businessman   Aged 13*

At long last, on 7 May 1945, as my mother was bashing the stems of some wisteria, we heard on the wireless that the Germans had surrendered.

"Pinch me," she said, "so I know I'm awake."

Why was she crying? She'd never cried before except when Jamie was put down. Had we lost after all? Then she laughed and dried her eyes on her apron, and we ran into the street. People were cheering and hugging, and hanging out flags, a little crumpled after five years in the attic. Then suddenly the bells rang out, from Cobham, Oxshott, and Leatherhead, echoing across the flat black-earthed Surrey landscape.

We had a great party in the evening at one of the big houses on the hill. I had a bath beforehand and, used to washing with only a sliver as thin as a communion wafer, was amazed my mother didn't scold me for leaving a new bar of pink soap in the water.

The weather was muggy and warm. Carrying a red jelly and a shepherd's pie containing our entire week's meat ration, we walked to the party. Every house was ablaze with lights and strewn with union jacks and bunting. The scent of lilacs and the tang of nearby pine woods mingled with the smell of hundreds of bonfires and beacons turning the sky to rose.

We had a huge bonfire nearly twelve feet tall at the bottom of the garden. Perched on top was an effigy of Hitler with mad staring eyes, slicked black hair, a little black

Bonfires, ringing church bells, blowing horns, banner headlines, cheering crowds, dancing, and street parties such as this one in Camberwell, south London marked VJ Day and the end of the war. London, 15th August 1945.

moustache and swastika armbands. At last the great pyre roared into golden flame. After two thousand days of blackout, the brilliance was breathtaking. Birds disturbed by the unaccustomed brightness sang their heads off. Insects freaked out, moths bashing against the lights, colossal may bugs bombing us like doodlebugs.

Jilly Cooper   *English Writer   Aged 8*

*M*y Dad returned home in July of 1945. We received a telegram saying he was flying into Newcastle, Delaware, via the Azores, from Paris. We knew he would be taking the train from Newcastle to New York City and then a taxi home to West Orange, New Jersey. On the day of his expected arrival, I sat out on the front curb, in front of our house, from early morning until late afternoon. I was 10 years old then and my mother and grandparents waited inside. My mom brought my lunch and cold drinks out while I waited. I hung a great big American flag from a large maple tree limb and held the gold star flag, that we had in our front window, as I sat on the curb. Finally, he arrived and jumped out of the cab. As he threw his arms around me, the feeling I had was one of great joy and even today, somewhat indescribable. He looked great and had a musette bag and a

Dutch (upper left) and American (upper right) children celebrate the end of the war. Perhaps none celebrated quite so fervently as these young survivors at Dachau (below right).

large canvas travel bag that I remember as being filled mostly with German military souvenirs and war type memorabilia.

Perhaps my fondest memory took place shortly after my dad returned home. He took my brother and I to Ebbetts Field to see the Dodgers play the Giants. We were very loyal Dodger fans, as my dad was born in Brooklyn. We travelled from West Orange, NJ, via the Erie Lackawanna RR to Hoboken, then took the PATH to NYC, and finally the subway to Brooklyn and the Ebbetts Field. It was my first experience going to a professional baseball game. The Dodgers won and we had a great time, and left Ebbetts Field with every conceivable souvenir available. My dad was in uniform and looked great with his newly acquired Major insignias and all of his ribbons and stars.

As we were headed to the subway entrance, we were stopped by a taxi driver who inquired if we needed a ride. My dad explained our route back house, via public transportation, and the cabbie started to ask questions of my dad about his service experience and after he heard that he *had just arrived home from Europe, the driver insisted that he drive us all the way home to New Jersey. My dad accepted the offer and off we went.*

We made one stop so my dad could call home and tell my mother what was happening. When we arrived home, dinner was waiting and the cab driver came in and joined us. The conversation was all about sports and World War II. It was unbelievable and my dad loved to tell this story afterward. I'll never forget the cab driver's names, it was Abe Schnitzer. We never saw him or heard from him again, but he has been spoken of and remembered often.

Larrie S. Calvert
American President, PCI Inc. Aged 10

sister, but a reflection of the joy that the adults must have been feeling at the ending of the war.

Years later, a strange thing happened. Whenever I've claimed to remember the war, my mother has always dismissed whatever I've offered. "You aren't old enough to remember that," she'd say. Talking to contemporaries I find this has happened to them too. I don't know whether this is because our parents *wanted* us to have been too young to be scared or because they preferred to keep as much of the pain as they could to themselves.

Helen Fletcher   *English   Schoolmistress   Aged 3¹/₂*

I grew up in Clapham in south London. During the war, the local authorities either drained the local swimming baths* altogether or kept them filled with water. The ones they kept filled with water were re-named Static Water Tanks. No one went swimming in them of course. The council also built Static Water Tanks on cleared bomb sites. They were used as an alternate water supply when there were air raids.

When people were "bombed out," they'd have no place to store their furniture or possessions so it became usual for people to store what remained of their possessions in the empty swimming baths. When schools were damaged they'd bring in their books and store them there too. After the war, as people tried to get life back to normal, they'd come to the swimming baths, burrow around, and take what they needed to re-furnish their own houses whether it

Though I cannot remember being told that the War in Europe had ended, I can identify the date with certainty, as my sister was born on VE Day. We were led down solemnly to see her and I can still recapture the feeling of intense and total happiness as I took my turn to stand on tiptoe and peer into the crib, which was hung with a soft yellow material, spotted with tiny blue flowers. As by then I had several baby cousins, and didn't think much of them, I can only deduce that this happiness was not just excitement at having a new

belonged to them or not. The schools used to come and recover their books and take a few more besides. It was hard to prove ownership – and often the owners were dead or missing in any case. I understand that they used Alexandra Palace in north London for storage too which

may have been a bad choice since it was a primary target for the bombers.

Jean Holder   *Retired Deputy Head Teacher English   Born 1933*

I had no particular feelings about the Germans or the Japanese during the War. I certainly didn't hate them. In any case I'm part German myself. All the same, I suppose the barrage of propaganda we were all subjected to during the war must have stuck in my unconscious somewhere. Plus, just after the War, most of the Nazis in films were homicidal maniacs. It wasn't until the sixties that film Nazis became all sensitive and filled with *angoisse* ("Ach, Hans, why are we doing zis? What does it all mean?")

At any rate, a dozen or so years after the War, I was ski-jumping at a meeting where there was an entry of German jumpers. I was standing at the top putting on my skis when one of the German jumpers came climbing up behind me, his skis over his shoulder. He was very Aryan looking, straight out of central casting as an SS officer. As he got to the top, he slipped, grabbed my shoulder long enough to steady himself, then smiled and muttered an apology.

In the half second or so this took, something like an electric shock zapped through my nervous system. A real live German had touched me! I actually jumped a little. I think my subconscious half-expected him to call me a schweinhund or something. I suppose my expression must have been pretty rum too because he quickly jerked his hand away. His smile turned to a rueful grin almost as if he had read my thoughts. Twelve years after the war, but it still took me a second or two before I could grin back.

Charles Perkins   *American   Publisher   Born 1935*

Left: An American Marine befriends a Japanese youngster on Saipan, 1944.
Below: A hero's welcome for Hector who had been a prisoner of war in the Far East. He is greeted by wife, child, and a new pre-fab home. London 1945.

My wife Margot lived with her parents and a baby sister in Essen, the industrial heart of Germany. A second sister was born in their apartment during an air raid. Her father was a turbine and rocket engineer, and he was usually away from home up north. Essen was spared heavy bombing for most of the war, but when the word went out that the Krupp Works were now fair game, her family was moved to a rural area near Braunschweig. They lived there, and in Alsace-Loraine, for the rest of the war. After the surrender, they returned to find the bombed-out remains of their apartment building. A few family possessions were dug out of the rubble.

In 1962 my bride and I visited Yellowstone, where I introduced her to a ranger acquaintance of mine. He detected an accent and asked her where she was from.

"Germany."

"Oh? I was there during the war. What part?"

"Essen. Maybe you know it?"

"Know it? Why, I bombed hell out of it!"

He said it in such a good natured way that it came out sounding like a joke, so we all laughed. Later, though, I think Margot and I wondered about the curious contrast of our different histories.

Wayne Hamilton   *American   Geologist, retired   Born 1936*

During evacuation my mother had raised the issue of religion. I suppose she must have objected to my being taken to church on Sunday morning, which is weird because my favorite occupation now, (and my wife's – who is not Jewish), is to spend the weekend drifting around the tiny English churches. I think it is a part of English culture that most English people don't know about. It always surprises me. Our favourite haunts are around the Cotswold churches which are an easy day's drive.

I've loved that part of English culture, as long as I can remember. Anyway, there was some kind of altercation, so I didn't go to church on Sunday any more but they had to do something with me so they put me in the barn. It always struck me as being a weird response to not going to church meant that you had to go somewhere else. So here was this little Jewish boy put in among the chickens every Sunday morning until I finally said, "Do you mind if I come to church with you?" Because I liked to. It didn't either convert me to Christianity or destroy my Jewish instincts.

I listen to choral evensong in the afternoon and my wife has always found that very odd but there is something about the ritual of the church that I think dates back to that time that I find fascinating. I found religious rituals were always interesting. It doesn't convert me. It's just that I find choral evensong and that steady chant in the voice and the beautiful use of music in the Anglican Church is quite fascinating.

Bernard Cohen   *English   Artist, Director of Slade School of Fine Art, UCL   Born 1933*

In 1945 we children had a clear sense of the war drawing to a close. Every morning at nine o'clock an English plane was seen flying along the coast so low that the Germans could not hit it from the fort at Haarr, and there were air attacks on

Not all reunions at the end of the war were joyous. Here a Finnish boy lays flowers on the grave of a father he will never know.

trains transporting oil tanks.

One warm sunny day in May the church bells started ringing. "What's that?" Andreas and I asked. "Peace" replied our uncle. When we came home in the evening a strange sight met us, something I will always remember. Attached to the top of the stables was an oar to which, blowing in the wind, was attached the Norwegian flag. The flag was rather washed out in color, except for one corner which was still bright red. It was the old flag from the time when the Union with Sweden was broken in 1905, and which Ane had never used until now. This was, she felt, an appropriate occasion even if there wasn't a real flagpole.

Of course some memories are still today clearly etched in my mind – more clearly than I had imagined. When I was in West Germany for the first time at the end of the '60s I got a shock when I saw the German police wearing uniforms exactly like those the Nazi officers had used, and I realised that these caps were quite different from any I had seen elsewhere on military personnel in Norway or other countries. When I had to do my national service I was frozen stiff when I first saw Norwegian soldiers marching in boots reminiscent of my childhood experiences of the Germans marching in the fort at home.

Lars Haarr   *Norwegian   Born 1938*

Until we meet again. The grave of Caroline Woollett's father is in the center foreground of the photograph.

My father was killed on active duty in northern France when I was a few months old. I never knew him except as a photograph in his battle dress which my mother always kept on display. My mother never re-married and it was difficult for her to bring up two young daughters on a widow's pension. She had a bit of help from her family but it was still quite a struggle. She kept chickens to help make ends meet. My mum never talked about my father much. It was hard for her to talk about him, I think, so I never asked although I would have liked to.

I knew my father was English but that he had been born in Australia: that he had come back to England to be educated; that he had a qualification in mining engineering; that he married my mother in 1937 and joined up when the war broke out. And that was about it. I knew that much but I had no memories of him at all. He was my father but he was also a stranger.

At any rate, a few years ago [1995] I decided to visit his grave near Zillebeck in Belgium. I have to confess that it started out for me almost as an intellectual exercise. I was removed from it; it was impersonal, a middle-aged woman visiting the grave of a man she'd never known. But I wanted to do it. . . to visit him and to take photographs for my sister and for my father's surviving sisters who had never been able to visit his grave. Or maybe it was for my mother who had died not too long before. She hadn't ever been able to visit his grave either. Maybe. . . I don't exactly know what

my motives were but I remember that it was a beautiful day and that we had difficulty in finding the right place because there were so many military cemeteries around Zillebeck. But at last we found the right one. My father had been buried in a section of a World War One cemetery along with comrades who had been killed in the same action.

There was a memory book there which told me my father had died defending the line of the Ypres-Comines Canal nearby. This surprised me because I had always understood he'd died at Dunkirk. We went to search for his grave and the closer we came to it, the more my emotions took over. When at last I was face to face with him, confronting the reality of his gravestone, I began to weep. I couldn't stop. I was just overwhelmed. I sat on a nearby bench with my face in my hands. It was a long while before I could look up and begin to take in details around me. I saw how beautifully strangers had kept his grave all those years. I saw the words my mother had chosen to be carved onto his headstone: "In memory of my husband Dick. Until we meet again." She never told us she'd done that. Then I noticed the date of his death on the headstone. My mother had died on exactly the same day forty-nine years later. . .

Caroline (née Cholmondeley) Woollett   *English*
Social Worker   Born 1940

RETURN TO KARELIA

400,000 Karelians were driven from their homes and re-settled elsewhere in Finland.

Then in 1944 the Russians invaded again – the Continuation War* and this time we were forced to leave Karelia for good. In the peace settlement, Karelia became part of Russia and Finland had to cede other territory to the Russians as well. Some people have said that Finland was pro-German during the war, but we weren't. We were simply anti-Russian. And with good reason! We weren't permitted to see our farm for fifty years and when we did go back in 1993, we had to obtain a passport and visa in order to visit our own farm!

When we left Karelia, we weren't sure that we would be permitted to return so we took as much as we could with us. We were evacuated by train. It was a long journey. One woman had a baby on the train. I remember sleeping on the luggage racks above the seats. We were taken right across Finland. In this part of Finland, they are Swedish-speaking people. They don't know Finnish and only a few can speak it. We were taken to schools and community houses where the local farmers would come and pick the ones they wanted. "I want this family. I don't want *that* family. Too many children." That was us of course. Five young children, most of us ill after our long journey. And my mother was ill too – an infected hand from a tiny splinter because there was no medicine.

At the end of the war, there was no place for us to go back to. Our home was now in Russia. The Finnish government had to find homes for nearly 400,000 displaced persons who had once lived in Karelia. Eventually, they found a small house for us, and for the next three years I worked in the fields for other farmers. For a while I was the sole support of our family. I was paid just enough to keep us all from starving.

In 1993. . .[pause]. . . in 1993, we went back. . . back to our home even though we needed a visa to do so. It was. . . [long silence]. . . wonderful to go back. . . wonderful. . .

Sirkka-Lüsa Rantanen   *Finnish   Housewife   Born 1931*

When peace came there was an enormous sense of relief. Our gang rode in triumph round the streets ringing our bicycle bells. Blackout was banished and lights hung in every doorway. A street party happened impromptu where four roads meet, and our staid grocer neighbor wheeled his piano out onto the pavement for the occasion. At home, the Morrison Shelter was dismantled and the dining table polished and restored to its place.

The celebrations in London were wonderful. Crowds of happy people gasping at the fireworks over the River, public buildings floodlit, the Abbey looking like a cardboard cut-out against the night sky. On VE Day, processions of victorious soldiers, sailors, and airmen marched through London to be acclaimed by the crowds. My father chose our vantage point for this event. We stood on the steps of the Royal Artillery Memorial at Hyde Park Corner. With that regiment my father had fought in France in the First World War, and I knew he hoped that day the this Second War would really "do the trick" and bring peace.

We felt thankful that we had come through it all united, and had not been broken or divided by the war. To celebrate peace felt like a proper thanksgiving.

Margaret Roake   *English   History teacher*   *"Aged 8 at the start"*

The actress, Deborah Kerr, at the end of the war. Her family kept chickens in order to supplement rations.

Air raid alarms were the only kind of parties I knew at the turn of 1944 and 1945. Even at the risk of sounding outrageous to everyone who survived bombing in London or in German towns, I admit I looked forward to them. This is easily explained by the fact that until February 14, 1945 not one single bomb had fallen on Prague. (On that day a "mistaken" raid by several pilots who had mistaken Prague for Dresden, having lost their way, killed 413 people and wounded another 1,450). Most Praguers therefore in late 1944 considered alarms a mere nuisance.

The reason why I looked forward to them and was glad when sirens sounded at night was simple. Here I was, a little over fourteen, living alone in our family's four-room flat. My father was in an internment camp, my mother had been deported to Theresienstadt concentration camp, and my sister worked in a factory near Prague. I had been more lucky. On the day of my fourteenth anniversary I had to stop going to school as first-class mongrel (*Mischling*, i.e. part-Jew). The factory I had been assigned to work in was the Prague-based Deutsche Lufthansa repair shop for flying instruments, and, though we worked from 6 a.m. to 6 p.m., I could easily live at home.

Though I know now, and knew even then that I had nothing to complain about, being fed at the factory canteen and having not only a roof over my head, but even all my familiar things, the problem was that the evenings were long and there just was nobody to talk to. And there were always people in the shelter. It seems strange, that nobody ever wondered why I was always alone, but stranger even that the Nazis, who had everything meticulously organized, didn't bother to confiscate the flat and dump me in some camp.

So there I was, with all that was left of our family's money, jewels, my mother's makeup and my sister's clothes, and could play grown-up. Just once I tried to go to a pub, but since I looked even younger than my age, they didn't let me in. So in the end I started dressing up to go to the shelter, but nobody noticed anyway and the only time anyone ever spoke to me there was, when a woman asked me whether I thought that this was a damned party and I told her I did. But she probably didn't care because she never even answered.

Hannah Rehakova   *Czech   Administrator   Aged 14*

I was born in Germany in 1938. Shortly after my birth, we escaped Germany by my parents crossing one border into Switzerland with my two year old sister while, Hena, our baby nurse, crossed a different border with me. We came to America in 1940. Our baby nurse, who also is Jewish, came with us and always has been a member of our family.

When I was two, my parents became the foster parents of Tony [name changed], who was also two years old. Tony was English and had been sent to his grandparents in America to escape the Blitz. An active two year old was more than his grandparents could manage, so he lived with us and his grandparents visited weekly. Hena looked after us all with equal love and affection.

Although we always knew that Tony had different parents and one day would return to London, we all grew very close to him. He was my constant companion. I loved him. We could have been twins. I recall riding bikes with him and roller skating.

After the war, when it was time for Tony to return to England, my mother began training his hair to "part on the other side" which she thought made him look more like an English boy. He packed all of his little matchbox* cars and left for London on the same day I was leaving for summer camp. I remember waving goodbye to him and feeling sad. When I returned from camp and Tony was no longer there, I felt a deep sense of loss.

Hena was also very close to Tony. When he returned to London, Hena corresponded with him until Tony's mother asked her to stop writing. Separated from his parents at so young an age, he had formed deep attachments to us, then lost us when he returned to parents who were little more than strangers to him. His mother felt that Hena's letters were causing him more pain. Tony never understood that sending him to America had been an act of love and sacrifice. He called my mother years later to ask if she thought of him as her son. My mother, in what may have been a misguided effort to help Tony connect with his own mother, said, "Of course I didn't think of you as a son. You weren't my son." Hena might have given a different answer.

We lost touch but I know that Tony became a gifted playwright and even had one of his plays produced on Broadway. He has had a difficult life, troubled and unhappy as both an adolescent and an adult. It's hard to equate this image with that of the charming, care-free "twin" I loved.

Evelyn Fuchs Starobin   *American   Florist   Born 1938*

The United States and Norway jointly celebrate the Victory.

Civilians were ordered to hand over to the Germans all our silver, precious metals, our radios. Late in the war we had to hand over a certain number of blankets. I went with my father to hand over the blankets and they were not satisfied. They were very old; everybody took their oldest blankets and maybe they didn't have enough of them either. There was an argument with the German soldier in charge of collecting the blankets and my father talked to him in German; my father told me that later. Fortunately, my father taught German in the High School. He also had a story why he didn't hand over the radio. My father had hidden it but we didn't know where. He never told us. He had told us that the radio was gone to the Germans. But he had hidden it and he could never use it. That was the problem, when you hide it you can't use it. After the war the first thing he did was dig it up. That was typical during the Occupation.

Hans Hilbers   *Dutch   Director, European Bank for Reconstruction and Recovery   Born 1934*

GHOST TOWN AM MAIN

Frankfurt am Main and the Düwel family at the end of the war. Now for the task of rebuilding the peace.

We were six children. Our father had been drafted into the war and our mother had to care for us all on her own. The war was very painful for all of us. With terror, I think of the bombing nights which ripped us from our beds, dressed as we were, when we left the house, often entirely alone, amidst the sound of sirens, to walk through the graves to reach the air-raid shelter. At the time, our mother was expecting another child, our seventh, a girl. She delivered the baby in the small cellar beneath our house, all on her own without outside help.

We survived many more bombing raids in which our family home was badly damaged. After all these terrors, we were glad when the first occupiers arrived. The occupying troops were kind and gave us something to eat. We were starving and emaciated as a result of the war events. Our mother was particularly badly affected. She got typhoid caused by starvation. After her slow recovery, she did laundry for the occupying troops and was given food for us in return. Gradually, order in events was restored, thank God! Today I still recall those times of my youth with terror and hope that such times again will never come again for us or our children.

Helga Düwel   *German   Shop Owner   Born 1938*

9th August 1945. I was in the bomb shelter under my father's factory with the rest of the family. My father went above ground to check on the situation, realizing that our town or the factory was not the target that day. After a while, he came back down into the shelter and I overheard him telling my mother in a hushed voice that he just saw a new kind of bomb exploding in the direction of Nagasaki, a gigantic explosion the kind of which he had never seen. When he realized that my sisters and I had heard him, he told us sternly not to say a word of it to anyone else.

Mamoru Mitsui   *Born Japanese, naturalized citizen of the United States of America   Architect   Aged 7*

I was taken to Trafalgar Square by my eldest brother on VE-Day and I remember Churchill coming through in his open car, cigar and the whole bit – but then another memory of the eve of VJ-Day when the news hit the headlines that an atom bomb had been dropped. I remember, vividly, that the people in the area where I lived didn't know what it was and couldn't say the word so it was "a tonic' rather than "atomic." People would go around saying things like, "Well, they've got this bomb that blows people to atoms," and I suppose in a way that that was the end of one's childhood nightmare, or a nightmare of innocence and the beginning of another nightmare of awareness.

Bernard Cohen   *English   Artist, Director of Slade School of Fine Art, UCL   Born 1933*

As the war in the Pacific neared its end, atomic bombs were dropped on Hiroshima and Nagasaki in Japan, each time killing 100,000 people. These events severely tested my religious faith, as I could not understand how a kind and benevolent God could allow such a horrible thing to happen. At the time, I asked my father if he thought it was possible that someone could set off a chain reaction that would blow up the world. He said, "No, I don't think so, but if it is, you can be sure that some damn fool will do it."

Gil Upton   *American   Lawyer   Aged 11*

On 14th August 1945, our father sent the family to the farm house and told us to spend the night there. The following morning, we heard newscasters say repeatedly that the Emperor would be addressing us, His Majesty's Imperial subjects, over the radio at noon. Since our family had one of only a few working radios in the village, many neighbors joined us in our living room shortly before the appointed time.

The voice of the Emperor, which no one there had ever heard before, was high-pitched and tended to be obscured by frequent static noises. He started his speech using the traditional opening words used in most Imperial Decrees, "Chin omouni," which meant, "In accordance with my divine thoughts." The entire speech was recited in the special Imperial Decree language that was virtually incomprehensible to the fourth grader that I was. As it turned out, between this unfamiliar language and the static-ridden broadcast, about half of the farmers who gathered there thought the Emperor was urging us to "endure the unendurable" and fight on. The others sheepishly suggested that they thought they heard some words to the effect that we should put down arms. After they left, still shaking their heads and trying to fathom the essence of the Imperial Decree, our mother told us that the latter was the case.

Mamoru Mitsui   *Born Japanese, naturalized citizen of the United States of America   Architect   Aged 7*

Rebuilding the peace. Hiroshima, Japan. While one of their teachers fans herself, these students are hard at work in their bomb-damaged school. The smiles of the two boys on the left say much about the irrepressible spirit of children. The ruins of Hiroshima can be seen in the background.

We heard about the end of the war from over the radio. The voice of the Emperor Hirohito was broadcast. Obviously it was a pre-recorded tape and his voice was extremely fragile and very difficult to hear. It was difficult to identify what he was trying to convey to his faithful, obedient citizens and farmers. After the broadcast my uncle murmured in a low voice, his shoulders sagged and he said, "Oh, we have finally lost the war."

We all cried and as you must have seen in Japanese newspapers, some people in Tokyo rushed over to the Emperor's palace and they bowed and they cried and apologized for their inability or lack of effort which caused the loss of the war. That's how I felt, like everybody else in Japan, about the loss of the war. The streets were dead silent.

Masachika Onodera   *Japanese   Executive Secretary, The Japan-British Society   Born 1930*

One effect of the war on me is that I am a scavenger. I learned to be a scavenger in the camp. Whatever you had was terribly precious and I can't pass things without picking them up. One of my greater pleasures is inhabiting the local refuse dump, which is a great embarrassment to my wife, finding things that are useful in it which I regularly do. I have no inhibitions whatsoever. Not so long ago I found an armchair and a sofa and I had with me my stepdaughter and a friend from a rather snooty girls boarding school. I explained to them this was a fun thing to do. It was a freezing cold day and I could only get one of these two objects in the back of my car so I left the two children sitting on the other one lest anybody nicked it. Drove the first home and returned later to find them shivering on the second. My further embarrassment was only made worse because the sofa wouldn't fit through the front door of the house.

Three times running, we lost everything. Everything. My father was alleged to have been in hospital in Hong Kong when he noticed in the road on the tarmac outside, his entire family silver being steamrollered to make it easier for packing. It left a sort of disdain for possessions. My mother's disdain for possessions was almost total. They are not important. I don't think anything daunted us much. We became enormously self-reliant. What I learned from the war is that life is for living and looking back is quite a waste of time. I live in a manner of living each day as it were my last.

Major General Sir James Templer   *English   Army, retired   Born 1935*

I was born in 1940, the youngest of seven children, and spent the four years that we still had in Hungary in the country. Life seemed to be quite normal in our Victorian-type household. We children ate in the nursery and saw my parents once or twice a day. Of those early years I only remember festivities like Christmas and Easter when the family gathered together to celebrate; at Christmas around a ceiling high Christmas tree smelling deliciously of pine and oranges, apples and spicy German cakes [Oblaten] which hung from the tree. At Easter we hunted around the garden, looking for the Easter bunnies' nests under rose bushes and hedges to find multi-coloured Easter eggs and toys.

Our family had always owned horses, both race horses and Lippizaners. The Lippizaners were used to draw our carriages. We left Hungary without them. Our Stud Manager, who could not bear the thought of us being without our horses, walked them over the border to Austria. They were mostly Lippizaners and one race horse, a mare, who later became the mother of them all. A few horses died on Vienna West-Bahnhof in the railway trucks in the cold winter of 1944/45. They were stranded for eleven weeks. In the end the Stud Manager promised the railway officials a large ham if they let the horses travel on to Bavaria. The next day the ham did the trick. They joined us in Sünching, Bavaria.

Through my father's British connections, we finally managed to leave Germany and in 1947 moved to London. Our Lippizaners also came to Britain. Eventually we, and later the horses, emigrated to South Africa.

Being an overly sensitive child, the fear that permeated throughout the war years, stayed with me throughout my school life in South Africa. I would have recurring nightmares about war and invasion and death up to the age of seventeen, and would burst into tears if I heard an airplane fly overhead at night.

It was the dreadful drone and the sight of those pinprick size aircraft overhead that always filled me with terror as a child. I don't recall that there were such things as enemies and Allies, all soldiers were enemies, and every day brought new dangers and fears. For example, we could not go into the woods mushroom picking because of possible snipers. We were told not to pick up toys in the street in case they were disguised bombs. We were not allowed to speak Hungarian in public (I only spoke Hungarian and German), in case the Communist secret service overheard us, as my father and we were on their hit list.

We were the lucky ones. We may have lost every material possession, our home, our country, our nationality (we were stateless) but we remained alive and together as a family. In retrospect, the war gave us the opportunity to widen our horizons and knowledge of humankind, by forcing us away from what had been for generations a comfortable, self-contained, and protected way of life.

Countess Hanna Jankovich-Besan   *Hungarian   Therapist   Born 1940*

TO THE MEMORY OF THE 13,000,000 CHILDREN OF
OUR GENERATION WHO DIED IN WORLD WAR II.

Allen, Fred American radio comedian, especially popular during WWII.

Anderson shelter Outdoor bomb shelter. Sand bags were piled on top of a corrugated iron frame for protection.

Armstrong, Jack "The All-American Boy." A radio adventure popular with young listeners.

ARP wardens Air raid patrol wardens.

Askey, Arthur British comedian; best known for the BBC radio show "Band Wagon."

Benny, Jack Popular American radio, stage, and later television comedian. Benny was famous for his alleged meanness.

Black Country The English industrial Midlands.

Black Pudding Sausage-type sweetmeat made from the blood of pigs, suet, and mixed with oatmeal.

Bowl Pitch. How the ball is delivered to the batsman in cricket.

C of E Church of England.

Chiang Kai-Shek (Jiang Jieshi) Chinese Nationalist leader who led his country during the war.

Conkers British schoolboy game in which horse chestnuts suspended on string are alternately smashed against each other until one breaks, hence, "oners" have won one fight; "twoers" have won two fights, and so on.

Continuation War The second phase of the Russo-Finnish war. The Finns were defeated and had to concede much territory.

Coronation Street British television soap opera set in a working class district of Manchester.

Doodlebugs Popular name for the V-1 flying bombs, launched by the Germans against the English.

Doolittle raid On 18th April 1942 the US launched a daring bombing raid on Tokyo led by General (then Colonel) Doolittle.

DUKWs American amphibious trucks.

Flannegan and Allan British vaudeville comedians.

Flying Bombs see Doodlebugs above.

Handley, Tommy British comedian who had his own popular radio show.

Home Guard A civilian defence unit comprised of men who were either too old or medically unfit for more active service.

Hurling An Irish game resembling field hockey.

Jinricksha (or Jinrikisha) A light, two wheeled vehicle drawn by a man. First used in Japan in the 19th century.

Kennington Oval Cricket ground in south London.

Lucky Strike green dye A precious metal in the green dye was needed for war production.

Morrison shelter An indoor bomb shelter. Essentially, a heavy gauge metal plate used as a roof – although more often than not the kitchen table had to suffice.

OPA tokens The Office of Price Administration administered rationing in the United States.

Paraffin Kerosene.

Pasties Cornish meat pies.

Peabody's An apartment building in the East End of London which was badly damaged during the London blitz.

Phoney War September 1939 to May 1940. War had been declared in Europe but little fighting was taking place.

Pram Baby carriage.

Prefecture A regional district of Japan.

Prep school An English preparatory school (usually a boarding school for boys aged 8-11).

Puttees Cloth wrappings wound around lower leg.

RAMC Royal Army Medical Corps.

Radley An English Public School (a private, fee-paying school for children aged 11-18).

Rounders Ball game similar to baseball.

Sinterklass Santa Claus.

Sky King A popular radio adventure program for youngsters.

Schloss Large German house, akin to a castle or chateau. Sometimes fortified.

Swan Vestas British brand of matches.

Swimming baths Public swimming pools and wash houses.

Terraced (house) A house attached to neighboring houses on both sides, as opposed to detached or semi-detached.

Tonypandy The mining town in south Wales where troops were called in to end the miner's riots of 1910. In fact, Churchill, then Home Secretary, had the troops replaced by London police before they reached Tonypandy.

UNRA United Nations Relief and Rehabilitation Administration. An organization which helped with the re-settlement of people made homeless by the war.

Vauxhall A district of south London.

VE Day Victory in Europe Day. 8 May 1945.

VJ Day Victory in Japan Day. 15 August 1945.

WVS Women's Voluntary Service.

White Pudding Irish sweetmeat similar to black pudding but made with pork and a base of barley oats.

Winter War The first phase of the Russo-Finnish war. November 1939-March 1940.

Zero Popular name for the Mitsubishi A6M Japanese fighter aircraft.

LIST OF CONTRIBUTORS

I would like to give my most heartfelt thanks to the individuals who have helped make this book possible. All of them have given freely of their time. Many have trusted me with often deeply personal memories, and with treasured photographs. I can only hope that the book does justice to their trust and to their expectations.

This is an alphabetical list of the interviews that appear in this book. For reasons of space, we have been unable to use all the interviews which have been so kindly and generously given. The editor apologizes to all those contributors whose memories do not appear in these pages.

ACKNOWLEDGEMENTS

I should like to thank the following individuals who helped with the book.

Rebecca Blond; Laura S Creith; Margaret Crowe; WN DeWitt; Stephen W Dunn; Harrison C Dunning; Clive Goodman; Dennis Goodman; Larry Hampton; Catherine Souza Harris; President Vaclav Haval; Harold Henderson; William R Herring; Dr Franklin Kometani; Mary Lou Erdman Larsen; Sue Libovitch; Jane Manaster; Diane MacDonald; Mary Mazza; Gail Taylor Miller; Martha Wysard Monahan; Simon Parry; Mr and Mrs Robert Perkins; Charles Pinkerton; Radomir Putnikovitch; Alice Read; David Robinson; KC Robson; EMC Rowe; John M Ryan; Maurice Schneerson; Sumner Sharpe; Robert L Slaughter; Barbara Swenson; Count and Countess Andrew Hubert von Staufer; Margaret Walker; Michael J Walker; Priscilla Weatherwood; Fyn White; Linda White; Sue Wood; Ernst Zwick.

I should also like to thank the following individuals and organizations.

Kay Baggett of the *Middlesex Chronicle*; Elizabeth Blight of the Manitoba Provincial Archives; LaVaughn Bresnahan of the State of Wyoming, Division of Cultural Resources; J Stephen Catlett of the Greensboro Historical Society; Emily Clark of the Chicago Historical Society; Charlene Dahlquist of Lyman House Memorial Museum, Hawaii; Mary Degenhardt of the Girl Scouts of America; Dorothy Tuttle Frye, Archives of Michigan State University; Soteris Georgallis and Maria Phani of the Cyprus High Commission, London; Mary S Judd of Punahou School, Hawaii; Marge Kemp of the Bishop Museum, Honolulu, Hawaii; Eileen M Kennedy of the Museum of the City of New York; Rebecca Kohl of the Montana Historical Society; Barbara Lonnborg and Terry L Hyland of Boy's Town, USA (and a very special thank you to former residents of Boy's Town who donated their memories to the book: Commander Lloyd Bucher, Charles Carriger, George Karleskint, Leo Magers, Edwin Novotny, and Joe Trudeau); Waverly B Lowell of the National Archives – Pacific Sierra Region; Stephen E Massingill of the North Carolina Department of Cultural Resources; Claire Maxwell of the Austin History Center; Joan Morris of the Florida State Archives; Eric L Mundell of the Indiana Historical Society; Steve Nielsen of the Minnesota Historical Society; Anne Osteendarp of the Dartmouth College Library; Susan Pagani of the State Historical Society of Wisconsin; Sickan Park, the Finnish Cultural Attaché, London; Simon Parry of Air Research Publications, London; Gerald I Reilly of the Mansion Museum, Wheeling, West Virginia; India Spartz of the State of Alaska Historical Collections; Bonnie Tregobov of the Jewish Historical Society of Western Canada; Curtis Tunnell of the Texas Historical Commission; Merek Web and Krysia Fischer of the Yivo Institute; The Christmas Archive, Ross-on-Wye, England; The Cyprus Veterans' Association of Nicosia, Cyprus; The Embassies of Belgium, China, The Czech Republic, Germany, Japan, and Russia (London); The Japanese Information and Cultural Center, London; The Public Library, Manchester, New Hampshire.

Particular thanks are given to Marco Banti, Monica Bloxon, Kleo Kleanthous, Gerschon Hepner, Mirja Liukkonen, and Ginger van Hasselt for translation help in a variety of languages and to Hanna Jankovich-Besan for help with typing and transcribing.

Some of the overseas material has been gathered on our behalf. We should like to offer special thanks to Anne Holden Rønning (Norwegian Editor); Curtis Tunnell (Texas Editor); and Paul L Wysard (Hawaiian Editor).

We would like to thank the following for permission to quote brief extracts from material first published elsewhere. Norman Bowler and Caroline Woollett for permission to print material from interviews in her book, *A Child's Eye View of West Hampstead; ES Magazine* for permission to quote from Albert Roux's "Cher Albert" column; Maria and Andrew Hubert for permission to quote from the Hughes and Moran interviews in their publication, *A Wartime Christmas* published by Alan Sutton Publishing.

PICTURE ACKNOWLEDGEMENTS

The Jacket: The Children of Lidice. The 82 children of the Czech village of Lidice represented in sculptures which took twenty years to complete by the Czech artist, Marie Uchytilova. Photograph, the Czech News Agency, Prague. Private Collections: 14, 19, 27, 34, 35, 39, 41, 48, 51, 66, 73, 74, 79, 83, 94, 96b, all 98, all 108, 113, 114, 129, 131, 132, 133, 134, 144, 145, 148; Associated Press Picture Library: 10b, 96a, 140a; Barnaby's Picture Library: 47 (A. Bruce), 91, 93e; Bundesarchiv, Koblenz: 9, 16a, 45, 93c, 119a; Corbis/Bettemann/UPI: 22, 42, 43, 44b, 65, 68, 70, 71, 107, 111, 124, 135, 149; Cyprus Veteran's Association: 105b; Czech News Agency, Prague: Jacket; Finnish Defence Forces Education Development, Helsinki: 18, 36a & b, 64, 95, 115, 116, 122, 143, 145, 148; Finnish Press Agency, Helsinki: 37, 57, 61; Getty Images: 3, 11, 54, 102b, 140c, 141, 142b, 151 (repeat of p.3); Michael Grossman: 77, 78; Imperial War Museum: 93b, 93d; Japanese-American Historical Society: 127; London Transport Museum: 90; Mary Evans Picture Library: 46, 112 ,120 (Meledin); Mirror Syndication International: 9, 44a, 63, 67, 123, 125; Museum of History and Industry, Seattle, USA: 26; Nordfoto, Copenhagen: 40, 64, 66, 80, 81, all 82; Popperfoto: 1, 2, 8, 10a, all 12, 15, 16b, 17, 20, all 21, 24, 26, 28, all 30, 33, all 49, 62, 102a,c & d, 105a, 109, 110, 118 a & b, 122a, 126, 135, 141a, 142a; Public Record Office Picture Library: 117; Rijksinstituut voor Oorlogsdocumentatie: 106; Topham Picturepoint: 31, 88-89, all 92, 136, 138-9, 146; US Library of Congress: 22, 27, 55, 58-59, 64, 84, 86, 93a, 97, 100, 110a, 140b, 147; US National Archives: 52, 53, all 56, 108a, 119b; The Vintage Magazine Company: 38.

The index is divided into three parts – a General Index plus separate indexes
for Persons and Places. Page numbers in bold refer to illustrations.

ABOUT THE EDITOR

Charles Perkins spent the war years as a schoolboy in New Hampshire, collecting waste paper and tires, buying savings bonds, and successfully guarding Hillsborough County from attack by enemy parachutists. He has enjoyed a varied career as writer, assistant professor, schoolmaster, editor, and publisher. His other writings include military history, science fiction, westerns, poetry, and literary criticism. He is married and lives in London, England.